Outlines of Psychology

AN ELEMENTARY TREATISE
WITH SOME PRACTICAL APPLICATIONS

BY

JOSIAH ROYCE, Ph.D., LL.D.

PROFESSOR OF THE HISTORY OF PHILOSOPHY
IN HARVARD UNIVERSITY

3221/5

New York
THE MACMILLAN COMPANY
LONDON: MACMILLAN & CO., Ltd.
1906

Norwood Press
J. S. Cushing & Co. — Berwick & Smith Co.
Norwood, Mass., U.S.A.

𝔗eachers' 𝔓rofessional 𝔏ibrary

EDITED BY NICHOLAS MURRAY BUTLER

Outlines of Psychology

PREFACE

A NUMBER of years since I was a contributor to a large volume entitled, *In Sickness and in Health* — the joint work of a number of authors. The volume was intended as a popular guide regarding various aspects of public and private hygiene, of nursing, and of related topics. The treatise, however, contained introductory statements, composed by different writers, and setting forth the most general outlines of Anatomy, of Physiology and of Psychology. It was my own task merely to contribute to this volume the sketch of some of the elementary principles and practical applications of Psychology. The later essays of the volume were the work of physicians. The introductory statements were accordingly very strictly limited, as to their plan and as to their contents, by their relation to the highly practical treatise in which they formed so subordinate a part.

By the consent of the publishers of the work thus prepared, I have been able to use the material of this, my former very summary sketch of Psychology, as the core of the present elementary book. I have indeed revised such of the former discussion as I here use; and I have added a proportionately large amount of new text, and have endeavoured to give the present volume its own unity. What remains from the original sketch is, however, especially the tendency to make a number of practical applications of psychological theory at various

v

places in my discussion — a tendency which may be of service to some readers who, like myself, are fond of defining a good many of the problems of teaching, and of practical life, more or less in psychological terms, so far as they are able to do so. Otherwise, as I hope, the present work speaks for itself.

This is not a book upon the Philosophy of Mind, nor does it deal with any philosophical problems. Such problems I have indeed discussed at length in other publications of my own. But the reader of my various philosophical inquiries will already know that I make a sharp difference between the business of the student of philosophy and that of the psychologist. In the present volume, I am concerned solely with certain problems of the natural history of mind; metaphysical issues are here not at all in question. On the other hand, this volume is indeed no effort to summarise the more technical results of modern Experimental Psychology, although I believe thoroughly in the importance of Experimental Psychology, and personally take no small interest in following, so far as I can, the labours of my colleagues of the laboratories; and although I hope that this book shows a good many signs of my having profited by such an interest. My plan has led me, however, to concern myself here with elementary principles rather than with technical details, and to attempt, to some extent, practical applications of these principles, rather than statements of the fascinating, but complex special researches of recent laboratory Psychology.

For the same reason, this volume makes no attempt to deal with the special Psychology of the senses, with the details of the theory of space-perception, or with any of the other special regions where modern Experimental Psychology has already won its greatest triumphs. I do not, indeed, undervalue what has been accomplished in those fields. But I have no desire to try to compete with the numerous recent expositions in which the later conquests of Experimental Psychology have been summarised. On the contrary, I hope that my reader's curiosity may be aroused in such wise that he may be led to look elsewhere for what I do not pretend to give him. My own purpose, and my chosen limitations, assign to me another task.

I presuppose, then, a serious reader, but not one trained either in experimental methods, or in philosophical inquiries. I try to tell him a few things that seem to me important, regarding the most fundamental and general processes, laws, and conditions of mental life. I say nothing whatever about the philosophical problem of the relations of mind and body, and nothing about the true place of mind in the universe. Meanwhile, I try to view the matters here in question in a perspective which is of my own choosing. The treatment of mental phenomena, under the three heads of Sensitiveness, Docility, and Initiative, is especially characteristic of the plan of my book. This arrangement and classification of well-known facts involves a point of view which seems to me to possess a certain relative novelty. The entire subordination of the usual distinctions of Feeling, Intellect, and Will, to these deeper distinctions, which my own division of the phenomena of mind is intended to emphasise, — the persistent stress that I lay upon the unity of the intellectual and the voluntary processes, which, in popular treatises, are too often sundered, and treated as if one of them could go on without the other, — these are also characteristic of the present discussion. Furthermore, in the chapter on the Feelings, I have presented views which are in some respects of my own devising. The traditional view makes Pleasure and Displeasure the sole elementary qualities of Feeling. Wundt has recently insisted upon the existence of three different "dimensions" of feeling; *i.e.* he has maintained that there are three "pairs of opposing qualities," to be found amongst the elementary feelings, — pleasure and its opposite together constituting *one* only of these pairs. I have here attempted, provisionally, a *two*-dimensional scheme of the elementary feelings. The interest of my hypothesis, if it has any value, lies in the statement which it makes possible concerning the relation of Feeling and Conduct. I am able to define, in terms of my view, the possibility of certain forms of conduct, and of certain tendencies of the attention, which the customary pleasure-displeasure theory, as I think, is unable to describe.

In addition to these matters, relating to the theoretical

aspects of my book, there is one further topic which may interest some more technical readers. In the chapter on Mental Initiative, I have, namely, stated certain views regarding the origin of novel modes of conduct, and novel forms of consciousness, — views which, as I hope, are worthy of some consideration, and which are, in some respects, relatively independent. They are introduced into this book especially for the sake of their practical bearings. But they also have a theoretical aspect which may interest the more professional reader of this volume.

To my mind, namely, an interesting side-light has been shed upon the well-known controversies between the associationists on the one hand, and the school of Wundt, and the partisans of "mental activity" generally, on the other, by the stress that Professor Loeb has recently laid upon the part that what he calls "tropisms" play in the life of animals of all grades. By a "tropism," Loeb means a response, on the part of an organism, to some type of physical or chemical stimulus, — a response taking the form of some characteristic movement, which may or may not be adaptive in any particular case, but which is determined by the nature of the stimulus and of the organism. Loeb's "tropisms" are exemplified by the actions of such organisms as turn toward the light, or as flee the light, or as find their way into crevices, or as do any other characteristic thing, with a mechanical certainty, whenever they are

stimulated in special fashions by light, by the touch of
solid objects, or by other stimuli, *e.g.* by chemical
stimuli. The moth's flight into the candle-flame is an
instance of such a "tropism." As thus appears, the
"tropism" need not, in any one case, prove to be an
adaptive response to the environment, although the
resultant of all of the "tropisms" together must in
general, in any organism, tend to the survival of the
type of organism in question.

Now it is especially notable that the "tropisms" of
Loeb are not, like the "reflex actions" of the usual theories, modes of activity primarily determined by the
functions of specific nerve-centres. Furthermore, they
are more general and elemental in their character than
are any of the acquired habits of an organism. At any
one moment when they are called into activity, they may
run counter to the acquired habits. In brief, Loeb's
concept of a "tropism" is different from the ordinary concept of a reflex action, and is different, too,
from the concept of an acquired adaptive habit of action.
Loeb has insisted that the new concept is more fundamental than the old ones, and that both habits and reflex
actions must ultimately be explained as results of "tropisms." Now it has occurred to me to maintain, in substance, that the factor in mental life which Wundt's
school define as "Apperception," and which others so
often call "spontaneity," "active attention," "conscious
activity," or, sometimes, "self-activity," may well be

treated, from the purely psychological point of view, as the conscious aspect or accompaniment of a collection of tendencies of the type which Loeb has called "tropisms." These tendencies appear at once as elemental, and at the moment at which they are aroused, as sovereign over acquired habits and associations of ideas; in other words, as directive of the course of our conscious life.

In thus reducing the physical accompaniment of the process which Wundt calls "Apperception," and which others call "self-activity" to the type of what Loeb calls "tropisms," I am able to explain, in so far as the point of view of the psychologist requires such explanation, the frequent appearance in our mental life of a factor which (1) is more general than is any specific mental function due to our acquired habits, and which (2) seems at any moment to be capable of directing the course of our associations, rather than to be merely the result of experience and association. Yet in order to explain the presence of such a factor, I am not obliged to go beyond the presuppositions which determine the point of view of the psychologist. Wundt has insisted that his "Apperception" is no disembodied spiritual entity. I conceive that Loeb has indicated to us, in the concept of the "tropism," how a power more or less directive of the course of our associations, and more general than is any one of the tendencies that are due, in us, to habit, or to specific experience, can find its embodiment in the most elemental activities of our organ-

ism. Wundt's opponents, on the contrary, insist that all
our activities must be due to inherited reflexes, modified
by experience, and organised by the law of habit; and
that consequently the law of association must determine
the sequence of all our mental states. Loeb shows how
the " tropisms " are more elemental than the reflexes, and
how they are capable of suddenly modifying our habits.
The result must be, as I maintain, that the associa-
tionist view of mental life must have its limitations.

Upon the basis of the ideas thus indicated, I have
sketched, in Chapter XVIII of my text, a theory of how
the apparent " originality," or " spontaneity," or in
another phraseology, the Initiative, of the organism, and
of the individual mind, are to be treated from the point
of view of the psychologist. Meanwhile this theory
has indeed deeper relations, in my own mind, to certain
philosophical views of mine as to the real nature of
individual choice and originality. These views I have
elsewhere in part already set forth; but they are not in
place in a book dealing with Psychology. And they are
indeed far enough from the views which Professor Loeb
has in mind in his researches.

I have thus indicated, not only to those readers to
whom I especially appeal, but also to the more technical
student, wherein lie some of the more characteristic of
the features which this little book possesses. The less
technical reader, however, for whom my text, especially
in its more practical discussions, is chiefly intended,

need not trouble himself as to what is mine or is not mine, nor as to the deeper problems of theory which I touch upon, nor as to how my views are related to those of other students. I have tried to help such a reader, who may often be, as I hope, like myself, a teacher, to understand some of the best known of the results of psychological study, and at the same time to view those results in a light that may sometimes justly appear to him to be novel. I have also tried to help him a little to apply his knowledge in practice.

I have still to acknowledge my constant indebtedness in this book, first, to the one who was amongst my earliest guides in the study of Psychology, namely, to my honoured friend and colleague, Professor William James, and secondly to Professor Baldwin, to whose treatment of the problems of Mental Evolution my own discussion of Mental Initiative owes not a little, and whose discussions of the social factors in mental development have also much influenced my own.

The fact that I have been forced to correct the proof-sheets of the present volume, during a temporary leave of absence from my usual place of work, and while at a distance both from my publisher and my library, may help to explain some of the errors which may have crept into the printed text, and which may have escaped my notice.

JOSIAH ROYCE.

MARCH 30, 1903.

CONTENTS

CHAPTER I

PAGE

INTRODUCTORY DEFINITIONS AND EXPLANATIONS 1–19

§ 1. Definition of psychology. Contrast between mental and
physical phenomena 1
§ 2. In what sense mental phenomena are internal . . 3
§ 3. A science of mental phenomena is made possible by the
fact that mental phenomena have physical *expressions* 5
§ 4. Such a science is further made possible by the fact that
mental phenomena occur under physical *conditions* . 9
§ 5. These physical conditions include certain nervous processes 10
§ 6. Nervous functions that are attended with mental life and
those that are not so attended; their general relations 11
§ 7. The three essential undertakings of psychological study . 12
§ 8. Psychological methods: (1) The study of the expressive
signs of mental life; (2) The study of the relations
between brain and mind 13
§ 9. Psychological methods: (3) Introspection; (4) Psychological experiment 16

CHAPTER II

THE PHYSICAL SIGNS OF THE PRESENCE OF MIND . . 20–57

§ 10. The signs of mental life. The discriminating sensitiveness of beings that possess minds 20
§ 11. The forms of this sensitiveness: (1) The signs of feeling 22
§ 12. The forms of discriminating sensitiveness continued:
(2) The signs of sensory experience 24
§ 13. Practical uses of the foregoing class of signs of mental
life. Difficulty of estimating these signs correctly . 27

PAGE

§ 14. The signs of sensory discrimination may seem to be present where there still may not be the corresponding consciousness. The heliotropism of plants and Loeb's general conception of a "tropism." Practical consequences as to these signs of mind 28

§ 15. The signs of mental life continued: The signs of the influence of former experience upon present conduct . . 32

§ 16. Inherited instincts and acquired habits. The latter as furnishing the signs of the influence of experience . 34

§ 17. Relation between the signs of the influence of experience and the signs of sensitiveness 36

§ 18. General definition of docility 37

§ 19. The signs of mental life continued: The signs of what seems to be spontaneity 38

§ 20. Difficulty of asserting the existence of spontaneity in the actions of any being. Docility may lead to what seems spontaneity 39

§ 21. Examples of what seem to be more genuine instances of spontaneity 42

§ 22. Provisional definition of the concept of mental initiative . 46

§ 23. The relation of the signs of initiative to the signs of docility 51

§ 24. Initiative in relation to what is often called "self-activity," and to the questions as to the influence of heredity and environment 53

§ 25. Summary: The signs of sensitiveness, of docility, and of initiative as the three classes of the signs of mind. Division of the later discussion 55

CHAPTER III

THE NERVOUS CONDITIONS OF THE MANIFESTATION OF MIND   58–80

§ 26. The structure of the nervous system. The neurons . 58

§ 27. Sensory and motor nerves 61

§ 28. Characteristics of cerebral processes: Habit, localization of function, generalized and specialized habits. "Set" of brain 64

§ 29. Relation of the cortex to lower nervous centres. Guidance, coördination, inhibition 70

PAGE

§ 30. Inhibition considered more in detail. Its importance . 70

§ 31. Examples of inhibition in relation to mental processes. The hierarchy of functions 73

§ 32. Practical applications of the principle of the inhibitory character of the higher nervous processes . . . 75

CHAPTER IV

GENERAL FEATURES OF CONSCIOUS LIFE 81–118

§ 33. What cerebral functions are attended by conscious life ? . 81

§ 34. The "stream of consciousness" and its "contents" . . 82

§ 35. The "unity of consciousness." What it means and its general relation to the variety of our conscious states . 85

§ 36. The variety of our conscious states as an essential condition of our consciousness and of its unity . . . 89

§ 37. Difference and sameness as inseparable relations amongst the various states present within the unity of consciousness. The relation of sameness and difference to unity and variety and to one another 90

§ 38. Practical applications of the principles regarding the relations of sameness and difference. How we teach people to note resemblances and differences . . 94

§ 39. The unity of consciousness as not only simultaneous, but successive. The "present moment" as possessing a finite length 95

§ 40. The question whether our mental life is a complex consisting of certain ultimate elements. The concept of elementary sensations and feelings 97

§ 41. The concept of mental elements more generally stated. Mental elements in relation to cerebral functions. The "blending" of mental elements 100

§ 42. Psychological experiment as a means of isolating and defining the mental elements 103

§ 43. Examples of the analysis of conscious states. The analysis of musical sounds and of other complexes . . . 104

§ 44. Criticism of the foregoing theory of the constitution of our conscious life. The "mental elements" exist when they are consciously observed, not otherwise. Analysis alters the consciousness that is analysed . . . 107

PAGE

§ 45. And nevertheless the theory of the mental elements expresses important truths. What the experimental analyses do show concerning our consciousness . . 112

§ 46. The law that for any ordinary state of consciousness an analysed state or series of states can be *substituted*. Significance of this law 115

§ 47. Classification of the subsequent discussion . . . 117

CHAPTER V

SENSITIVENESS. *A*. SENSORY EXPERIENCE 119–147

§ 48. The concept of a sensation 119
§ 49. The relation of consciousness to sensations . . . 120
§ 50. Sensations as relatively simple mental states experimentally producible 122
§ 51. Every grade and form of normal consciousness is affected by the accompanying sensory experience. Practical consequences of this principle. Examples . . . 123
§ 52. External and internal sensory experience and their general relationships 129
§ 53. Organic and dermal sensory experience 131
§ 54. Sensory experiences of taste, smell, sight, and hearing . 134
§ 55. The attributes of sensation. Quality and intensity . . 136
§ 56. Extensity as an attribute of sensory experience. The bases of our knowledge of space. The relation of space to the reactions of orientation 139

CHAPTER VI

SENSITIVENESS. *B*. MENTAL IMAGERY 148–162

§ 57. Definition and characteristics of mental images . . 148
§ 58. The classes of mental images. Galton's inquiries. The types of imagery characteristic of different minds . 151
§ 59. Relations of mental images to consciousness in general, to current sensory experience, and to motor processes and tendencies. Practical considerations concerning mental imagery 157

CHAPTER VII

PAGE

SENSITIVENESS. *C.* THE FEELINGS 163–196

§ 60. The feelings in general. Their traditional relation to the
intellect and the will. Their place in the present study 163

§ 61. Elementary feelings not as extensively to be studied by
experiment as are elementary sensations. The "subjective" character of feelings 165

§ 62. The classification of the feelings into those of pleasure
and those of displeasure. Apparent difficulty about
this classification. Usual answer to this difficulty . 167

§ 63. The antagonism of pleasure and displeasure. Their relation to conduct 171

§ 64. Further difficulties in the way of viewing the foregoing
classification as exhaustive. The "mixed" feelings
and their complexity 173

§ 65. Wundt's "three-dimensional" classification of the feelings 176

§ 66. Hypothesis of a *two*-dimensional classification of the feelings. Two pairs of opposed tendencies in feeling:
(1) Pleasure and displeasure; (2) Restlessness and
quiescence 177

§ 67. Characterisation of pleasure and displeasure. Characterisation of restlessness and quiescence . . . 179

§ 68. The quiescent and the restless states of displeasure and
the restless and quiescent pleasures 182

§ 69. Relation of the two pairs of antagonistic feelings to consciousness in general 184

§ 70. The four types of mixed feelings more exactly defined
and illustrated 185

§ 71. The relatively simple states of feeling. Relation of restlessness and quiescence, and of pleasure and displeasure, to the attention 189

§ 72. Review of the whole survey of conscious processes up to
the present point. Question as to the completeness of
the classification, thus far given, of our present conscious states. Is the will such as to include still other
sorts of mental states? 192

PAGE

§ 73. The place of the will in consciousness. The relation of
will to sensory experience, to imagery, and to feeling.
Result as to the completeness of the classification up
to the present point   193

CHAPTER VIII

THE GENERAL LAW OF DOCILITY   197–217

§ 74. The evidences of docility are furnished by facts that have
to do both with knowledge and with conduct   .   .   197
§ 75. The cerebral law of habit and its relation to our conscious
processes   198
§ 76. The process of formation of a new habit; simplification;
welding of partial processes into unity. Training welds
simultaneous as well as successive functions   .   .   200
§ 77. The law of association as the expression of the law of
habit in mental terms. Inadequacy of this expression.
Simultaneous and successive association   .   .   .   203
§ 78. Consequences of the inadequacy of the mental process to
represent the complexity of the cerebral process. Association by similarity. Its reduction to the law of
habit   205
§ 79. The theory that association binds mental elements together. Criticism of this theory   208
§ 80. The traditional forms of association   209
§ 81. Inadequacy of the general law of association to determine
what one of various possible associations shall prove
effective in any one case   210
§ 82. Vividness and recency as factors which determine the
course of association   212
§ 83. Factors which determine the course of association (con-
cluded) : The present " set " of the brain   .   .   .   214

CHAPTER IX

DOCILITY. A. PERCEPTION AND ACTION   218–228

§ 84. General plan of the following discussion   218
§ 85. General relation of perceptions to actions. Illustration
from the life of infancy   218

PAGE

§ 86. Perception and action in adult life 221
§ 87. The feelings which accompany perception. The feeling of familiarity 224
§ 88. Practical consequences of the relations between perception and action 225

CHAPTER X

DOCILITY. *B.* ASSIMILATION 229–247

§ 89. Assimilation, differentiation, and the social aspect of docility as the remaining aspects of docility to be treated in this discussion 229
§ 90. The assimilation of new habits to old ones as a consequence of the law of habit 231
§ 91. The mental aspect of the process of assimilation . . 234
§ 92. Illustrations of mental assimilation. The Herbartian "Apperception". 235
§ 93. Illustrations of mental assimilation (continued): Our memory of the past as an assimilative process. Errors of memory which result 236
§ 94. Further illustrations of defective memory . . . 239
§ 95. The assimilative process is never the only aspect of our conscious relation to our experience 242
§ 96. Assimilation in its relations to the thinking process. "Explanation" and reasoning as assimilative processes 245

CHAPTER XI

DOCILITY. *C.* DIFFERENTIATION 248–273

§ 97. The general nature of the differentiation which accompanies the development of the mind 248
§ 98. The derivation of our consciousness of simultaneous variety from our consciousness of successive variety . 250
§ 99. Illustration from our consciousness of space . . . 252
§ 100. Education as an instance of differentiation. Practical importance of the dramatic element in instruction . 254
§ 101. Judgment, and the thinking process in general, as a process of differentiation. Analysis and synthesis . 255

                                                            PAGE
§ 102. Practical consequences 257
§ 103. The process of attention as an aspect of the process of
            differentiation 258
§ 104. The limits of differentiation and the "psycho-physic law" 264
§ 105. The psycho-physic law as a law not of sensation, but of
            the limitations of our docility 268

CHAPTER XII

DOCILITY. *D*. THE SOCIAL ASPECT OF THE HIGHER FORMS OF
            DOCILITY 274–298

§ 106. Human mental life as primarily social 274
§ 107. The bases of social consciousness: Imitation . . . 275
§ 108. The bases of social consciousness: The love of opposition 277
§ 109. The general relations of the thinking process to social
            stimulations and habits. Why language becomes so
            significant for the development of the thinking process 280
§ 110. The formation of general ideas 285
§ 111. General ideas as "plans of action" 288
§ 112. Social activities as the means of bringing these plans of
            action to clear consciousness 290
§ 113. Judgment as dependent for its development upon social
            conditions 292
§ 114. The social aspect of the development of the reasoning
            process 293
§ 115. The social aspect of the development of self-consciousness 296

CHAPTER XIII

THE CONDITIONS OF MENTAL INITIATIVE 299–332

§ 116. The problem as to the possibility of mental initiative
            stated 299
§ 117. The early imperfection and the slow development of the
            manifestations of our inherited tendencies to action . 302
§ 118. Consequences of these facts for the early training of the
            individual 304
§ 119. The persistence of the young organism in acts that are
            not yet adaptive 306

PAGE

§ 120. Illustrations of the restless persistence in acts that are so
far not adaptive in the case of adult animal organisms   312

§ 121. Illustrations of a similar restless persistence in adult
human beings   315

§ 122. Such restless persistence in advance of adaptation as
the one source of significant initiative in conduct and
in mind   318

§ 123. Illustrations from the plays of children   319

§ 124. Illustrations of a similar initiative in the activities of
youth   324

§ 125. Illustrations of restless persistence in case of the social
tendencies toward individualism   326

§ 126. Ordinary active attention as a process of restless persistence in advance of adaptation. Attention and the
"tropisms" of Loeb   328

§ 127. The bases of all initiative are to be found in "tropisms"
that lead to a restless persistence in types of action
which are not yet adaptive. Practical consequences   330

CHAPTER XIV

CERTAIN VARIETIES OF EMOTIONAL AND INTELLECTUAL LIFE   333–363

§ 128. Recapitulation and survey of further practical applications   333

§ 129. The nature of the emotions   335

§ 130. The relation of the emotions to their physical expression   337

§ 131. The practical aspect of the life of the emotions. Emotional variability. The emotional "undertone"   .   340

§ 132. Abnormal emotions. The sexual emotions and their
abnormities. Practical considerations as to the abnormities of emotional life in general   .   .   .   343

§ 133. The intellectual life in general. Principles that preside
over its practical guidance   349

§ 134. The abnormities of the intellectual life. Secondary
impairment of the intellectual life   .   .   .   352

§ 135. Primary intellectual disorders illustrated. Hallucinations
and delusions   355

§ 136. Eccentricity of intellectual life. Practical rule for judging "original" characters and persons   .   .   .   360

CHAPTER XV

PAGE

THE WILL OR THE DIRECTION OF CONDUCT 364–379

§ 137. The will, in the wider sense of the term, as our whole
        consciousness of our activity 364

§ 138. The relation of attention to volition. Choice, and the
        will in the narrower sense 367

§ 139. Conscious choice and its unoriginal character. The will
        in the narrower sense takes its rise in "involuntary"
        action 369

§ 140. Illustration of volition by the case of the growth of the
        speech-function 371

§ 141. The practical aspect of the training of the will . . 373

§ 142. Abnormities of volition 375

EDITOR'S INTRODUCTION

As Psychology has taken on something of the aspect of a natural science, it has presented new difficulties to the student. The natural sciences are based on an elaborate series of presuppositions, none of which are tested or examined by those sciences. The older form of psychology began by setting forth its presuppositions, many of them crude and untenable, perhaps, but nevertheless it made the fact clear that the superstructure had a foundation of some sort. Psychology as now expounded is as chary of stating its presuppositions as is physics, with consequent loss of clearness and cogency to the philosophically minded student. As a result, there is constant need for a summing-up and interpretation of the results of special inquiries and investigations. Without this summing-up and interpretation, the student of psychology in its newer forms is lost in a maze of details, whose interrelations he comprehends very imperfectly, if at all.

It may be assumed, I think, that the fundamental fact to be grasped in psychology is what has been called the "isolation of the individual mind." Professor Royce refers to this in his opening paragraphs. When this viewpoint is clearly held, then the function and value of the several methods used in psychology, as well as the significance of the departments into which its facts are classified, become plain. Genetic, comparative, and social psychology are then terms with a real meaning, and such qualifying words as "rational," "experimental," and "physiological" are seen to have reference primarily to methods of study, rather than to varying data.

The student of psychology must put to himself these questions and others like them, and must search in his study for the grounds on which correct answers to them rest:—

How and by what warrant do I pass from a knowledge of my own mental states to a knowledge and interpretation of the mental states of others? What are the primary evidences of mind? Into what and how few simplest units can my own complex mental states be broken up? What are the processes of mental growth and development, and what laws govern them?

If he gains clear and reasonable convictions on such points as these, he has not studied psychology in vain.

There has been much useless and misleading discussion as to the special value of psychology to the teacher. I fail to see how the proposition that a knowledge of psychology is of use to the teacher is open to discussion at all, unless through a juggling with the plain meaning of words. That the average teacher need not spend much time in mastering the more technical details of modern psychology, is obvious; but it is equally obvious that the average teacher should be familiar with what may, perhaps, be called general psychology, particularly in its genetic aspects. No process is known to man by which knowledge will surely be converted into sympathy and insight; but sympathy and insight, however great, are invariably made greater when knowledge is added to them.

In this belief, Professor Royce's exposition of the main facts and principles of psychology is gladly included in a series of volumes intended particularly to meet the needs of studious teachers.

NICHOLAS MURRAY BUTLER.

COLUMBIA UNIVERSITY, NEW YORK,
April 15, 1903.

OUTLINES OF PSYCHOLOGY

CHAPTER I

INTRODUCTORY DEFINITIONS AND EXPLANATIONS

§ 1. Psychology, in a general way, has the same sort
of relation to the functions of the human mind that
physiology has to the functions of the human body.
Psychology is, namely, the doctrine which attempts to
describe our mental life, and, as far as possible, to discover its conditions and its laws. And by our mental
life, as opposed to our physical life, we mean a certain
collection of states and of processes with which, from
moment to moment, each one of us is, in his own case,
very directly or immediately acquainted, while, on the
other hand, it is impossible that any one else besides
the original observer, whose mental life this is, should
ever get this immediate sort of acquaintance with just
this collection of states and processes. Herein, then, lies
the essential characteristic of our mental life. Others
may learn, from observing our acts and our words, a
great deal *about* this, our own mental life; but each one
of us is the only being capable of becoming directly
aware of his own mental states. On the other hand,

B   I

however, our physical life, in its external manifestations, may be observed by any one who gets the opportunity. And thus the fact that the mental life of each one of us can be directly present, as a series of experienced facts, to one person only, may well be used as a means of defining the difference between our physical and our mental life. Thus physical facts are usually conceived as "public property," patent to all properly equipped observers. All such observers, according to our customary view, see the *same* physical facts. But psychical facts are essentially "private property," existent for one alone. This constitutes the very conception of the difference between "inner" psychical or mental, and physical or "outer" facts — a conception behind which, in the following discussion, we shall not seek to go.[1]

---

[1] This method of defining the general nature of the mental world, and of distinguishing the mental from the physical world, is founded upon philosophical considerations which I have more fully explained elsewhere. Cf. my *Spirit of Modern Philosophy* (Boston, Riverside Press, 1892), Chapter XII; the essay on "Self-consciousness, Social Consciousness, and Nature," in my *Studies of Good and Evil* (New York, Appleton & Co., 1898); and the second and fourth lectures in my *Gifford Lectures; The World and the Individual, Second Series* (New York, The Macmillan Company, 1901). The present is no place for developing these metaphysical considerations. It may, however, interest the philosophically disposed reader to know that my own philosophical position is that of Constructive or Absolute Idealism, and that, accordingly, the distinction here made between the mental and the physical worlds is, to my mind, only a relative distinction due to the special conditions to which our human knowledge of both these worlds is subject. None the less, for

§ 2. It is this fundamental difference that leads us often to speak of the mental as the "internal life" or the "inner world," and to oppose it both to our own physical life and to the "external physical world." This way of expressing the distinction between mental facts and all others is fairly good, but must be carefully guarded against misinterpretation. The physiological processes of our bodies are physical, but are indeed also often viewed as "internal," since they go on within our bodies, and are in general mainly hidden from direct external observation. But our mental life is "internal" in quite a different sense. Digestion, circulation, and the changes of our tissues are processes which are actually altogether hidden from many forms of outer observation, and which, at best, can only be observed very partially, and for the most part very indirectly, by observers who view us from without. But, on the other hand, these processes, in the case of each one of us, are also very ill known to us ourselves, and are in large part not even indirectly represented by any of our own conscious mental states. So that, when we speak of our physiological processes as internal, the word "internal,"

human experience, in so far as it is concerned with the special sciences, the distinction here made is of paramount practical importance.

My colleague, Professor Münsterberg, whose philosophical position is not the same as my own, has nevertheless quite independently reached the same definition of the fundamental contrast between the mental and the material phenomena. See his *Psychology and Life* and his *Grundzüge der Psychologie*.

although it here generally implies "hidden, in whole
or in part, from actual outer observation," does *not*
imply "directly felt by us ourselves." But when we
speak of a pain as an "inner" mental fact, we mean
that while nobody but the sufferer can possibly get any
direct acquaintance with its presence, the sufferer himself can do so, and is aware of the pain. Furthermore,
the fact that other observers cannot directly watch our
inner physiological processes, is itself something relatively accidental, dependent upon the limitations of the
sense organs, or upon the defective instrumental devices,
of those who watch us. But the fact that our mental
states are incapable of observation by anybody but ourselves seems to be not an accidental, but an essential
character of these mental states. Were physiologists
better endowed with sense organs and with instruments
of exact observation, we can, if we choose, conceive
them as, by some now unknown device, coming to
watch the very molecules of our brains; but we cannot
conceive them, in any possible case, as observing from
without our pains or our thoughts in the sense in which
physical facts are observable. Were my body as trans-
parent as crystal, or could all my internal physical
functions be viewed and studied as easily as one now
observes a few small particles eddying in a glass of
nearly clear water, my mental states could not even
then be seen floating in my brain. No microscope
could conceivably reveal them. To me alone would

these states be known. And I should not see them from without; I should simply *find* them, or *be aware* of them. And what it is to find them, or to be aware of them, I alone can tell myself.

§ 3. Mental life has thus been defined by pointing out its contrast with all that is physical. Now, psychology is to undertake the study of mental life for the sake of trying to describe and, in a measure, to explain its facts. But this undertaking may, for the first, appear to be quite hopeless. How can one describe, with any sort of accuracy, where the facts to be described are in any case open to the inspection of one observer only? Successful description, made with any scientific purpose, seems to involve the possibility of comparing together the various attempts at description made by different observers in view of the same facts. When astronomers observe celestial objects, they compare the results of the various observations of different astronomers. Upon the multitude of trained observers, occupying, upon occasion, widely different positions on the earth's surface, but all looking at the same heavenly bodies, the possibility of the growth of astronomical science seems to depend. How, then, shall psychology progress if, in our various mental lives, no two observers can ever take note of precisely the same facts? Is it not as if there were as many real moons as there are astronomers observing the heavens, and a different real moon for each astronomer, which nobody but himself could ever see? In such a case, one may ask, What would become of astronomy?

Without in the least going into the extended and interesting philosophical problems suggested by these questions, it is enough here to point out at once that, while no two persons among us can ever observe the same series of mental facts and processes, psychological study is nevertheless made possible by the fact (a fact of the most fundamental importance) that we all of us not only have our mental states, but also appear to *give these mental states a physical expression* in certain bodily acts, viz., in what may be called our expressive functions. The mental states themselves each one of us observes for himself alone. Their physical expression is something that, like any other physical fact, is patent to all observers.

Now, any one of us can often observe for himself what sort of physical expression some given sort of mental states gets in his own case. Thus one can sometimes observe how, by cries or by groans, he himself gives expression to his own pain; or how, by appropriate bodily attitudes, he expresses the mental states of attentive interest which we call "looking," "listening," "watching," and the like; or, finally, how he adapts the familiar words of his mother-tongue to the expression of multitudinous inner moods, and other personal experiences, for many of which, in fact, we have no definite and conscious bodily expression at our voluntary disposal *except* such words as chance to occur to us as appropriate at the moment when these states are passing. Cries, groans, sighs, tears, gestures, attitudes, words, and other far less easily observable expressions — some voluntary, some involuntary — are thus found to accompany our mental processes. But all these expressive movements are themselves facts in the physical world, and are, as such, matters both for common observation and for exact scientific scrutiny. Most of these expressive acts show marked similarity, either in several, in many, or in all men. And meanwhile, what states in each one of us they express, the individual observer experiences for himself. In attempting to describe our mental experiences to one another we therefore constantly make use of the names of familiar expressive functions, such as laughter, weeping, and the like.

Some of our expressive acts, like the ones just named, viewed apart from their names, are of instinctive origin and are only partially under the influence of conventions. Other expressive acts, like the use of the words of our mother-tongue to embody or to describe our mental states, are of purely conventional origin, and have only become moulded by slow degrees to a certain sort of uniformity as regards their relation to similar mental states in many people. Whether one person means by the word "love" a state very closely similar to the state that another person means by the same word may be, and often is, a very difficult question to decide. Yet the use of the words of our common mother-tongue to express our mental states, guided as this use has been since childhood by the effort to conform our expressions to the comprehension of our fellows, is often brought to a point which enables us to be decidedly sure that the states which many people agree in describing in given words are themselves in pretty close agreement. With some caution, the same may be regarded as true, within limits, as to the states described in various languages by parallel words and phrases.

While we are then unable to make our mental states objects of common observation, in the sense in which the astronomers are said to observe the same star, we nevertheless can observe in common our natural and conventional, our simple and complex, our voluntary and involuntary, our more subtle and our less subtle motor expressions of our mental states, whether in our outward deeds or in the permanent products of these deeds (as in works of skilful art), or in our words, or in our momentary gestures, or, finally, in our established habits of behaviour. The inner meaning of such expressions each of us can, by more or less attentive scrutiny, discover for himself. Their agreement in many persons enables mental facts, private though they be, to be indirectly submitted to a comparative study in many people, and to some sort of generalisation, classification, and even explanation.

§ 4. While this outward physical expression, which our mental life gets, makes psychology, as a comparative and more or less scientific study of mind, possible, our study itself is very greatly aided by a further consideration, viz., that we not only express our minds through our movements, but seem to ourselves to be *dependent*, for at least very much of our mental life, *upon more or less definable physical conditions*, which we recognise, even apart from any special study, as matters well known in daily life, and as matters which we can study in common. Thus the private mental condition is noticed by its one observer to vary with the presence or absence of physical facts that he and his fellows can observe together. That one cannot see in the dark, that one feels cold at a time when the thermometer reveals the physical fact of a low temperature, that violent physical exercise makes one weary — these are facts which have, at the very same time, their psychical aspect manifest to one observer, and their physical aspect manifest to all observers. A more scientific study, moreover, shows us that not merely some, but all of our mental states vary with physical conditions of one sort or another. Now, this sort of union of the public and the private, of the generally accessible and of the purely individual, gives us many means for indirectly comparing and classifying mental facts and for studying their conditions in various people.

§ 5. But both the expressive movements and the physical conditions thus far mentioned prove, upon closer examination, to have a character as physical processes that makes them still further the topics of a scientific scrutiny; for we possess, as a most important part of our physical structure, *our nervous systems*. And it may be shown that the expressive physical functions (acts, gestures, words, habits, etc.) in which our mental life gets its outward representation and embodiment, are all of them, as physical events, *determined by physiological processes that occur in our nervous systems*. In other words, the functions of the nervous system, while they include many other processes as well, still also include, as a portion of themselves, precisely those functions by which, from moment to moment, our mental states get expressed. Thus the scientific study of our expressive functions becomes linked to the general study of nervous physiology. On the other hand, however, those numerous physical conditions, both without and within our bodies, which have been mentioned as appearing to determine in some way our mental states, prove to be conditions that are effective *in so far as they at the same time physically influence our nervous systems*. Thus in two ways the scientific study of mental life may get aid from the study of the nervous system.

§ 6. Now the physical functions of the nervous system are capable of a very extended comparative and experimental investigation. Those of the nervous functions which are not closely related (as apparent conditions or as expressions) to our mental processes, appear, in the light of such study, to differ from those nervous functions which are so related, chiefly in respect of the relative simplicity of the nervous functions which are not thus closely related to the mind, when compared with the relative complexity of those nervous functions which are more intimately related to mental processes. But no one easily definable dividing line appears between the two, except the familiar fact that the nervous functions most closely related to our mental life are localised, so far as concerns their central stations, in the cortex or grey matter at the external surface of the brain, while the nervous functions that have no discoverable mental accompaniment are, for the most part, directed from centres placed below the level of this brain cortex. Otherwise, as we shall see from time to time hereafter, it is hard to prove any essential difference in kind between the physical functions whose nervous conditions are centred in the cortex and those which are centred lower down. The higher functions are, indeed, often vastly the more complex. They change much more during life, and under the influence of our experience, than do our lower nervous functions. They show more signs of what is often called "spontaneity"—that is, of a certain relative (although never complete) independence of the present external physical surroundings in which our body chances to be placed. But these, although large differences, are differences of degree. Physically speaking, and despite vast differences in detail, the same general or fundamental types, both of structure and of function, are observable, both high up and low down in the nervous centres.

§ 7. Yet one must insist that the study of neurological facts has, although very great, still only relative value for the psychologist. For one thing, what the psychologist wants to understand is mental life, and to this end he uses all his other facts only as means; and for the rest, *any physical expression of mental life* which we can learn to interpret, becomes as genuinely interesting to the psychologist as does a brain function. A pyramid or a flint hatchet, a poem or a dance, a game or a war, a cry or a book, the nursery play of a child or the behaviour of an insane person, may be a physical expression of mental life such as the appreciative psychologist can both observe and more or less fully comprehend. The study of such facts, and of their physical causes and results, throws light both upon what goes on in minds and upon the place which minds occupy in the natural world. To be a student of psychology thus involves three essential things: (1) to observe carefully the signs which express mental life, and to interpret these expressions as far as possible; (2) to examine those physical processes which in any case appear to condition mental life or to cause its expressions to occur; and (3), with constant reference to the foregoing classes of facts, to describe by means of a self-examination, or "introspection," the one series of mental facts which can alone be directly observed by the individual psychologist. Studies of the sorts (1) and (2) can be made by all properly equipped observers together, and in presence of what are called the "same" external facts. Studies of the sort (3) each psychologist must make alone for himself; but by the aid of the facts acquired through studies of the sorts (2) and (3) he can indirectly compare his introspective results with those of other psychologists. The first two sorts of study are very greatly furthered by what we know of the nervous system, but are by no means confined to this region of knowledge. Psychology is by no means a branch of neurology. On the contrary, wherever, in the physical world, any mind gets intelligible expression, or any physical conditions appear to determine mental states, the psychologist finds what he wants, in so far as he seeks means of comparing his introspective observations with the experiences of other minds.

§ 8. The foregoing conditions already serve to define the principal methods of psychology, whereof we may next name the most important.

(1) Our first method — *the study of the expressive signs of mental life* — is in some forms extremely familiar to the popular mind. Every person of any experience is his own psychologist in judging almost constantly the ideas, moods, and intents of his fellows, by watching not only their faces, but also their whole range of voluntary and involuntary expressive movements. The relatively scientific use of such study as a method of more careful psychological investigation depends both upon extending the range of its application, and upon rendering more minute the scrutiny employed. The naturalist employs this method when he studies the minds of animals through an observation of their behaviour and of their skill. It should be carefully remembered, however, that not merely the passing functions of the moment, but the established habits and the permanent physical productions of any animal, are of importance as outwardly expressing its mind ; and a similar thing holds of physical facts and processes that express the coöperative work of many intelligent beings. Works of art, institutions, languages, customs, faiths, cities, national life in general — all these things and processes are instances of complex expressions of mental life in outwardly observable physical forms.

The inevitable dangers and difficulties of this, the most constantly employed of all the methods of studying minds, are meanwhile, in part, well known. The facts to be studied are very numerous and complex, and easily misjudged, especially in case of minds that are markedly different from our own. A good example of this difficulty is the common failure of even very intelligent men to understand a good many among the expressive functions of women, or the similar failure of women to comprehend a great many among those of men. The barrier of sex will probably prove a permanent hindrance, in some important directions and regions, to the progress of the scientific study of the human mind, so far as that study seeks to make the mental life of one sex fully comprehensible to psychologists who belong to the other.

(2) The second method of the psychologist begins by proceeding backwards from the study of the outwardly expressive functions, in which our mental states get a sort of embodiment, to the scrutiny of their nervous conditions. These, once found to be, as they are, centred in the organisation and in the functions of the brain, this second method develops into that of the *study of the relations that exist between mental life and brain processes.* This method is necessarily an indirect one. It takes very numerous special forms. One of these is furnished by the study of nervous diseases, with reference to those changes, in the expressive signs of mental life, which are the result of whatever form of nervous disorder is each time in question. In so far as the phenomena of insanity are already, despite our defective knowledge, traceable to otherwise known and

definable physical disorders of the nervous system, the study of such phenomena for the purpose of the psychologist also obviously belongs here. A further extension of the present method is offered by those experiments upon the nervous systems of animals which involve any noteworthy and intelligible changes in the signs of mind which these animals show. And it is thus that the functions of the brain have been frequently and very fruitfully studied during the last twenty-five years, despite the difficulty of drawing exact conclusions as regards the human brain and the human mind from the interpretation of such experiments. Nor does the use of the present method cease here; for, apart from disease and from vivisection, we are able to perform an experiment upon the functions of the brain whenever (as by stimulating our sense organs in particular ways) we can harmlessly bring about any physical change in a living man, whose mental life can indirectly be studied through his own accounts of it, while the physical effect that the experiment has upon his brain functions is meanwhile capable of a more or less determinate estimate. It is in this way that we study what is sometimes called "the physiology of the senses."

§ 9. (3) In close connection with the first, and in frequent connection with the second of the foregoing methods, stands the *method of introspection*, by which the individual psychologist *undertakes to observe his own mental states and processes.* If carried on alone, without constant reference to the physical conditions of the mental life observed, and without a frequent comparing of notes with one's fellows, introspection can accomplish little of service for psychology. But, in union with other methods, introspection becomes an absolutely indispensable adjunct to all serious psychological study. The man who has never observed within will never be able to interpret the minds of others. The student of neurology can directly contribute to psychological science only in case he learns to scrutinise carefully his individual mental processes, even while he indirectly learns about their nervous conditions. Introspection is, however, for the scientific psychologist, despite its importance, rather to be used as an auxiliary of the other methods than as a method capable of leading the way. For psychology is concerned with what is common to many or to all human minds. We are guided in our search for these common characters of minds by studying the expressions and the conditions of mental life. Introspection helps us mainly to an *interpretation* of the common features. However expert a man may be in his own mental states, it therefore takes a wide intercourse with his fellows, an outwardly observant examination of the signs of mind in others, and a careful study of the physical conditions in which given mental states arise, to reach any conclusions worthy of scientific consideration. The truly great " introspective psychologists " of the past, from Aristotle down, were none of them, as psychologists, at all exclusively devoted to the study of their own personal experiences. They were, for instance, greatly influenced both by the traditional views of their social order, and by the popular psychology which lay more or less concealed in the languages that they used.

(4) A centrally important modern method, which unites or may unite features belonging to all the foregoing methods, is the method of *psychological experiment* in the stricter sense. This method involves *bringing to pass mental processes of greater or less complexity* (acts of attention, simple acts of will or more complex acts of choice, associations of ideas, processes of memory or of computation, emotional states, etc.) *under physical and mental conditions which can be exactly controlled or determined.* Then, according as he wishes, the psychologist studies one or more of the various noteworthy aspects of the situation that has been experimentally brought to pass. Thus one can examine by direct introspection what goes on in a single observer under the circumstance of a given experiment. Here one takes advantage of the definiteness which the experimental devices may give to the whole experience. Or again, in a series of related experiments, one can introspectively note how the mental states or processes alter as the physical conditions undergo certain determinate variations. Further, through comparing the reports, or the other expressive signs which various subjects give

of what goes on in their minds under similar experimental conditions, one can get results as to the relations that exist between the mental life of various people. In some cases it is also possible to determine, to a certain extent, what physical changes in the central nervous system are produced by the experiment, and thus our knowledge of the relations of particular nervous and particular mental states may be furthered.

Very important results have also flowed from the careful noting of the various time relations of any or of all the foregoing classes of facts as they occur when exact experimental conditions have been established. The problem, how long a given mental process takes, and how this time element varies with given variations in the situation, is one of great interest to the psychologist.

Experimental psychology is the most recent of the branches of psychological work. For the most part it has to be carried on in special laboratories, where there are instrumental means for measuring time relations, as well as for determining precisely the physical conditions under which the mental processes to be studied take place.

CHAPTER II

The Physical Signs of the Presence of Mind

§ 10. In view of what has now been said about methods, we may best begin our analysis of the general characteristics of mental life by asking what are the most general classes of expressive signs by which the living beings that have minds manifest to us their mental life. How, then, do those animals which are high enough in the scale to seem to show us that they certainly possess mental life differ from those living beings which, like the plants, give us no such manifestations?

The most general answer to this question is, on the whole, not very difficult. When a cat watches for a mouse, when a dog finds his way home over strange country, we do not doubt that here are real signs of the presence of mind. When a tree that is cut with the axe shows no sign of feeling the blow, we note that here signs of mind are absent. To be quite certain just where to draw the line between living beings that seem to have no minds and living beings that possess minds, does indeed involve us in great difficulties. But there are some general signs of mind which we all usually regard as unmistakable, and some cases of lack that seem to us to exclude the presence of any functions such as the psychologist studies.

In the most general way of viewing the matter, beings that seem to us to possess minds show in their physical life what we may call *a great and discriminating sensitiveness to what goes on at any present time in their environment.* And by this their sensitiveness we here mean something which, though a sign of mind, is itself purely physical, viz., a capacity, observable from without, to adjust themselves by fitting movements, or by their internal physical functions, to what takes place near them. This sensitiveness is called *discriminating* because it is never a mere tendency to respond to every sort of change at random, or to all effective changes in the same way; but it is a tendency to respond to *some* changes (*e.g.* light or sound) rather than to others, and to *various* changes in *various* fitting ways. To be sure, plants also show very many signs of well-adjusted responses to the changes in their environments. And even so those functions of animals which need show no signs of any mental accompaniments (*e.g.* gland secretions, or the regulation of the body's temperature) are also discriminatingly sensitive, in the physical sense, to external conditions. But the matter is here first one of degree. Greater, quicker, or else more highly elaborate is the sensitiveness of the beings that appear to have minds, as it is shown in their expressive functions. Duller, or slower, or else simpler, appears the physical sensitiveness of the non-mental being or function when the environment changes.

But it is not merely this very general difference in degree which we note when we consider this discriminating sensitiveness as a general sign of the presence of mind. If we come closer to the facts, we next note that the general sensitiveness of the beings that have minds determines itself, as we watch it, in various special ways, and expresses itself in conduct, whose relation to the *former experience* of the creature in question, and whose apparent *spontaneity* and *variability* it concerns us to study. Let us, therefore, examine a little more closely the various classes of signs of mind.

§ 11. (1) The sensitiveness of the psychically endowed beings first manifests itself by what, with a ready sympathy, we easily interpret as signs of *satisfaction* or of *dissatisfaction*, of *pleasure* or of *pain*, and of various emotions. These signs, in their simplest forms, are so well known that we need hardly describe them. Where, as in the earthworm, we can detect nothing that we ordinarily call intelligence, we seem to be able to note the signs of pain. Writhing, withdrawal from a source of injury, and other simple movements of an obviously protective character, are such elementary signs of dissatisfaction. Still other movements, even in very low forms of life, seem to indicate satisfaction. Higher up in the animal scale we meet

with reactions of fear, of anger, of joy, of the more
elaborate forms of desire, and, in the end, of numerous
other emotional states. We may for the present class
all these as the SIGNS OF FEELING. The beings that
have minds thus seem to us, from the first, *to show
signs of more or less immediately valuing, or estimating, their own state, or their own relation to their
environment.*

It must be remarked that we are not here at all concerned with the question whether our usual interpretation of these kinds of feelings in case of lower animals,
and especially in case of animals far distant from ourselves, is an actually correct interpretation. In case of
human beings, our interpretations of such signs of mental life are subject to a social control that makes us
able to criticise, with more or less success, their accuracy. But in case of lower animals, such control is
no longer possible. Nevertheless, the signs of mental
life that we seem to get, the movements that we are
disposed to interpret as of psychical significance, in
case of organisms decidedly distant in character from
our own, are often so simple as to suggest at once a
certain useful analysis of our own mental processes,
when we compare the latter with the mental processes
which these creatures seem to exhibit. For the human
being shows us signs of feeling that are inseparable
from the signs which he gives us of his intelligence or
of his volition. Hence we do not at once so easily dis-

tinguish between his feelings and the rest of his mental life. The lower organism that shows no indications of higher intelligence, but that simply indicates what we readily take to be a state of feeling, may indeed not be exhibiting to us any genuine sign of consciousness whatever. Or, at least, if the signs do stand for a genuine consciousness, the psychologist may be unable to interpret the facts with the clearness possible in case of human beings. Yet the analogy of these simpler reactions to certain aspects, present in the behaviour of human beings, are useful to us for the purpose of beginning an analysis both of the functions and of the mental processes that appear in connection with higher organisms. Hence the use of these symptoms that, while extremely simple, still seem to us to manifest mental life. We cite them here, not because their interpretation is psychologically certain, but because they attract our attention to an aspect of mental life which we shall henceforth distinguish, namely, the aspect of the feelings.

§ 12. (2) The second manifestation of the sensitiveness of beings that appear to us to have minds takes the form of tendencies on their part *to discriminate between the various kinds of physical facts and processes in their environment, to react to some and not to others, and to react in such a way, to those by which they are influenced, as seems to show us that they discriminate between these various classes of physical facts.* The manifestations of sensitiveness which thus appear are very closely bound up with those signs of feeling, that is of satisfaction and dissatisfaction, which we have just characterised. On the other hand, these signs of sensitiveness to the physical differences of the environment tend from the very first to a far greater *specialisation* than is possessed by the mere signs of feeling as such. Thus, the creature endowed with what we take to be mental characteristics may appear to be sensitive to the presence of light, and sensitive to differences in intensity of light or in the colour of the light. Or it may respond to considerable jars and shocks which occur in the physical environment. Or again, it may behave differently according to whether the more delicate form of vibration which constitutes a sound is present or not, or according as it is touched or not by an external physical object. Its reactions in the presence of such stimuli may take the simple form of approaching the source of the stimuli, or of otherwise moving so as to increase the stimuli, as if the resulting experiences were agreeable. Or the reactions may seem to express dissatisfaction with some stimulus, through a tendency to remove the organism from exposure thereto. But on the basis of these more fundamental and simple reactions of approach and retreat there develop, in all higher creatures, a very richly varied collection of responses for which the only general description is *that they tend to be different for different stimuli, and the same for the same stimulus.* Thus, the reactions to light tend to include the acts which we interpret as *looking.* They may also tend to involve a vast number of reactions which we interpret as involving discriminations of colours and shades. And similar varieties exist in case of other senses.

Now it is true that, in all the higher animals, such discriminating sensitiveness shows itself, at least in the animal that has for some time been exposed to disturbance, principally in connection with the signs of mind that we shall mention in our subsequent enumeration — that is, in connection with the signs of what is called recognition, of intellect, or of choice. Yet all the higher and more complex reactions of an animal must depend upon its power to discriminate between the various disturbances that come to it from without. Whatever habits it may acquire, however much it may seem to be independent of its present situation, and dependent upon its past experience, still its present behaviour is, in all normal cases, sure to be decidedly influenced by its present relation to its environment. The signs of mind thus obtained are the SIGNS OF SENSORY EXPERIENCE; and so the discriminating sensitiveness of any creature to the impressions which the environment is constantly making upon its organism is, quite apart from the relation of this sensitiveness to the signs of feeling, a highly important factor in determining our estimate of the sort of mental life that the creature possesses.

§ 13. It seems well to add here some words as to the psychological uses and the limitations of the present class of the signs of mind. In our intercourse with human beings we sometimes too readily overlook the importance of the present relations of the organism to the environment as determining what goes on in mental life. Thus, a teacher may be disposed to charge a pupil with stupidity, when a closer examination reveals the fact that the defect in the child's conduct is due to some slighter derangement of sense organs. So the short-sighted or the astigmatic pupil may be accused of stupidity, or inattentiveness, or even of malicious unwillingness to study, because his defect of vision makes him unable to discriminate objects seen on a blackboard at a certain distance, or in certain relationships to one another. Similar accusations may be even more easily made with injustice in case a pupil suffers from a slight deafness. In all such instances the failure to make a correct diagnosis of mental life depends upon not observing, or upon not interpreting correctly, the signs of the presence or absence of a certain condition of sensitiveness to present impressions, on the part of the organism in question. In other words, the signs of mental life are misinterpreted, in such wise that what is due to a defect of sense organs is judged as a defect of the intellect, or of the will, in other words, as a defect in the habits and in the self-direction of the pupil. It follows that the study of mind *must always take account of the difference between what is due to the present relation of the creature to its environment, and what is due to the relation between its present experience and its past acquisitions.*

§ 14. Meanwhile it is indeed also important to note, in the case of this form of the discriminating sensitiveness, quite as much as in the signs of feeling, that *we are unable to conclude from the mere presence of a certain kind of reaction to sensory stimulation that the creature in question is certainly possessed of such mental life as we ourselves* have when similar discriminations take place in us. The general rule already mentioned holds, that decidedly low organisms and that in general the plants may respond in what seems to us a decidedly discriminating way to disturbances of the environment, when nevertheless the psychologist finds it of no service to his science to attribute mental life to the organisms in question.

In recent biological research a tendency has consequently appeared to describe the apparently sensitive and discriminating reactions of lower organisms in terms of a phraseology that does not presuppose the existence of any mental life whatever. In such cases one names the stimulus that proves to be effective, such as light, colour, the touch of a solid object on the surface

of the organism, or something of the kind.   One names
also the kind of reaction which this stimulus provokes
in a given organism.   Thus, some organisms turn themselves towards the light when they are exposed to the
light, or else go through certain reactions that end in
getting them away from the light.   Other organisms
respond in a highly sensitive way to the presence of
moving objects in their environment.   In the researches
here in question the effort is made to describe these
characteristic reactions in terms of certain purely physical and chemical processes which occur in the organisms exposed to the stimulations.   And the reactions
receive names accordingly — names intended merely to
describe the relation of the organism to the stimulus,
and perhaps to define the hypothetical nature of the
physical or chemical process to which the reaction may
be due.   Thus, in botany, the term " heliotropism " has
been used to name a well-known, typical reaction of
certain plants when exposed to sunlight.   Professor
Loeb in a well-known book [1] has used the general term
"tropism" to name *any* uniform and characteristic reaction of an organism to its environment such as is
the turning of a plant to the light, or the flying of a
moth into the flame.   Such a "tropism" Loeb explains
as due to physical and chemical processes.   From this
point of view, the presence of what we call discriminat-

[1] Loeb, *Comparative Physiology of the Brain and Comparative Psychology.*   New York, Putnams, 1900.

ing sensitiveness in the responses of an organism, is, by itself alone, only a proof of the presence of certain physical processes occurring in the organism when it is disturbed in a particular way. From the point of view of Loeb it is not even any essential character of these "tropisms" that they involve a nervous system. Simple organisms that possess no nervous system also show these "tropisms." Organisms normally possessed of a nervous system may retain a considerable part of their discriminating sensitiveness even when, by experimental interference, their nervous mechanisms have been put out of function, so far as the "tropisms" in question are concerned.

Furthermore, even in ourselves, in whom our power to discriminate between the various disturbances that affect our organs of sense, is certainly bound up with our conscious and mental functions, it nevertheless remains the case that the activities of our sense organs are due to physical and chemical processes of the same general kind as those that occur in organisms so low that the followers of Loeb would regard them as showing no sufficient evidence of the presence of mind. It follows that *discriminating sensitiveness to the present disturbances of our sense organs is never by itself alone a sufficient sign of what the psychologist is obliged to regard as a mental process. Nevertheless, in beings that for other reasons we regard as possessed of mind, there is no doubt that this discriminating sensitiveness possesses*

*a very great importance for the interpretation of what
mental life is taking place.*   Here, as so often elsewhere,
the higher involves the lower.   If we merely see a creature respond to the lesser differences in his physical
environment, we are indeed not sure what sort of mind
this creature possesses, or whether he possesses any
mind at all, so far as the psychologist can hope to study
his life.   But, on the other hand, if a creature does possess a mind, we can never understand this mind unless
we know what discriminating sensitiveness is present.

It also remains true that *where we are sure of the
presence of mind, we observe a very highly developed and
varied sensitiveness to sense impression to be present,
whenever the other signs of mind grow numerous and
important.*   Thus, the artist is distinguished from other
men not merely by his acquired habits, and by his voli-
tions, but by his sensitiveness to certain special disturbances of his sense organs.   He responds to colours or to
tone, either in a more discriminating way, or in a more
emotional way, than other men show.   In general, the
genius of any type is such because of the sort of sensitiveness that he exhibits to certain kinds of present
experience, as well as because of the habits and the
voluntary tendencies that he ultimately develops on
the basis of this peculiar sensitiveness.   The mechanic,
the naturalist, the business man, the administrator, the
philosopher, no matter how highly developed their other
functions may be, differ from one another by virtue of

the sorts of discrimination that they show in dealing, from moment to moment, with the condition of their environment as it passes before them.   Where one's senses do not discriminate, one's thought is incapable of forming abstract ideas such as are adequate to the facts.   Persons who do not possess certain senses may develop a very high degree of intelligence.   But the character of this intelligence is profoundly affected by the defects of sensation to which such persons are subject.   While the relation between sense experience and acquired habit will become a little clearer farther on, it is already possible to say that, to adapt an old phrase, *there is nothing in the intellect which is not affected by what occurs in the region of the senses;* so that as our sensitiveness to present stimulations varies, our whole mental constitution, even on the highest level, is affected.   Hence, the signs of discriminating sensitiveness remain among the most important of the evidences that we can use in analysing mental life, and in discovering the laws that determine its development.

§ 15. We have now considered *two* aspects of that discriminating sensitiveness to present stimuli which the beings that seem to us to have minds manifest, viz., the signs of feeling and of sensory experience.   But we said above that the relation of a creature's sensitiveness to its *former experience* would also interest us.   In fact, a still more remarkable aspect of animal sensitiveness than the ones yet noticed appears, in simple forms, decidedly low down in the scale, becomes in certain lines of evolution rapidly more and more important higher up, and reaches its highest expression in man. *The animal, and especially the vertebrate animal, in proportion to its elevation in the mental scale, shows a disposition to be determined in its present action by what has happened to it in the past.* That is, it is not merely sensitive in particular ways to particular changes; *but it seems to learn by experience.* What response the organism makes at any given time is determined not merely by its inherited structure, nor yet by present sensory disturbances, but, in addition, by the results of former stimuli, which have affected it during its intercourse with its world. This capacity to be moulded by experience greatly elaborates the discriminating sensitiveness of the organism that is able thus to appear to learn. Wherever this capacity assumes its higher and more complex forms, the signs of such plasticity, of such power to be taught by the world in which the animal lives, constitute, when taken together, the signs of intelligence, as well as the signs of habitual voluntary conduct.

It is true that, in ourselves, nervous functions which seem to have no mental aspect, are still often moulded by experience. Not every case then of this sort of plasticity is itself a sign of mental life. In fact, all the so-called "acquired characters" of animal organisms plainly involve, in some measure, a capacity to be moulded by physical experiences. But, once more, the

D

matter is one of degree. The power to show the effects of past experience is, in its more elaborate forms, the most persuasive of all the signs of the presence of mind. Especially convincing is this sign when it appears as a power to apply the results of former experience in the adjustment of an animal's actions to decidedly novel conditions. When wild animals, after having experienced something of the nature of traps, become especially skilful in detecting and avoiding new sorts of traps, we do not easily doubt that this is a sign of some sort of intelligence. When (as is narrated in an account quoted by Romanes) an elephant, taught to pick up articles and pass them to the man who is on his back, detects at once the character of some novel article (*e.g.* a sharp knife), and guided by some subtler indication, handles this novel article carefully, or with a careless haste, we are sure that this acquired skill indicates the presence of mental life of some highly developed kind.

§ 16. Decidedly different is the case where the actions of an animal show great apparent present skill in their successful adjustment to surrounding conditions, while, nevertheless, the adjustment in question seems to be largely an inherited function of the animal, which is only in part, perhaps in very small part, moulded by the animal's own past experience. In this case we call the actions that we observe cases of relatively unmodified instinct. The signs of unmodified instinct cannot of themselves be regarded as signs of what, from the psychologist's point of view, is identical with intelligence or with conscious volition. The most marvellous developments of unmodified instinctive functions occur in invertebrate animals, especially among the insects (*e.g.* ants, bees, and wasps). While these instincts get in some respect readjusted to passing experience, they are sometimes remarkably perfect apart from the influences of any past experience. The instincts of the higher vertebrates are generally a good deal moulded by the experiences of the individual animal, so that although an important aspect or portion of the functions may be directly inherited, the mind of such an animal is nevertheless subject in its growth to the laws of the intelligence and is here seldom free from great modifications during the life of its possessor. In man the inherited instincts, although they lie at the basis of all our intellectual life, get so much modified and moulded by our experience that we generally fail to recognise their presence as instincts. Yet, as James and others have shown, man has, at the outset, an extremely large number of elaborate and inherited instinctive predispositions to given sorts of conduct.

In so far, however, as we leave out of account the relatively unalterable inherited instincts, we can then say that by the signs of intelligence and of the presence of voluntary although habitual conduct, we mean those signs which *show an animal's plasticity in the presence of*

*experience, and especially its skill in adjusting the results
of past experience to the meeting of novel situations.*

§ 17. It will be observed that, in case of the class of
signs of the presence of mind here in question, all such
signs are intimately bound up with those described
under the previous head, and cannot exist apart from
them. The animal which at present shows that its conduct is affected by the results of former experience,
generally displays this influence by being sensitive to
aspects of its environment to which it would otherwise
not adjust itself. Furthermore, as we shall see when
we come further to examine the mental processes which
accompany intelligent behaviour, many of these processes involve certain mental states called images, or
ideas, or called by similar names. Such states we shall
find to be similar to these which present external disturbance of sense organs would arouse. And, as we
shall also find, the existence of these various states and
processes proves to be explicable only in case we lay
stress upon the relation between the animal's present
external sense disturbances and its former experiences.
In other words, even its present sensitiveness involves
mental features which, whenever it is really intelligent,
are different from what they would have been in case
certain other experiences had not preceded them. We
are consequently unable to deal with the mental processes involved in genuinely intelligent actions, without taking account of something more than the present

discriminating sensitiveness of the animal's organism. Yet this something affects the present state of its consciousness. Hence the study of phenomena of the present class is very naturally distinguished from the study of the phenomena, physical or mental, which have to do with the present disturbance of the animal's organs of sense, and is nevertheless very closely bound up with the latter study.

§ 18. There seems to be need of a name whereby we may distinguish and characterise the group of signs of mind here in question. We have already used the name "plasticity." But this name naturally suggests present modifications of an animal's behaviour, as well as the relation of its present behaviour to its former life. The name "intelligence," which we have also used, implies distinguishing certain mental processes as having to do with the knowledge about its world which the intelligent animal shows. While this name is indeed applicable in case of all the functions here in question, it does not, so expressly as we could wish, lay stress upon the fact that the intelligent activities are always due, in creatures such as ourselves, to the influence of former experiences upon present habits and upon present consciousness. Moreover, all these intelligent activities are also more or less expressions of will. They constitute conduct as well as show intellect. Furthermore, we need at this stage of our inquiry a name that lays stress quite as much upon the externally observable character of certain signs of mind as upon the inner character of the accompanying mental processes themselves. I suggest therefore as a good name for the present type of signs of mental life the term DOCILITY. *By the docility of an animal we mean the capacity shown in its acts to adjust these acts not merely to a present situation, but to the relation between this present situation and what has occurred in the former life of this organism.* The same term "docility" we shall also come to apply later to the mental processes which accompany these external manifestations of the tendency to profit by former experience. The term "docility" is chosen therefore as a convenient name *both* for the physical manifestations of the animal's power to profit by experience, and for the mental processes that accompany this same power.

It will be noticed that we do not here distinguish signs of the possession of intellect from signs of the possession of a will. As we shall hereafter see, the so-called will and intellect of ordinary psychological study are but two aspects of a single process.

§ 19. We now come to still another group of the signs of mental life. The adjustment of an organism to its environment involves everywhere not merely the reception of impressions from without, *but the occurrence of responses which are in some sense initiated within the organism.* All the signs of mind without exception include the *reaction* of the creature that possesses the

mind to the world in which it lives.   Yet in some cases
our attention, as we study an organism, is more attracted
by what happens to the organism, that is, by what comes
to it from without ; in other instances *our attention is
more attracted by the novel character of the response itself
which the creature makes to the conditions in which we
find it*.   In the one case we are disposed to say that the
animal which we are observing merely shows signs of
being disturbed.   *In the other case, we are likely to say
that this animal shows " spontaneity" of movement*.
Now when we speak of " *spontaneity*," we speak of
what common sense regards as one of the most characteristic signs of the presence of mind.   Yet before we
can estimate the value of this sign, we have to consider
somewhat carefully in what sense spontaneity is ever
observable in the actions of a living creature, and in
what sense this spontaneity, when it appears to exist,
can be of any use to us as a mark of mental life.

§ 20.   The discriminating sensitiveness with which we
began the series of the signs of mental life generally
does not seem to us to be something very noticeably
spontaneous on the part of the animal that shows it.
When a creature is disturbed by an external cause, and
shows signs of pleasure or of pain, we have indeed its
own reaction to its world — a reaction which may be
very characteristic of its own special type of life.   But,
on the other hand, the particular reaction seems to us
to be rather directly due to the disturbance than to be

something initiated from within the animal organism. Yet in some sense such relative initiation from within always takes place. For what the disturbed creature does, depends on what nervous centres it has. On the other hand, when, in the absence of any disturbance that, at the moment, seems to us notable, a living creature moves about (as so often happens in very various grades of animal life), we then speak of "spontaneous movements," and easily think of them as initiated directly from within the organism. If an animal is obviously disturbed by light or by sound, and shows merely the usual signs of seeing or of hearing, we are likely to regard this mainly as a direct response to an outer impression. But when a dog, in the absence of his master, begins to show signs of restlessness, and, running to the window, looks out in a way that we regard as indicating a desire to look for his master's return, this we are disposed to consider a relatively "spontaneous activity." Or when a man, made angry by a blow, returns the blow instantly, we may regard this merely as an instinctive response to a present disturbance. But when another man, after brooding over an injury, writes a challenge to a duel, or when he plans the murder of his enemy, common sense regards this as a relatively "spontaneous activity," and may attribute it to what is called the "free will" of the individual in question.

But our estimate of this contrast between the so-called "direct response" of a living being to its environment, and the apparently "spontaneous activity" of the same or of some other living creature, appears in a somewhat different light if we consider, not merely what we have called the present discriminating sensitiveness of the creature in question, but that *docility* of a higher organism upon which we have now insisted. We know that what an animal at present does may be a result, not merely of the momentary stimulation, but also of great numbers of past habits. These habits may affect present conduct in such wise that what is now done is rather a repetition of some former act than a fitting response to a present situation. Thus, when a tune "runs in one's head," the singing of the tune may seem to an external observer a very "spontaneous" kind of action. Closer examination may, however, show how the singing of the tune is due to the past habit of singing it, and to the fact that this habit has been reawakened in some way through its accidental connection with a passing present experience. It results that, *when we take into account the combined effect of sensitiveness and docility, we have very much to limit the extent to which we can judge the activities of any animal to be even relatively spontaneous.* And from this point of view the so-called spontaneous movement of the undisturbed animal may turn out to be habitual adjustments to stimuli — and to stimuli that we have failed to notice in our observations of the creature in question. Thus, when we take into consideration both the present impressions and the habits of the being in question, the whole appearance of "spontaneity" may seem to vanish; and we may come to regard the reaction as a purely "mechanical adjustment," determined by current events and previous habits. From this point of view, even the plans of the revengeful man, slowly maturing, and resulting in his challenge or in his crime, may now seem to us to involve no new evidences of mind besides those which we may characterise in terms of sensitiveness and docility. For his enemy has aroused him, and he is by habit a fighting man.

§ 21. Nevertheless, when we follow the activities of beings high up in the scale of mental life, and even when we follow some of the processes which occur lower down in the animal kingdom, where the evidences of mental life seem doubtful, we do meet many signs which we fail thus easily to describe in terms either of the present discriminating sensitiveness, or of the gradually acquired habits of the organism, or of both combined, so far as we can at the outset judge of them. In case of our own minds, we also observe a good many processes which we cannot readily reduce to the discoverable laws of our docility, and which we are equally unable to explain by a reference to the present disturbance of our sense organs. That all such phenomena must conform to some sort of law, every psychological investigation naturally presupposes. For a scientific inquiry is concerned with what one hopes to reduce to rule. On the other hand, the explanation of such phenomena may actually have to be sought in other directions than those which we follow when we consider *merely* our sensitiveness and our docility.

This is not the place to determine as yet whether such special explanations of the processes in question will finally prove to be necessary. We are considering, thus far, merely the signs of mind. What interests us is that there are phenomena which, *prima facie*, suggest that something at least *relatively* spontaneous is occurring — something due to what goes on *within* an organism, and something not easily describable *either* in terms of the present disturbances of sense organs *or* in terms of the already acquired habits of the organism. Phenomena of this kind appear most prominently in such cases as the following. First, an animal may be in a situation where it will have to learn a new art of some kind, in case it is to become suitably adapted to its environment. For example, an imprisoned animal may have to learn how to get out of the cage, in case it is to reach food or comfort. Its present sense impressions do not lead to successful responses. Its already acquired habits may prove, at first, inadequate to guide it to successful escape. It is, namely, not intelligent enough to adjust these habits to the novel situation through any sort of direct examination of the facts before it. The animal may struggle for a good while, and then finally escape. In thus escaping it may establish *new* habits, which will lead it to escape more readily if imprisoned again. In this case, it indeed does not occur to us that the process is one involving anything incapable of reduction to law. But, on the other hand, we may have to take account of other factors besides the simple docility of the creature, and of something over and above its inherited instincts, before we can fully understand the process whereby this art was learned. The description of what happens, in so far as we can get such description, does indeed turn out to be, in the supposed case, comparatively simple. A process of "trial and error" seems to take place, and this process results, after numerous failures, in a chance success. Yet this very process certainly involves features that are somewhat different from those by which an animal which has been repeatedly fed learns the place where its food is customarily given to it. And it may therefore prove to be worth while to give a special name to the kind of process which this series of trials and errors involves.

Or, in the second place, on a very much higher level of mental life, an inventor, or a scientific investigator, may long stand baffled in presence of a problem belonging to his art or science.   He may finally solve the problem.   In doing so, he may at the same time invent a new method of procedure which henceforth becomes applicable, by himself or by other men, to similar problems.   The process of discovering this original solution of the problem may well involve elements that need a name of their own.   Neither one who observes from without the activities of such a person, nor one who examines from within their psychological characteristics, may be able to describe what happens wholly in terms of the discriminating sensitiveness to experience which the organism manifests, or which the mind possesses at any one moment.   Nor may such an observer be able to reduce the process to the laws governing the ordinary docility of this organism or of this mind.   In such a case the signs of mind visible to an outward observer seem to need a name of their own.   The mental processes involved seem to stand somewhat by themselves, and to suggest, if they do not necessitate, peculiar modes of describing their laws.

Or, finally, a man in a perplexing situation, a statesman in the presence of some new political problem, a reformer at some crisis in social affairs, may, after long deliberation, resolve upon some highly original mode of conduct.   In such cases the result may be momentous for the whole subsequent history of one or of many nations.   We may or we may not be wrong to refer the decision in such a case to what common sense calls the "free will" of the man in question. It may or it may not turn out that the act of choice was as necessary as is sneezing or digestion. But whatever the result of inquiry may be, the act as it stands possesses for any observer characteristics which seem to indicate a peculiar kind of mental life. This type of mental life may need a name for which our former terms, "sensitiveness" and "docility," appear distinctly inadequate.

§ 22. In all these classes of cases it will be observed that we need not suppose anything of an entirely novel character to have occurred, and that in fact we need not make any presuppositions as to whether any *essentially* novel factors are involved at all. But it is also certain that such learning of new arts, such inventions, such apparently original decisions, are phenomena that have a very considerable importance as symptoms of mind, and that tend to suggest to us a type of mental life somewhat distinct from any other. As to the fitting name to give to responses of this kind, we have already pointed out that they very readily suggest the word "spontaneity." The imprisoned animal, apart from its previous training, appears "*spontaneously*" to learn how to escape. The inventor "*spontaneously*" solves the problem. The man at the practical crisis shows what we call his power of "*spontaneous*" choice. Yet the word "spontaneous," although in common usage, has unhappy suggestions attending it. It seems to imply that something occurs apart from any conditions what-

ever.   And as we have seen, psychology has no interest in recognising uncaused events.   And very obviously
we can never observe that a given event has *no* causes,
while here we are merely endeavouring to find a name
whereby to characterise a type of observed events.
For the same reason, the term "creativeness" has
false suggestions.   The most of the phenomena that
are here in question have very prominently some of
the characters which common sense has in mind when
we speak of "acts of will" or of "voluntary" processes.   Yet, as we shall later see, the term "will" is so
variously used by common sense as to make it convenient for our present purpose to avoid determining our
classification of the signs of mind by means of a use
of that word.   Much that is relatively habitual is also
voluntary.   All voluntary conduct depends in part on
docility.   And so far as we are at present concerned,
these relatively novel acts, these signs of apparent
spontaneity, which we are defining, may prove to be
either what common sense calls voluntary, or what are
to be regarded as involuntary.   Their novelty, and the
fact that they cannot be reduced by any direct observation to the signs of the two former types, that is, to
the signs of the sensitiveness or to the signs of docility
— this is here what we are concerned to emphasise.

We are aided in finding a name for such processes
by remembering that, in the modern theory of evolution, a difference has long been recognised in the char-

acteristics possessed by living organisms, between what
is due to *heredity* and what is due to *variation*. The
characters of any organism are, namely, either *repetitions* of ancestral characters, or else characters that
appear in the *individual organism*, without having
been due to such repetition, unchanged, of ancestral
traits. And of the *variations*, that is, of the new individual characters that appear in an organism, some
may be *acquired during the life of the individual* in
question. Such variations, in fact, are all those due to
injuries and mutilations, and all those due to the fortunes and experiences of the individual organism. But,
on the other hand, some of the individual variations
may be due *to congenital causes ;* so that, in addition to
what it inherits from its ancestors, the organism has
from the very beginning relatively *independent variations*, which are characteristic of itself, and which
are not repetitions of anything which its ancestors
possessed.

Now in that portion of the life of an organism which
interests the psychologist, the successive activities that
appear fall into classes which somewhat roughly correspond to the classes of phenomena in which the theory
of evolution is interested when it considers the relation
of the life-history of each organism to the race from
which the organism sprung. To the process of heredity in the race corresponds, in the individual, what
we have called its docility; for by heredity an organ-

ism of one generation repeats the characters of its ancestors, while the docility of an individual involves the tendency of its present acts to repeat its past conduct. On the other hand, to what the evolutionists call the variations of the individual organism when compared to its race, there correspond, in the life-history of each individual, the relatively novel acts and experiences of this individual — the acts and experiences, namely, which are not repetitions of its own former acts and experiences. Now some of these novelties in the life of an individual seem to us to be more directly due, as we have seen, to external disturbances. But, in case of the facts that we are now considering, we come to variations in the conduct of an individual which seem to us to be due, in part, neither to external disturbances nor to the effects of former habits. These new acts play the same part in the life of an individual that what the Darwinian theory calls spontaneous variations play in the life of a race. Just as congenital variations are due, not to the external disturbances that come to an organism, but to the processes that brought it into existence, so here, in the present class of the signs of mind, we have to do with variations or novelties of conduct that cannot easily be referred either to the former habits or to the present sense experiences of the organism in question.

In consequence the characteristic of the signs of

E

mental life which we have here in question might well be summed up by speaking *of the variation of conduct in general*, or by using the term "variability," or the other term "spontaneous variability," to characterise the process in question. Yet in order to avoid the various confusions to which the term "spontaneous variation" has given rise in evolutionary theory, and in order to avoid also the indefiniteness that attaches to the otherwise used and extremely general terms "variation" and "variability," it seems better to find still a new, although a closely related term, for the particular *kind* of variability here in question.

I propose then to call the signs of mind which are here in question, signs of INITIATIVE, or more particularly of MENTAL INITIATIVE. The word "initiative" suggests that where initiative is present there is at least considerable apparent novelty of behaviour on the part of the creature that exhibits initiative. The word is not meant to convey the conception that the initiative in question involves independence of definite causal connection. We have no difficulty in speaking of a new organism as "initiated" by the process of genera tion. Yet it does not occur to us to suppose that the new organism is disconnected from its ancestors, or that its ancestors are not the cause of its initiation. To speak of the beginning or of the initiation of anything, is simply to call attention to an observable fact, and is not to make any presupposition as to the presence or absence of lawful connection between this fact and previous phenomena. In speaking therefore of mental initiative, I merely *call attention to the fact that there are certain of the signs of mind which are presented to us by the appearance of relatively novel acts in the life of an intelligent creature, in cases where these novel acts cannot be directly referred to the present external disturbances to which the organism is subject.* The acquisition of new ways of behaviour, which are not merely impressed upon the organism from without, the appearance of inventive activities, the novel deeds of genius, the momentous choices, upon which so much in the life of individuals and of nations may depend — these are all instances of the signs of mental initiative.

§ 23. It remains, even in this introductory sketch, to compare the signs of initiative with the signs of docility, as evidences of the existence of mental processes, and to indicate the significance of the signs of initiative. It must be distinctly admitted *that it is only where the signs of mental initiative appear in close connection with the signs of docility* that they are of importance for the psychologist, or furnish any notable evidence of the presence of significant mental life. The mere fact that an organism does something which it has never done before, and which is not wholly describable in terms of its present sensitiveness to external disturbances, is in itself, apart from its relation to intelligent activities, no sign that a valuable mental function is going on. Thus, the first epileptic fit which should appear in the life of one who was to be henceforth an epileptic sufferer, would not be by itself any sign of a psychologically important process, although there might be some reason to speak of it as an apparently " spontaneous " physiological occurrence. For the epileptic fit is not, like the new invention, *a variation of the already significant intelligent habits of the organism.* In any case, the act which manifests mental initiative must have the character of a real adjustment to the environment, and must not be, like the epileptic fit, a failure of adjustment. Furthermore, even a new adjustment to the environment, in so far as it possesses simply the character of a coming to light of an inherited instinct, which has not previously entered into or been affected by the habits of the organism, is a change possessing no such psychological significance as an invention or a novel choice may possess. In the lives of human beings the sudden appearance of instinctive functions not previously connected with the acquired habits of the organism occurs, except at some points in the early development of childhood, only in decidedly modified form. But in such changes of behaviour as occur when a child first walks, or when it rapidly passes to a new stage in the acquisition of language, or even when later in youth new relations to the opposite sex are determined by

instincts which previous experience has not at all adequately wrought upon — in all such cases the variability of mental processes involved has a decidedly
different significance from that possessed by the forms
of mental initiative just exemplified. *The sort of mental initiative which is especially in question in the present
discussion is that which appears when already acquired
and intelligent habits are decidedly altered, or are decidedly recombined, in such fashion as to bring to pass
a novel readjustment to our environment.*

§ 24. Yet if inventions and critical choices are
classic instances of mental initiative, our instance of
the struggling animal, striving to escape from its
cage, has already shown us that the elementary forms
of mental initiative appear decidedly low down in the
scale of animal activities. We shall find hereafter that
the processes in question are very widely prevalent,
in all the manifestations of mind. A general understanding of how such processes are to be explained,
despite the fact that they are not mere instances of
docility, and that they are not directly due to present
sense impressions, will throw no small light upon what
are usually regarded as amongst the obscurest questions of psychological theory. Every teacher, in these
days, hears a great deal of "self-activity," and of
the supposed principle that every human mind in a
very large measure determines its own choices, its
own beliefs, and its own destiny. On the other hand,

every student of mental phenomena becomes early acquainted with the view that *all* of our mental life is due to environment and to training. Our environment impresses us, because we are discriminatingly sensitive. Our training becomes significant to us because of our docility. To say that environment and training suffice to determine our mental life inevitably involves denying the presence in us of that "spontaneity" upon which the partisans of mental activity love to lay stress. But there are also many students of mental life who add to the factors called environment and training the now so well-known hereditary factor, which is expressed in the original constitution and in the permanent tendencies of our organism. But heredity appears, from the customary point of view, to be as decidedly opposed as are training and environment to the existing of spontaneity. And those who regard heredity, environment, and training as the sole factors determining our mental life, are usually regarded as necessarily opponents of those who look to "self-activity" as a significant factor in our growth. Plainly a decision as to the relation of all these factors, and as to the possible existence of anything worthy to be called "self-activity," depends upon a study of that side of mental life which the signs here in question bring to our notice. What we so far see is, that while some of the apparently spontaneous activities of animals and of men can indeed be explained by a more careful study of their present sensory disturbances, or of their past habits, some of these seemingly spontaneous doings involve processes that seem more stubbornly to resist a reduction to the two other types. It seems worth while to give these classes of phenomena, at least provisionally, their separate name. Plainly they include much of what is often referred to "free will." Plainly they also include a great many phenomena of mental variability which seem to be of a much less startling and momentous character. But in so far as inventiveness also is included among the manifestations of the type here in question, these phenomena appear to include much of what is usually described as ingenuity, and so involve what is usually regarded as the intellect as well as what is commonly conceived to be the will.

Here, therefore, as in the case of docility, the phenomena of mind which are under consideration include both those usually classed under the intellect, and those usually considered under the head of the will. For we show initiative both as to our knowledge and as to our conduct.

§ 25. Under four headings we have now discussed what amount in sum to *three* provisionally distinct types of the signs of mind. The *first type* possesses two sub-types, whose difference is, for the psychologist, of great practical importance. We accordingly discussed these two sub-types separately under our first and second heads. They were respectively *the two sorts of signs of discriminating sensitiveness;* namely, the signs of FEELING, that is, of satisfaction and dissatisfaction; and the signs of a tendency to discriminate between the various SENSORY DISTURBANCES that come to our organism from without. The signs of these two types consisted throughout *in modes of behaviour of the organism;* for we are never able to distinguish the signs of any sorts of mental states, apart from that reaction of the organism to its environment which accompanies these mental states. On the other hand these signs, so far as they went, directly indicated to us merely the organism's *present state,* and the relation of this state to *external disturbances.* The *second type* of the signs of mind, discussed under our third head, consisted of the signs of DOCILITY. They are especially useful to the psychologist as indicating the presence of what is called Intelligence and of what is called Conduct. They are inevitably mingled with and inseparable from the signs of the first type. But they are signs of docility so far as they show us *that what the organism now does depends upon what it has done and upon what has happened to it in the past.* On the higher level we regard these signs as convincing indications of the presence of mind; and therefore the analysis of these signs and the study of their laws becomes of great aid to us in the comprehension of mental processes. The *third type* of the signs of mind we have defined as the signs of MENTAL INITIATIVE. They are suggested to us by such variations of intelligent habits as cannot readily be explained either by the present sense disturbances or by the former experiences and habits of the organism in question. While they are often suggested to us by the phenomena that manifest what is often called the will, they also appear in case of the processes of the type of thoughtful invention; and their relation to what is usually called the intellect, as well as to what is usually called the will, must form the topic of our later study. But by analysing these signs, even in this preliminary way, we have enabled ourselves to map out in advance the territory which psychology must attempt to study.

CHAPTER III

THE NERVOUS CONDITIONS OF THE MANIFESTATION OF MIND

§ 26. The organic conditions for all these manifestations of mind is the presence of a nervous system.
At all events, such signs of mental life as some have
believed to be present in organisms too low to show us
any differentiated nervous systems are such as to need
here no further mention. The externally observable
discriminating sensitiveness which everywhere accompanies all the higher manifestation of mind is, physically speaking, a property of nervous tissue.

Leaving to the anatomist and the physiologist every
extended description of the structure and functions of
our nervous system and of its instruments, viz., the
sense organs and the organs of muscular movement,
the psychologist can here only try to show very sum-
marily what characters of the nervous system most
interest his own undertaking.

The nervous system consists, for our purposes, of a
vast collection of "elements," each one of which is a
"nerve cell" that, in addition to its minute central mass,
possesses prolongations which are either "nerve fibres"

58

or else are other so-called "processes," viz., minute and multiformly branching extensions of the substance of the nerve cell. These processes, extending, in the central nervous system, from one cell to the immediate neighbourhood of other cells, form an extremely complex network of finely divided threads of mosslike or of mouldlike collections of short and long threads and branchings. A current and authoritative but not perfectly certain opinion holds that the processes of one cell probably never really unite either with the processes or with the central substance of any other cell. Thus each cell, with its processes, lies it would seem side by side with other cells, whose processes, intertwining like the foliage of neighbouring trees with its own processes, still never grow into its own substance, so that all these "elements," *i.e.* cells, each with its own extensions, are anatomically independent. The nerve fibres proper, which grow out of what are called the axiscylinder processes of cells, run often for long distances unbroken through the nervous system, either reaching their various terminal organs in the outer or "peripheral" portions of the body, or else coming to an end in tuftlike branchings in the immediate neighbourhood of the cells whose functional relation to their own parent cells they are destined to determine. Nerve fibres often divide into branches of equal value, or else send off, in their course through the central regions of the nervous system, many accessory branches, which may terminate as does the main fibre, but at points often far removed from one another. Thus any given fibre, with its branches and accessories, may serve to bring its parent cell into some sort of relation to many other regions of the central nervous system. On the other hand, the anatomical independence of the elements which has thus been probably made out suggests that every cell has some sort of relative and subordinate independence of function. When it has once received any disturbances, it probably sends out, through its processes and its fibre, its own sort of excitation; but very possibly this excitation does not pass over from the terminations of the cell branches to any other nervous element without considerable alteration in form, and perhaps in degree. It has been suggested by the experimental work of several neurologists that what a cell does to its neighbours or to the more distant cells with which its fibres bring it into relation must be somewhat analogous to "induction" as known in case of electrical phenomena. From this point of view the excitation of a cell through the excitation of its nerve fibre or by any other means may "induce" other cells, with which the first cell stands in relation, to give out, in their turn, their own form of excitement, which they then pass over by induction to yet other cells. In any case, the known general structure of the nervous system seems especially adapted (1) to the manifold propagation of excitements in various directions, (2) to the con-

stant variation of the form of this excitement as it passes
from element to element of the nervous system, and (3)
to the most complex influence of the excitations of one
part of the nervous system upon the independently
aroused excitations which happen to be present in other
parts of the system.

§ 27. The best-known division that exists in the
functions of the nervous system is that between *the
sensory and the motor functions*. Beginning in the more
external or peripheral regions of the organism, disturbances are constantly passing inwards from the sense
organs, where the fibres of the sensory nerves have
their outward endings. These sensory fibres carry physical disturbances of some still unknown form to the
neighbourhood of more centrally situated cells, which
in their turn may, and in general obviously do, send the
excitation or its induced resultants to very various parts
of the still more centrally situated nervous tissue. The
rate at which the nervous disturbances are carried in
nerves is in general known, although not so accurately
in the sensory as in the motor nerves, and is from thirty
to forty metres per second. In the meantime, centrally
initiated physical disturbances are constantly passing
outwards over motor nerves to the terminations of these
nerves in muscles, glands, etc., where these disturbances
produce complex effects upon the organs of voluntary
and involuntary movement, upon the circulation, and
upon the secretions. In general, the sensory nerves, in

view of their actual relations to the rest of the organism, are so disposed as to carry disturbances only inwards, and the motor nerves so disposed as to carry only outwards, although this law seems to be not absolute, but only a resultant of the usual conditions. The sensory nerves terminate outwardly, as has just been said, in sense organs, which are in general so constructed as to expose their nerve fibres to only one sort of physical excitation (as the fibres of the optic nerve are normally exposed to the effects which light produces upon the retina, the auditory nerve to the effects of sound-waves, etc.).

This division between sensory and motor nerves is, in the first instance, a purely physical matter, and does not by any means name functions that must have any direct relation to our mental states. For disturbances travelling inwards over sense nerves need not be passed on through the nerve centres until they reach the level of the cortex of the brain; and unless they do reach the cortex, we have no sensory experience, and the sensory motor process then goes on without mental accompaniment. Just so, very numerous motor currents pass outwards from centres — *i.e.* from groups of cells situated wholly in the spinal cord or elsewhere below the level of the cortex — and are in no wise due to excitations aroused in the cortex. In such cases the motor processes in question have no relation to our will. A pigeon deprived of its brain hemispheres can fly, avoiding obstacles; can perch, balance, walk, etc., when stimulated to such acts by appropriate sensory disturbances. It, however, no longer shows hunger, fear, love, or similar sorts of discriminating sensitiveness, and gives no sufficient signs of such intellectual life as would characterise an uninjured pigeon. If left alone, it rests in apparently absolute repose and indifference to its environment. Driven from one perch, it merely flies till it finds another. Thus the sensory excitations which reach the brainless pigeon's nervous centres produce, probably apart from any definite mental life, physical disturbances of cells, such as stimulate in an always rigidly determined serial succession (through the intermediation of motor nerves) just the right muscular fibres which are needed to produce each time the pigeon's acts of balancing, flying, or perching. Yet all this appears, in the end, to involve none of the watchful, often hesitant, tremulous, emotionally busy sensitiveness of the normal pigeon. The brainless pigeon seems like a delicate but strictly determined machine, which never really seeks to escape, and never shows the least normal concern for its own preservation, but merely perches when it touches a perch, flies when it is in the air, balances when it begins to fall — and all this with the stubbornness of a steadily working clock.

So far, then, a sensory impression has appeared in our account as a physical disturbance that passes inwards from a sense organ over a sensory nerve. In the cen-

tral masses of cells such disturbances, occurring as they
do, at any moment, in great numbers, produce changes
that are often far-reaching, but that are usually determinate as regards their total outcome, and that often
are so quite apart from any signs of intellect, of feeling,
or of will. In most cases, however, the outcome, if definite, is some sort of "adjustment to the environment,"
i.e. is of a nature to be, in general, serviceable to the
life of the organism. The adjustment is modified by
the endless interchange of excitations throughout the
central nervous system, whose enormous numbers of
relatively independent "elements," mutually inducing
different forms of excitement in one another as soon as
any of them are disturbed, tend both to the multiplica-
tion and to the control of the effects of every disturbance. The useful movements that result are such as
they are because, in the end, groups of muscle fibres
get excited in a definite serial order for every complex
act. And this serial order is determined by the total
structure and the consequent functions of the central
nervous system.

§ 28. But now, where the signs of mind are definitely
shown, the accompanying nervous processes are still of
the same fundamental sort as in the cases just discussed.
The difference lies in the place, in the complexity, and
in the significance of the central nervous processes involved. When, as in our own cases, the cortex of the
brain is present and is actively functioning, it functions

as it does because of the current sense disturbances which reach it. The result of the brain process is always an outward-flowing, but very highly orderly — a serially arranged — collection of disturbances which, acting through the coöperation of lower centres, result either in actual external movements, or in tendencies to movement, or, finally, in the prevention of movements which would be carried out, at the time, by the lower centres if the latter were not under the control of the brain. Intermediate between the ceaseless income of the sensory disturbances that reach the cortex so long as it is active, and the equally ceaseless outgo of the motor processes (or of the processes tending to the control of movements), that leave the cortex all through our waking life, there are central processes occurring in the form of an interchange of induced cellular disturbances among the elements of which the cortex of the brain is composed. As there are some hundreds of millions of these elements in the grey matter which forms the surface of the brain, and as the intertwining foliage of the branching forest of cell processes, together with the masses of innumerable winding fibres that wander from region to region of the brain, must determine an august multiplicity of interrelations among these elements, it is no wonder that these central processes should show a simply inexhaustible complexity. Still more marvellous, however, from a purely physical point of view, is the orderliness which reigns amid the

F

complexity. This orderliness is, in general, due to the great law of habit. *The brain tends to do the sort of thing that it has already often done.* The brain is, meanwhile, persistently retentive of its own once-formed habits regarding these interchanges of the activities of its various elements whenever they are excited in particular ways. And it is thus persistent to a degree which we can never cease to regard with more wonder the more we study the brain's functions. On the other hand, the cortex remains, to a remarkably late period in life, persistently sensitive to a great variety of new impressions, and capable of forming at least a certain number of specialised new habits—such as are involved whenever we learn to recognise and name a new acquaintance, or to carry out a new business enterprise. And all these things, it must be remembered, the cortex accomplishes as a physical mechanism. If we change — by experimental interference, by accident, by poisoning, by disease — any of the physical conditions of the cortex, we interfere with some or with all of these functions. Meanwhile, if we at any time were to cut off all sensory stimulations, the brain, as many facts indicate, would either soon cease to act at all, or would remain active only in a slight or in an almost utterly insignificant way. On the other hand, so long as the brain is active, it sends out motor stimulations, or stimulations that tend to control or to suppress the activities guided by lower centres. And it is precisely this motor outgo of the brain that determines the very signs of mind which we discussed above.

Furthermore, while the brain is, during waking life, full of general activity, it is now well known that every definite outflowing process, as well as every definite sensory stimulation, involves sharply localised regions of the brain. Eye and ear, arm and leg, have definite centres in the brain corresponding to the stimulation of the sense organ, or to the movements of the limb. *Each of the numerous habits of the brain means, then, tendencies to the excitement of localised tracts and paths under given physical conditions.* An excitement passing over one set of paths leads to one system of external movements, *e.g.* from eye centre to hand centre, when one sees and then grasps. If circumstances vary the paths, they vary the motor results. It is possible to have, in cases of localised brain disorder, the survival of a few very complex habits of movement in the midst of the utter wreck of all the other related habits of the same grade of complexity and of similar significance — as when a patient loses all power to remember his native tongue except for a few surviving words, chosen by the disease, as it were, either at random or in more or less typical fashion, to outlast the rest. In this case a few definite and localised habit-worn paths for the induction of activity remain after all the related paths of the region in question have been destroyed.

Meanwhile, what the brain at any moment does, in answer to the current sensory stimulations, is determined both by its entire past history and by its inherited "temperament" or original type of structure. For by heredity the brain has come to be just this vast colony of functionally united cells. And, on the other hand, whatever has happened to the brain in the past has meant some definite and usually sharply localised interchange of induced activities among its elements. Every such interchange has altered the minutest structure of all the elements concerned, has established localised paths between them for future inductions to follow. They can never act again precisely as they would have done had they not acted once in just this way. And this is what is meant by saying that the brain *forms its habits*. One must now, in addition, note that this formation of habits may occur in the most subtle fashions. Parts that have often functioned together tend to function more easily together again. This is true down to the minutest detail of localised functions. But what is still more significant for all our higher mental life is, that *general forms or types of activity, however subtle their nature, when once they have resulted from a given exchange of induced activities (due to sensory stimulations), may tend thereby to become henceforth more easily reëxcited, so that the habits of our brain may come to be fixed, not merely as to the mere routine which leads to this or to that special act, but as*

to the general ways in which acts are done. A given
"set" of the brain as a whole, that is, a given sort of
preparedness to be influenced in a certain way — yes,
even a given tendency to change, under particular conditions, our more specific fashions of activity — *may*
thus become a matter of relatively or of entirely fixed
habit ; so that, under given conditions, the brain, so long
as it remains normally intact, is sure to respond to certain sensory disturbances by assuming this " set," by
being ready for this relatively new influence, or by
actually seeming to change even its specific past habits
themselves in a certain general but habitually predetermined direction, whenever given sorts of stimulation are
presented. It is known, for instance, that " fickleness "
of conduct, irrational change of plan of behaviour, can
itself become a hopelessly fixed habit in a given brain.
There is, then, no type of activity so general that *some*
brain cannot be trained to become habitually and
fatally predetermined to just that type of interchange
of internal functions, and so to that type of outward-
flowing activity. On the other hand, it is indeed true
that, owing to the localised character of the phenomena
which determine single habits, the training of one
specialised cerebral function, in any particular case,
may not result in the training of some other specialised
function, even where we, viewing the matter from without, have supposed that these two functions were very
intimately connected. The question as to just *what*

effect the training of any one special function will have upon other functions, or upon the general tendencies of the brain, is therefore always a question to be answered by specific experience. This the teacher, in estimating the general effects of new educational devices upon the pupils, must always remember.

§ 29. Of the general relation of the activities of the cortex to those of the lower nervous centres, and of the relations between various activities of the cortex itself, it still remains to say here a few words. The brain cortex directs, by itself alone, and apart from the co-operation of lower nervous centres, no externally observable motor processes. What it does is partly to combine and elaborate, partly to guide by slight altera-tions, and partly to hold back or to *inhibit* the activi-ties which other centres, left to themselves, would carry out in response to the sensory stimuli which reach them. The brain also arouses the lower centres to act in its service by substituting its own stimulations for external disturbances. The character of the cortex as an organ for preventing or "inhibiting" the functions of lower centres is of very great importance, and well exemplifies the sort of hierarchy which obtains among our nervous centres. Within the brain itself a similar hierarchy exists, and a similar system of mutual inhibi-tions gets formed on the basis of our experience.

§ 30. Upon the process of "inhibition," *i.e.* of the prevention or overcoming of one form of nervous

excitement through the very fact of the presence of another, the organisation of all our higher life depends.
*What, in any situation, we are restrained from doing is
as important to us as what we do.* Tension, the mutual
opposition and balancing of numerous tendencies, is
absolutely essential to normal life. The brain receives,
at every waking instant, an enormous overwealth of
sensory stimulation. For instance, the habits of those
portions of the brain which receive the fibres of the
optic nerve, and of those portions which direct our
eye movements, are such that every object of the least
note in our field of vision actually acts as a stimulus to
incite us to look directly at itself. Consequently, if
the eyes are idle, the presence of any one bright light
in the otherwise indifferent field of vision is a physical
disturbance, to which the natural motor response is the
turning of the eyes toward that light. And so, if the
field of vision is full of interesting objects, all of them
thus tend to excite various motor responses on the part
of the eyes. In order to look steadily, for even a
moment, in any one direction, we therefore have to
inhibit all of these tendencies except the one whose triumph means seeing the preferred object. This is only
one among the countless cases where the accomplishment of a given act means the inhibition of other acts
to which the brain is meanwhile incited by the presence
of some habitually effective stimulation.

As every normal stimulation that reaches our brains

during our adult years is likely to appeal more or less
vigorously to some established brain habit, the need of
such suppression of possible motor processes is absolute and continuous. The problem of the inhibition
of those habits of movement whose presence at any
given moment would injure the useful adjustment of
our organisms to their environment is, despite its complexity, solved, in case of all the higher nervous centres by the presence of certain general and very
characteristic physical processes whose nature is still
very ill understood, but whose beautiful adaptation
to their purpose we can already to some extent estimate.   We have before spoken of what may be called
the general " set," or " sort of preparedness for a given
kind of excitation," which the brain at any moment
may be brought to assume.   This " set " is in general
itself the obvious result of a previous series of sensory
stimulations, and of an appeal to old habits, and it
may come to pass either suddenly or quite gradually.
Once assumed, any given " set " of the brain manifests itself by the fact that, for the time, one group of
sense experiences tends to arouse the motor habits that
have become attached to them in consequence of the
past experiences of the brain, while the motor habits
to which all other current sense impressions appeal are
in great measure inhibited.   Yet these relatively ineffective sense impressions certainly reach, in most
cases, their centres in the brain; for, if altered a

little from their current character, they may at once assert their presence by calling out movements that show concern in the alteration. A similar "set" may be given by the action of the brain to a group of lower centres, which then proceed to react automatically to external stimuli until the whole process is cut off by external stimuli, or by a new signal from the cortex; and while this "set" continues, all other motor habits of the centres in question are inhibited.

§ 31. Examples, both of inhibition in general and of its relation to the passing general "condition of preparedness" of the higher and lower centres, are easy to give. In general, all higher intellectual pro-cesses are accompanied by processes in the cortex which appear, when seen from without, enormously inhibitory. One absorbed in writing or reading lets pass without response countless impressions which pretty certainly reach the brain — impressions to which, under ordinary circumstances, he would respond by acts of looking, of listening, of grasping, or of other more or less useful or playful types of adjustment. Let him cease the higher activity, and he adjusts him-self more vivaciously to the lesser matters of his en-vironment. An absorbed public speaker, an actor, or a man in a formal social company, inhibits those move-ments, however habitual they are in other company, and however strong the momentary sensory solicitation to them, which his habits have taught him to suppress

as being here "out of character." This word "character," here names the mental equivalent of a given
"set" of brain. So long as one assumes the "character" the well-practised inhibitions triumph. If one
goes home, or changes one's company, those former
inhibitions may vanish as if they never had been, and
it may be even impossible to reassume them, except in
particular surroundings. In case of the relations of
higher and lower centres, the "set" of a group of
lower nervous processes is well illustrated by the activity of walking, which consists of a regulated series
of motor adjustments to sensory stimulation, — leg movements, acts of balancing, etc. This series is largely
under the control of relatively lower centres, both in
the cortex and below. It may be initiated by a signal
from above. Once begun, it is continued with a consequent inhibition of all inconsistent muscular movements, and with little or no guidance from the more
complex groups of brain centres, until the signal to
pause is given. Then other activities of adjustment
take the place of the ones that have come to an end.
Thus one pauses in a walk through a garden to survey more carefully the appearance of the flowers, to
do a piece of work that requires the skilful use of the
hands, etc. The rule of inhibition, as regards the
before-mentioned hierarchy of the nervous centres,
seems to be that *the higher a given function is, the more
numerous are the inhibitory influences that it exercises*

over lower centres. Intense brain activity of the highest sort is opposed, while it lasts, to nearly all the simpler functions above the level of the vital necessities, except the very few, such as reading or speaking, which training may have brought into the direct service of the highest activity itself. Excite a child's brain to anything approaching absorbing activity (*e.g.* by telling the child an interesting story), and for the time you "keep him quiet." Otherwise he runs about, looks here and there, laughs, wriggles, kicks, prattles — all adjustments to his environment, adjustments either useful or playful, but of a simpler sort. These may cease by inhibition when the story begins. The child may then sit for a short time with moveless hands, with optic axes parallel, *i.e.* with eyes "gazing far off," with legs hanging loosely, with falling lower jaw — all of them more or less inhibitory phenomena.

§ 32. The practical consequences of this general principle of the inhibitory character of the higher nervous processes are multitudinous. Absence of inhibitions is a familiar sign of nervous disorder or degeneration, and also, in children, of immaturity. "Self-control" is an essential part of health. This principle furnishes the reason why so much of our educational work has to be expended in teaching "self-control," whose physical aspect is always the presence of inhibitory functions. The moral law has often been expressed in the form of the well-known " *Thou shalt*

not." Such negative precepts always presuppose that
in the person who really needs to be taught by the
precept, a disposition or habit of brain preëxists which
involves, when left to itself, a certain sort of response
to a given environment, *e.g.* in an extreme case, a
tendency to the expressive acts called, in human social
relations, theft or murder. Instead of telling such a
man what positive motor activity to substitute for such
doings, the negative precept undertakes to point out
that, as a condition prior to any better adjusted conduct, these motor tendencies, at least, must be inhibited. But their inhibition is to be actually brought
about, in case of the successful moral precept, through
the influence of what is called in psychological language "suggestion." The physical efficacy of such
"suggestion" depends, however, upon its appeal to
brain habits, of a very high level, which, like the
other higher processes, have a general capacity to
act in an inhibitory sense, as against functions of
lower levels or of a more primitive simplicity.

But just as we often train habits of inhibition as a
preliminary to the more positive establishment of useful higher functions, it is, even so, true that, whenever
we can get higher functions of a positive sort established, we thereby train inhibitory tendencies. And,
on the whole, this is the wiser course for the teacher
of the growing brain to take, where such a course is
possible. Inhibition is a constant means, but it is still

but a means to an end. The end is the right sort of motor process. *You teach a man to control or to restrain himself so soon as you teach him what to do in a positive sense.* Healthy activity includes self-restraint, or inhibition, as one of its elements. *You in vain teach, then, self-control, unless you teach much more than self-control.* The New Testament statement of "the law and the prophets" substitutes "Thou shalt love," etc., for the "Thou shalt not" of the Ten Commandments. A brain that is devoted to mere inhibition becomes, in very truth, like the brain of a Hindoo ascetic — a mere "parasite" of the organism, feeding, as it were, upon all the lower inherited or acquired nervous functions of this organism by devoting itself to their hindrance. In persons of morbidly conscientious life such inhibitory phenomena may easily get an inconvenient, and sometimes do get a dangerous intensity. The result is then a fearful, cowardly, helpless attitude toward life — an attitude which defeats its own aim and renders the sufferer not, as he intends to be, "good," but a positive nuisance.

The practical problem as to the degree of inhibition which it is well to establish in our nervous life is one which wholesome people meet in part by the device of a duly changing or alternating activity of the central nervous system. *The strain of absorbing intellectual work is, in considerable part, pretty obviously either conditioned or intensified by two factors:* (1) *the actual nervous expenditure involved in the inhibitory processes themselves.* While one works, countless excitations tend to set free lower motor functions, and all these tendencies have to be held back by counter signals from higher nervous stations. This in itself involves a great deal of motor expenditure. "To sit still" is itself, in general, a motor process, and is often a very hard one, *e.g.* when one is in an exciting or harassing situation, and when prudence says, "Do nothing; wait and see." (2) *The indirect effects of non-exercise of the inhibited functions:* to sit still and think, to restrain ourselves, means to condemn many groups of muscles to inactivity. This means a tendency to disturbed nutritive processes, and so in the end an unequal development or an actual degeneration of the whole organism. We relieve the strain as well as favour the neglected organs when we substitute exercise for inhibition. Variation of labour is thus, in itself, and within limits, actual motor rest or recreation. "To let ourselves go," within the bounds of propriety, duty, and moderation, involves a rest from the heavy motor task of "holding ourselves still." This is especially true in children, in whom the inhibitory processes are ill-formed, and therefore the more laborious. Young children should never be asked to continue long any one type of inhibitory process. With them any one persistent "set" of the brain becomes very soon an injurious incident.

On the other hand, not every change of the "set" of brain is itself restful. The phcnomena of "worry" include many "changes of mind," *i.e.* of more special "set" of the brain. Yet the result is disastrous. But the effects of worry seem to be very largely due to the strong tension existing in the worried person between his abnormally numerous sensory incitations to particular acts and that general "set" of his brain which, so long as he is worried, survives all his actual changes of special "set" or plan, and tends to inhibit all suits of definite or connected activity. Whether he rushes about or lies still in pretended rest, whether his mood is this or that, he is all the while incited to act, and is busy holding himself back from effective action. His endless question, "What shall I do?" his motor rest-lessness, his petty and useless little deeds, all express his inability to choose between the numerous tenden-cies to movement which his situation arouses. Count-less motor habits are awakened, and then at once sup-pressed. In his despair he tries to inhibit all acts until *the* plan — the saving plan — shall appear. And so, ac-complishing nothing, he may do far more motor work than an acrobat. But let the dreaded calamity over whose mere possibility he worries actually befall him. *Then*, indeed, there is often but one course of conduct, perhaps a very simple one, suggested by his new situ-ation. The useless inhibitions vanish. One definite "set" of brain is, indeed, substituted for the preceding state, but the new one is free from the over-numerous and violent special tensions between higher and lower centres and functions which characterised the former. The recently worried man may hereupon become cool, may wonder that he can bear the worst so much more easily than he could the uncertainty, and may by contrast find not only rest, but a kind of joy in the relief occasioned by the cessation of useless motor processes. Where the man himself has worried, it is thus often the part of the seemingly most cruel fate to rest him; and this the latter then does by cutting off the extra inhibitions in favour of an easily accomplished response to definite stimulations.

Finally, in this connection, it may be observed that when a given series of acts, involving a certain number of successive inhibitions, has to be accomplished, much more mental strain is involved and more weariness results, according as the inhibitions themselves have to be made objects of a more definite consciousness or volition. And the degree of strain increases very rapidly with the attention given to the inhibitory side of the process. Hence the hard labour involved in learning new adjustments, in acts of voluntary attention, and in conscious self-restraint generally.

CHAPTER IV

GENERAL FEATURES OF CONSCIOUS LIFE

§ 33. A certain proportion of the foregoing functional processes are attended by mental states. In
general our mental life, or, as it is often called, our
consciousness, attends those processes which, while
involving the cortex, are of a decidedly complex grade
and of a relatively hesitant character, or which come
in consequence of the graver interferences on the part
of our environment. Our most perfect adjustments to
our environment are accomplished unconsciously, unless we chance to become aware of them through
their relations to what is actually concerning our conscious life. Our mental life, however, regularly attends (1) those of our habitual cortical functions which
are at any time considerably altered to meet novel
conditions, and which accordingly have, despite their
skill, a relatively hesitant fallibility about them ; (2)
those of our functions which are considerably disturbed
in their normal flow by the intensity or the novelty
of the external stimulation ; and (3) those of our functions which, in relation to the other functions present

in the cortex, have a physical intensity that exceeds the average of what is going on at the same time. For example, we are conscious when we think out a new plan, but we perform numerous acts of mere routine without noticing them. What we do very rapidly we fail to follow, in its details, with our mental life. What, as being somewhat novel, we do with "deliberation," we may follow very adequately. But the physical accompaniments of strong states of feeling, however swiftly they bring some reaction to pass, still imply a change in our consciousness. And intense experiences, such as disagreeable noises (the sound of a hand-organ or of a hurdy-gurdy), may long retain a place in consciousness which may be out of proportion either to the importance, or to the novelty, or to the complexity, or to the deliberateness of the motor functions which they arouse. Meanwhile, the precise conditions that mark the boundary between those functions which have no mental equivalents and those to which consciousness corresponds, is unknown. What we are sure of is that our consciousness is a very inadequate representative of what goes on in our cortex.

§ 34. The mental life which accompanies these functions consists of a "stream of consciousness" in which we can generally distinguish many "states" or different "contents" of consciousness. The "stream of consciousness" is the name frequently applied to what passes in our mental life, because, mentally speaking, we live in a state of constant inner change, so that no portion of our consciousness ever remains long without some alteration, while most of our contents are always changing pretty rapidly. On the other hand, the changes in our inner state are, in general, however swift they may be, still somewhat gradual when compared with the swifter physical changes known to us. A flash of lightning lasts very much longer for our sight than it does as a fact in the physical world. This is partly due to the "inertia" of the retina of the eye. But a similar "inertia" holds of all our central processes. Every mental experience always joins on, more or less, to subsequent experiences, and in general to previous experiences also. A new experience gradually wins our attention, reaches its height, and dies away as our attention is turned to the next; and even in very sudden experiences this relatively gradual character of the process can be noted, if not at the beginning then at the end of the experience, as it slips away into a mere memory. If one listens to any simple rhythm, such as the ticking of a watch, one can note how the succession of separate ticks is viewed by our consciousness in such a way that the successive beats do not stand as *merely* separate facts, but are always elements in the whole experienced rhythm to which they seem to belong, while the successive pres-

entations of the rhythm form a sort of stream of
events, each one of which gradually dies out of mind
as the new event enters. In consciousness there is
no such thing as an indivisible present moment. What
happens in our minds during any one thousandth of
a second of even the busiest inner life none of us can
possibly make out. The contents of mind, as we know
them in the " psychological present," constitute àt the
very least a considerable and flowing series of changes,
the least appreciable portion of which takes up a considerable fraction of a second.

As for these " contents " themselves of the stream of
consciousness, it is well to say at once that they never
form any *mere* collection of " ideas " or of other simple
and divided states. Consciousness is not a shower of
shot, but a stream with distinguishable ideas or other
such clearer mental contents floating on its surface.
What we find in any passing moment is a little portion
of the " stream," a " pulse," or " wave " of mental
change, some of whose contents may be pretty sharply
distinguished, by what is called our attention, from the
rest, while the body of the stream consists of contents
that can no longer be sharply sundered from one
another. If one listens to music, the notes or the
chords may, in their series as they pass, appear as
sharply separable contents. But these stand out, or
float, upon a stream of mental life which includes one's
estimate of the time sequence of the music as a whole,

one's pleasure in hearing the music, one's train of associated memories, one's general sense of the current bodily comfort and discomfort, and much more of the sort, which no man can analyse into any collection of separate or even separable states. In consequence, we are never able, by any device at our disposal, to tell with certainty the *whole* of what is, or just was, present to any one moment of our conscious life. The old question whether one can have "more than one idea at a time" present to one's mind is a question absurdly put. Present at any one time to one's mind is a small portion of the flowing stream of mental contents, in which one can in general distinguish at least two, and sometimes more, elements of content (perceptions, feelings, images, ideas, words, impulses, motives, hopes, intentions, or the like), while beside and beneath what one can distinguish there is the body of the stream or (to change the metaphor) the background of consciousness, where one can no longer distinguish anything in detail, although in some other moment one may easily note how the whole background has changed.

§ 35. In this general characterisation of the "stream of consciousness" we have already by implication answered certain questions that are of fundamental importance for psychological theory. Plainly the conscious state of any moment involves two characteristic features, the so-called "UNITY OF CONSCIOUSNESS," as it is exemplified at that precise moment, and the equally

obvious presence of a VARIETY of mental states, which
have to one another relations of similarity and of difference. By the phrase "unity of consciousness" we
mean the fact that, at any time, *whatever is present
tends to form an always incomplete but still, in some respects, single conscious condition.* If you look at your
open hand you see at once more than one finger. On
this page you see *at once* more than one printed letter.
If you look at a person who is speaking to you, you *at
once* see him and hear him. If bad news disturbs your
mind, you are *at once* conscious of certain ideas which
the bad news arouses, and of the distress which this
news occasions. In all these cases, the phrase "at
once" stands for the fact that we more technically
characterise as the present unity of consciousness. The
facts present to mind are not merely various, they occur
together. In what way they occur together, in what sense
we are "at once" aware of them, every person must
observe for himself. The unity of consciousness is
directly accessible only to its own single observer.
Nobody else can directly verify the fact that such unity
exists. But the agreement in the various reports given
of this unity by many observers constitutes the objective
evidence upon which the psychologist depends when
he makes his assertion. The phrase "at once" is of
common occurrence, even in popular language, as a
means of characterising the unity of conscious states.
When more careful examination is made for psychologi-

cal purposes the character of this unity becomes more precisely definable, yet, after having made proper provisions for securing exact observation, every one must judge for himself the aptness of any characterisation which may be offered in the effort to express the nature of the unity of consciousness.

This fact of the unity of every conscious state is one for which there is no precise parallel in the physical world, as we are ordinarily accustomed to conceive that world. There are many senses in which various phenomena of nature, occurring outside of our minds, may be regarded as forming a unity. Thus we speak of one forest, of one range of mountains, or of one ocean. In a similar way each thing in the physical world is regarded as in some sense a unity of many properties and states. Yet, in all such cases, the sense in which we speak of the physical object as one or as many seems somewhat arbitrary ; and changes with our own point of view as external observers of the facts. We sometimes say that the word "forest" is merely a collective name for the many trees, or even that the term "thing" stands for a collection of physical facts and processes which our subjective interests unify, but which "in themselves" are so many distinct facts. But the unity of consciousness is a fact constantly forced upon us whatever our point of view. For *no one can observe a mental variety of inner states without finding these states together in his one inclusive condition of mind.*

The unity of consciousness is sometimes compared to that of a living organism. Just as the various functions and organs of a living body constitute in some sense a single whole, so, as one often says, the various states present at once to mind have an organic unity. Yet the comparison is not altogether satisfactory. For the considerations that lead us to regard a living organism as a unity of many organs and functions are decidedly complicated, and are presented to us indirectly, so that we often have to think, with considerable doubt, whether or no we shall call some large organism a single individual, or a colony of many individuals. But the unity of consciousness we have always with us, not because we think out some reason why consciousness must be one, but because all that happens at any moment within our minds constitutes for us a single event, however complex this event may be. Furthermore, the reasons that lead us to call an organism one depend wholly upon coöperation and mutual support of various organic processes. But the unity of consciousness exists in some degree, however distracted our inner state may be, and however much the various tendencies present may seem to disturb or to oppose one another. Thus, if an intolerable discord breaks into the midst of a musical harmony (as when, while some one is playing beautiful music, a hand-organ begins outside, or the scraping of a file upon metal is heard), these various mental presentations seem not mutually to support one another in any organic way ; yet, so far as they are present at once, there is still a unity of consciousness, however distracted and incomplete this unity may appear.

§ 36. On the other hand, the fact of the VARIETY present to consciousness at any moment is equally obvious. *The one conscious state of the moment is always a unity consisting of a multiplicity.* The relation between these two aspects of the present consciousness is best observable in cases where the unity and the multiplicity involve a certain harmonious effect. This occurs when we listen to music, and are aware at once of several harmoniously related facts, such as tone, harmony, and rhythm. It occurs also when we enjoy decorative art, and are aware of a complex of lines, of forms, and of colours, composing a pleasing totality. Yet, as already pointed out, disharmonious and distracting conscious states contain the contrasting aspects of unity and variety, in so far as the most painful and distressing complications of the moment are experienced at once. There are some cases where the unity of the conscious state seems to be predominant, and where the element of variety tends to lapse. Such states occur on the borderland of sleep, or in conditions where for any reason we become aware rather of the total impression of the instant, rather than of the variety of experiences that occur within this instant. Yet the variety never wholly disappears, unless consciousness itself disappears. When the last differences lapse, then we become insensible. When we are aware only of unity, it appears that we then become aware of nothing at all.

§ 37. As the last statement made indicates, the variety present at any one instant of consciousness is a variety of *different* elements. To say this is to utter in one sense the barest of commonplaces. Yet, in another sense, the statement becomes important, because it attracts attention to the two most funda. mental relations which can exist amongst the various states that are present in consciousness. These relations are: (1) difference, and (2) similarity or partial sameness. Whatever these various states are, they are known as *different from one another*. The kind of difference that they possess may itself vary endlessly. Colours and shades differ from one another in the field of our visual experiences. Colours differ from odours, as we observe when we look at a flower and smell it. Mental states due to the direct disturbance of our organs of sense differ from images that we can observe in the absence of objects. Thoughts differ from one another, and from feelings or from decisions. And so on indefinitely. All variety of which we are to be conscious involves difference. And the experience of difference is amongst the most fundamental of the facts of mental life.

Yet difference itself is never found as a relation between two facts without there being present another relation which is of equally fundamental importance. *When we observe that one fact differs from another, we also are able to observe that these two facts have, as we say, something in common, or are similar to one another.* Colours differ from odours. But both the colour and the odour of a rose have in common the features that enable a psychologist to recognise that they are both sensations. The mental image that I can form of my friend's face when he is absent, differs from the mental image that I can form of the sound made by a violin, which I have heard somebody play. Yet if I have both images present to my mind at once, I can observe that they have in common something which makes me call them both images. *Thus, sameness and difference are inseparable characters.* Not only is this the case in the most general sense, but in special instances my consciousness of the similarity of two objects that are present to my mind helps me to become aware of their differences, and *vice versa ;* so that the consciousness of similarity and the consciousness of difference are, in certain cases at least, mutually supporting facts so that to become aware of one of these relations helps me to become aware of the other. Thus I can readily observe the difference between right and left as directions, because I am aware of their similarity as being both of them directions within the one space world of which at any moment I seem to be conscious. The relation of similarity between the successive chords and phrases of a musical composition helps me to become aware of the differences present in the musical experience. In the effects of decorative art the similarities present, for example, the symmetries, help me to appreciate more definitely and pleasantly those differences of experience upon which the decorative effect depends. On the other hand, in so far as a consciousness of difference seems to be present without much consciousness of similarity, this consciousness of difference itself acquires a characteristically baffling and puzzling effect, so that I am likely to say, in such cases, that I am aware of the difference, but am not aware wherein the difference lies. Thus, a sudden shock, such as a thunder clap, an explosion, or the experience of the discharge of a Leyden jar through one's organism, may give one a vague consciousness of difference, whose intensity still does not insure any clear consciousness of what the difference is, until, at the moment when we recognise the nature of the shock, we come to possess certain conscious states that are not only different from, but observably similar to, other states.

Thus the unity of present consciousness is indeed diversified by differences. But these differences are never without greater or less similarities amongst the different states. *Where the similarities and differences support one another*, so that we become aware of each by means of the other, and so that each makes the other precise, as is the case when we observe the object of decorative art, or the musical phrase, *then our consciousness acquires a character called* CLEARNESS, — a character which must, once more, be experienced in order to be appreciated. In this sense, for instance, an object upon which our eyes are focussed is seen clearly; or a series of sounds that are not too confusingly mixed with other sounds are heard clearly. And it is in this sense that the beauty of the object of art is clearly observable.

It is worth while also to notice that the Unity and the Variety of consciousness, at any moment, stand in a relation to one another that may be also called a relation of similarity and difference. For the unity of this present instant of consciousness is itself different from the variety of this instant. And on the other hand, the unity and variety are similar to one another, in so far as they characterise the same instant of consciousness. Meanwhile, in so far as the relation of sameness and the relation of difference are considered in themselves, it appears that the sameness, or the similarity, of the various conscious states present at any one moment, seems to bring these states rather into relation to the unity of consciousness, while the differences amongst the states seem rather to relate them to the aspect of variety.

§ 38. The extremely elementary but often neglected facts about the unity of consciousness which have thus been enumerated have, even when taken by themselves, a very important practical application. *If it is our purpose to make any one, as for instance a pupil, clearly conscious of some kind of difference between facts, we carefully choose facts that, while similar to one another in as many other ways as possible, clearly manifest just this particular difference. On the other hand, if we wish to make one observe a similarity, as happens when we desire to illustrate a law or a type or a class of facts, we carefully present different instances of this same type; that is, we illustrate sameness through difference, and difference through sameness. And in both cases we tend to succeed in proportion as we bring the differences and the samenesses that are to be studied into some single unity of consciousness, by presenting various objects at once.* If this simple rule is neglected, if for instance one merely presents objects with a view to their arousing the effect of difference, as when one tries merely to surprise a pupil by the shock of startling varieties, one produces indeed a vague consciousness of differences, and a consciousness that, even in the worst case, is sure to be attended with some consciousness of similarity. But this consciousness remains uninstructive, *because the similarities and differences presented are not so arranged as to support one another.* If on the other hand, for the sake of making one aware of certain similarities we present him a truc monotonous series of objects in which no difference can be detected, or at least no interesting difference, we tend to reduce the pupil's consciousness to the lowest level. And in so far we fail to instruct him. The rule for arousing the kind of consciousness to which the teacher appeals is similar to the rules followed in the decorative arts or in music : *present similarities and differences together in such fashion that each shall support the other.* Or, expressing the rule with reference to the unity of consciousness : *aim to secure the most complete unity of consciousness that is consistent with a desired degree of variety of experience, and* vice versa.

§ 39. But we now come to another aspect of the unity of consciousness, and to one which the foregoing account of the "stream of consciousness" has inevitably mentioned. We have here to call special attention to it afresh. *The term "at once," used with reference to the unity of consciousness, is inevitably ambiguous.* We always appreciate at once a variety of coexisting or of contemporaneous conscious facts.

We also experience "at once," but in another sense of the term "at once," a brief series of successive conscious states. As above stated, our consciousness knows nothing directly of an indivisible present moment, such as physical and mathematical theories assume to occur in time. We are aware at once of more than one successive tone or chord in a musical sequence, of more than one stage or state of our own action, when we are performing some rapid series of deeds. What the German psychologist, Wilhelm Stern, has called the "psychical present moment," what Professor James has called "the specious present" (herein following the usage of several recent English writers), is no infinitesimal instant of time, but always has an appreciable length, somewhat more than the tenth of a second, and apparently not longer than two or three seconds. The length of this "specious present" probably varies with decidedly complex conditions. It seems to be longest when we are following the succession of a decidedly regular rhythmic process, which is presented to our consciousness with the most favourable degree of complexity of structure. It seems to be shortest when the sequence of conscious facts contains a rapid series of distracting differences, whose similarities we fail clearly to grasp. What occurs within this psychical present moment is known to us in some sense as one, but nevertheless as a sequence, which contains within it successive various states, of which some are observed to precede, while others follow.

Every consciousness of change depends upon our power thus to observe " at once" a considerable, although also, from a larger point of view, brief sequence of mental states. Now it is in following such a *sequence* of states that we tend to become especially and most clearly aware of the differences which are there present. *The perception of sequence aids us in the perception of difference.* If two experiences are in any sense coexistent, that is, if their causes are presented to me at the same time, I may fail to notice the difference between them. But if they follow one after another, I shall be much more likely to note the fact that they are different, in case the succession is immediate, and without any interval between. *Hence, our discriminations, in a great number of cases, occur in a succession of acts.* This fact has great and obvious practical importance; and it partly explains why stories interest us more than mere descriptions, for the former constantly remind us of interesting sequences.

§ 40. The foregoing considerations have now prepared us to face a problem upon which modern psychological writers naturally lay great stress. This is the problem: of what elements does our mental life consist? and in what sense does it consist of elements at all? The example set by the physical sciences naturally makes many psychologists interested in reducing mental life, at the outset of the inquiry, to its simplest elements, just as the physicist and the chemist

H

reduce complex bodies, first to the relatively simple aggregates (such as solids, liquids, gases), or, in chemistry, to the chemical elements whereof they are composed, and then to the hypothetical molecules or atoms whereof these elements are constituted. Such analysis having proved so useful in the case of physical phenomena, the question arises whether the psychologist has a right to use this method. As a fact, this method has been very greatly used in modern psychology, and with very important results. An indication of the nature both of the processes used and of the results reached, is necessary in order that we should be able to estimate the theoretical and practical value of every such procedure.

When we look at an object, such as a rose, when we touch it, and inhale its odour, we plainly have a complex mental state; that is, there is a variety within the unity of our consciousness. Now of what elements does this variety consist? It is not difficult for even an untrained introspection to detect the fact that our total impression of the rose which is present to us is made up of the conscious seeing of colours, of the conscious smelling of odours, and of the equally conscious impressions of the sense of touch. Since these various kinds of conscious states are obviously due to the external disturbance of our sense organs, the name "sensation" readily suggests itself for them. In addition to these sensations we have also a feeling of pleasure in the

rose.   In addition, the rose arouses in us a consciousness of its name, and gives us various other mental
states of the type usually called "ideas" or "images."
Our consciousness of the rose thus appears to be a
unity of all these elements.   But a further analysis
seems to show that all of these states are themselves
enormously complex.   What we call the colour of a rose
is an experience made up of varieties that a closer
analysis soon begins to detect, since the various parts
of the rose do not give us exactly the same kind of
visual impression.   If we pursue still farther such an
analysis, by appealing to what can be discovered more
or less indirectly, and experimentally regarding the relation of our organ of vision to the rose that we see, we
seem able to discover that various portions of the retina
of the eye are receiving sensory impressions, any one of
which, if it were alone, would produce in our consciousness a particular sensation of colour, which we should
then localise at some one point of the visual field.   It
appears hereupon natural to say that our total impression of the colour of the rose is *a mental complex of many
different sensations*, no one of which we do experience
alone, but every one of which must be present *as a constituent of our total mental state*.

But now we indeed cannot by direct analysis discover,
in our total impression of the rose at the moment when
its colour and odour impress us, of precisely what ultimate
elementary sensations all the impression is composed.

For only indirectly, by experimental devices, can we
isolate one or another of the simplest sensations which
any one smallest sensible portion of the object, that is
of the rose, would give us, if that portion did alone act
upon our sense organs. There results the theory that
our total mental state is not only a unity consisting of
various conscious facts which we ourselves can by more
or less effort directly observe within this unity, *but is
also a unity consisting of certain ultimate sensations
and feelings that we cannot ourselves detect except indirectly, through experiments which isolate such elements,*
and which bring them before us in moments of consciousness when the original total impression is absent.
Hereupon we may be led to declare that these now
isolated elements somehow blended to form the total
impression that then we had.

§ 41. Generalising somewhat from such instances as
the ones just used, we can state in more universal terms
the theory of the constitution of our mental life which is
just suggested as follows : At any moment we have
a total mental state possessing the characteristic unity
of consciousness. This state we may call T. T consists, as we have already said, of a variety of mental
life which we can by direct analysis very readily
detect as present in the total condition. Let us call
the elements directly observable in this variety, *a, b,
c, d.* But now, according to the present theory, each
one of these relatively simple mental processes, *a, b,*

c, d, is, as a fact, enormously complex.   Thus a, let us say, is a totality of the sort such as our visual image of the rose when we remember it, or our visual perception of the rose when we see it, exemplifies.   But a is due to an excitation, of sense organs, and of brain tracts, or of brain tracts alone, or at least accompanies such excitation.   Let the brain centres, excited when a comes to consciousness, be denominated by 1, 2, 3, etc.   Through experiments of the nature of those already indicated we can in many cases produce an excitation of some brain centre in relative isolation.   In such cases we may discover that this excitation is accompanied with a conscious process s, which we shall suppose to be a conscious process due to as simple a brain process as we can hope to excite in any relatively isolated way.   A similarly isolated excitement of the brain process which we have called 2 would produce another conscious process, which we may call s'. The conscious states s and s' may be such that *when* we have observed them in isolation, we can detect an aspect of the original process T, namely, of our whole mental state, which we may regard as "due" to them, or to either one of them.   We may proceed in a similar fashion to isolate conscious elements that correspond to those other processes in the brain, which form parts of the original total brain processes.   Isolations of this kind we can carry out with especial success in cases where we are dealing with conscious states due to the excitement of sense organs. With somewhat greater difficulty we can approach such isolations of portions of the total brain processes in other instances also, namely, in case of brain processes that have to do with our images of absent objects, and also in some other instances. Where such processes of isolation cannot be actually accomplished, we can conceive them possible.

Since every complex brain disturbance thus consists of processes that could be excited in relative isolation, and since each one of these processes may be conceived as attended, when this process is excited alone, by some conscious process of a simple nature, and of the type of s, in the instance just mentioned, we are, according to the present theory, justified in asserting that the original mental state T consists of elements s, s', and many other such elements, of which it is said to be made up. These elements may escape in any single instance our direct analysis. But we may conceive them capable of isolation by some such process as that which has just been in general formulated. If we conceive each one of these elements of the type of s so simple that no further analysis of this element will be possible, we may call s, for the purposes of psychology, an absolutely elementary mental state. The theory here in question declares that all consciousness is made up of such elementary states. They are said to " blend " together, or to come into some sort of

" union," in order to form our total conscious state at any moment. The task of psychology is declared to include an exhaustive catalogue of these elementary mental states, and then a further examination of the laws according to which they blend, or otherwise unite, to form the more massive states of consciousness which we directly observe to be present at any moment. The parallel of such an analysis to the atomic theory, as the latter has been so successfully developed in modern physical and chemical science, is obvious.

§ 42. But the present theory lays claim to a basis in experience which has been frequently denied to the atomic theory, as the latter exists in chemistry.   For, as a general rule, the mental elements of which the modern psychologists make use are themselves facts which are capable of being observed in greater or less isolation by experimental devices, although we may fail to detect these elements in the conscious state in which they are said to enter, so long as we merely look to the sort of analysis which we can ordinarily make of consciousness at any one instant.   It is psychological experiment that enables us to get elements in relative isolation, and also to show that they correspond to disturbances of sense organs, and to resulting excitations of brain, which we can prove to be part of the physical accompaniment of those conscious processes into which these elements are said to enter.   Furthermore, when the elements have once been isolated by experimental devices, it very generally proves to be possible to detect their presence within conscious states closely similar to the very ones in which it was at first impossible to find them.　At all events, it is possible by analysis to find, in our total conscious state, at least traces of something similar to the isolated elements, when once we have observed the latter.　It is true that, even then, the conscious processes in which we find traces of the elements that we have once learned to analyse, through the experimental devices that have given us these elements in isolation, are processes which occur *after* our experiments have been made; and are therefore no longer identical with those states of our naïve and untrained consciousness in which we could not as yet discover any trace of these elements by any effort then possible to us.　Nevertheless, *the theory here in question supposes that all our conscious processes, even the ones whose elements we have never learned to observe in isolation,* are actually composed of such elements.　And because of the experimental results whose nature has been in general indicated, this view is commonly advanced as a strictly empirical conclusion.

§ 43.　A few further examples are still necessary to illustrate the way in which such a conclusion comes to appear to many so convincing.　When the unmusical person hears a musical chord, or listens to a complex harmony, he is unable, in general, to give any complete account of the elementary tones of which the harmonious sounds consist. He is indeed aware of a certain richness in the whole experience, which would enable him to say that he is listening to *something* complex. In the case of the harmony due to various instruments or voices, he is more or less able to distinguish, as he listens, what belongs to each instrument or voice, unless indeed the voices and instruments are numerous, when once more he quickly loses his power to analyse. The musician, accustomed to hear voices, instruments, and single tones, in isolation, as well as in harmonious union, analyses at pleasure the harmonious effect, and knows that the sound consists of a certain collection of tones, which even while they blend, constitute for him still a distinguishable collection. But physical and psychological experiments go still further in the analysis of tones than the ordinary musical consciousness goes. The physical disturbance produced by striking a single key on the piano is a highly complex, but analysable, system of sound waves. It is discovered that the more elementary constituents of which this system of vibrations consists can be experimentally isolated. In this case, such more elementary constituents of the total physical process, when they are isolated, produce certain sensations, namely, the " partial tones," of which the original tone is consequently said to consist. When once the ear has been trained, by listening to the partial tones in isolation, it then becomes possible for consciousness to discover, by analysis, the presence of these partial tones in what at first appeared to be the single tone of the piano. *In consequence the theory seems warranted that the original tone, viewed as a conscious state, was not simple,* but was a blending of various elementary states, corresponding to the so-called fundamental tone which determines the pitch of the note that the untrained ear hears, and to the various "partial tones," which sound along with the fundamental tone, and which constitute part of the total physical process upon which our original hearing of the tone depends. *It seems, at first sight, that we here have an empirical proof of how a mental state which seems to the untrained consciousness simple, actually consists of many mental elements.*

In a very different field we meet with a corresponding analysis of a complex mental state, in case of what has been called the "feeling of effort," which we observe when we make a movement requiring a considerable exertion of energy. Our ordinary consciousness does indeed indicate that this "feeling of effort" is a complicated state. But processes of isolation of the kind already illustrated gradually bring us to observe that such a "feeling of effort" is a complex state possessing a decidedly discoverable constitution, and due to various sensory disturbances produced by the contraction of our muscles, by the rubbing of our joint surfaces together, by stretching and pressure, occurring

in skin, tendons, etc., or finally to mental images suggested to us by the results of former sensory experiences of just this kind.   The "feeling of effort" is
consequently said by the present theory *to consist of
mental elements corresponding to these various elementary
excitations*.

§ 44. So much must suffice as a general indication
of the theory of the structure of consciousness here in
question.   No one can doubt the importance of the experimental evidence upon which it is based.   And no
one can doubt that this importance is partly a matter
of psychological concern.   We *do* gain a great deal
for the understanding of our conscious processes when
we discover that they accompany physical processes
whose complex structure can be studied, and whose
more elementary constituents can be analysed.   We
gain also when we learn that these more elementary
physical processes can be found to be accompanied,
when once they are isolated, by certain simpler mental
states.   We also advance in insight when we learn
that, when once our powers of analysis have been
trained, we can detect the traces of such simpler
states in the massive states of consciousness with
which we began, although these massive states at
first seemed to defy any minute analysis.   On the
other hand, it may well be questioned whether these
results of experience are *rightly interpreted* by the
theory that we have just been summarising.   Con-

sciousness, as we have already said, is not a shower of shot. *It does not come to us as consisting of these elementary states.* When what is called the "analysis" of the original unity of consciousness takes place through these devices of isolation, and through a comparison of the results of isolation with the complex mental states that we produce *after* studying the isolated elements, for the sake of verifying the results of our "analysis," then what is "analysed" *is not the original naïve consciousness, which was whatever it was found to be at the time when it occurred.* On the contrary, what we "analyse" is *a new sort of consciousness* that takes the place of our original and naïve consciousness — a more sophisticated consciousness, so to speak. Now the psychologist is indeed *equally* interested both in naïve and in sophisticated consciousness. But whatever the relations between the two may be, he is not justified in asserting of the naïve consciousness that it already possesses the structure which experimentally trained analysis can learn to find in the more sophisticated consciousness.

Whoever hears the chord and does *not* analyse it, has heard a certain whole in which he simply did not detect parts such as the later analysis detects in the chords that it examines. Now a state of consciousness exists when somebody is conscious of that state. When nobody is conscious of that state, it does not exist. When the musician observes the chord to be an unity wherein he finds an actually conscious and analysed variety, he finds what he finds. But what he finds is simply not present in the consciousness of the unmusical listener. The elements that analysis detects exist, as conscious states, when they are detected and not before. Not only is this true of the elements that can be isolated only by careful experiment or by means of technical training. It holds also of those elements which we can either find or not in a given present conscious state, according as we do or do not choose to attend to them. As has been said, we always observe in any conscious state unity and multiplicity. But the conscious state contains exactly such multiplicity as we do observe. *The multiplicity that we might observe, and do not observe, belongs to a possible mental state which, at the moment of our failure to observe, we do not possess.*

It now seems to us, therefore, wrong to say that a mental state consists at any time of elements which we ourselves do not distinguish in that state. When we assert that these elements are nevertheless there, although they are not distinguished, we are considering not the mental state itself, but either what we know about the complex external physical object of which we suppose this mental state to be the sign; or else what we know about the state of the brain; or again what we know about the meaning of this mental state, when the latter is regarded as a stage in a logically or morally significant process; or else, finally, we are referring to a more sophisticated state of mind which the psychologist, by his devices for analysis, has substituted for the original and naïve consciousness. The physical world contains countless aspects that at any moment we might observe, but do not. If this physical world is viewed as the object of which at any moment our consciousness is showing us some aspect, we can indeed quite correctly say that our consciousness *fails to observe the elements* of which its physical object all the time consists. In a similar fashion, a complex brain process consists of elementary processes. And just so every state of consciousness that we have is also a stage in a mental process that in the whole of our lives has a very rich meaning. Of this meaning we may become conscious afresh from various and countless points of view. We may accordingly quite rightly say that any conscious state means a great deal of which we are just then not conscious. If, by analysis, we can detect something of this meaning, we can then say that what our analysis discovers was present, *as a meaning*, in the state that we did not analyse. But the concept of the psychological element, present when it is not observed, but constitutive, along with other elements, of the mental state in which it was not observed, is a conception neither of a physical fact nor of a moral or logical or æsthetic meaning. Such elements are found only in those states of mind which result from habits of analysis.

If the musician says to the unmusical man, "You heard the chord; and, as a fact of your consciousness that chord was composed of these tones; yet of these tones you were not conscious," we can understand what the musician means if he intends to say something about the physical constitution of the sound-vibration. We also can easily understand him if he means to say something about the constitution of the process in the sense organ or in the brain centres of the one who heard the tone. And we can well understand his meaning if he intends to say something about the musically valuable fact, if for instance he implies something of this sort "the æsthetic reason why that chord was so rich to you or so beautiful depended upon the fact that it had this constitution." In this last case the musician may be analysing not so much the physical or the neurological complexity of the processes concerned, as the meaning which the whole state had for the one who admired the chord, but who did not analyse it. But if the musician persists in saying "the chord as a conscious fact consisted for you of mental states corresponding to its various constituent tones, but you are not aware of these mental states, because they blended into the one total impression," then indeed the musician seems to be asserting the existence of a mental state which was not

the mental state of anybody — not of the musician,
since he analyses the chord, nor of the unmusical
man, since the supposed element finds no place in
his consciousness that he himself, for whom alone
his mental facts can exist, is capable of observing.

§ 45. But what from this point of view, as one may
insist, becomes of the vast body of empirical evidence
whose existence we before admitted? We answer (as
the just cited case of the musical and the unmusical
experience indicates) : All this evidence exists indeed,
but it does not prove that our consciousness consists of
any other elements than of those which we at any time
observe as the variety present within its unity. Our
consciousness is what we find it to be. What the
psychologists can tell us about it must consist, *first*, of
a more careful restatement and generalisation of the
characters that, upon various occasions, various human
beings actually find there. It is the business of the
psychologists to note what the ordinary consciousness
forgets, namely, the various observations which we can
from time to time make, or do from time to time make,
upon the contents of consciousness. And now, *second*,
it is the business of the psychologists to discover what
ordinary observation altogether ignores, or at best only
fragmentarily notices, namely, the sequence and connection of our successive mental states. And, *third*, it
is indeed a very important part of the psychologists'
task to discover the laws that govern these sequences,

and their relation to their physical accompaniments and conditions.   It is especially in connection with this last great task of the psychologists that the experimental facts, which are usually supposed to prove the existence of mental elements, find their true place and significance.

What these empirical evidences *do* show is *first, the relation of our conscious states to their physical accompaniments and conditions.*   One of the most important of these relations is statable in the following terms : *when we have a conscious state which as a fact we do not analyse or discover to be various in its constitution beyond a certain point, this mental state is in general dependent upon very complex physical conditions.*   These physical conditions are in large measure due to stimulations of our sense organs.   They are also in large measure due to such central brain disturbances as are only indirectly connected with our sense organs.   Now these complex physical conditions are capable, in many cases, of being excited in relative isolation.   When this occurs we very generally find what has been already reported, namely, that *to the elementary and more or less completely isolated physical disturbance, there corresponds a relatively simple mental state.*   So much then for the thus discovered relations of mental and of cerebral processes.   We *further* discover that *if we get again a total mental state as similar as possible to the one which before we did not analyse* (for example, if we strike

I

again the same musical chord after having experienced one of its elements in isolation) *we can then, in a very large number of cases, detect in the renewed mental state the elements which we have observed in isolation, and which we did not observe in the original state.* In brief, by devices of this sort we can learn to *substitute analysed mental states for unanalysed mental states.*[1]

Since we can conceive this process of substitution carried much farther than our experimental processes have carried it at any particular stage of the process, we can form upon good empirical grounds a general theory of the type thus expressed : *To every unanalysed mental state there may be made to correspond an analysable mental state, or, in case of actual success, an actually analysed mental state.* The physical conditions of the new state agree in the main with the conditions of the original mental state, except in so far as these conditions include such habits of brain as have been acquired by the intervening experiments, or by other analytic devices. The mental expression of these habits is the habit of analysis itself. In the analysed mental state the variety that consciousness detects corresponds to a variety that may also be discovered in the physical or physiological conditions, both of the

---

[1] This substitution is not possible in *all* cases where an analysis of the physical disturbance into simpler physical disturbances is possible, *e.g.* in case of the colours of mixed light. But the remark in the text is true of a large class of cases.

original mental state, and of the analysed mental state. This is the summary of the empirical facts. The facts are important because they enable us to learn what we should otherwise miss concerning the constitution of the physical conditions upon which both our analysed and our unanalysed mental states depend. Furthermore, the whole series of phenomena shows an interesting and *uniform connection between analysed and unanalysed mental states.* Since, as we shall see, the whole development of our intelligent life involves an increasing *differentiation of our mental powers*, it becomes of the utmost importance to understand the conditions upon which such differentiation depends. The experimental processes that we have summarised form an invaluable contribution to this knowledge. *They show us by experiment how consciousness becomes differentiated,* in other words, *how a most important aspect of mental growth takes place.*

§ 46. Finally, if we choose another way of summarising these same facts, we may indeed say that since, in so many cases, an analysed state of consciousness can be made to correspond to a previous unanalysed state in the way pointed out, and since, where this process is not carried out, we have good reasons to conceive it possible, we may declare that every state of consciousness which is due to a complex collection of sensory and central processes may, when viewed with reference to its physical conditions, be treated *as if it were* complex of mental elements corresponding to certain more elementary physical processes, such that these more elementary processes, when isolated, are capable of producing elementary mental states, and such that these elementary states can be found by our attention as constituents of analysed states of consciousness. But when we use this mode of expression, we must remember that we are employing a *convenient fiction*. The mental state presented to the naïve consciousness is just then what it seems to be, and is, literally speaking, no more various than at the moment we find it to be. It can be treated as if it were composed of elements that we do not analyse, only in so far as we compare it in the before-mentioned way with the analysed mental states that correspond to it whenever our habits of analysis have been formed, and when we consider it with reference to its physical and physiological conditions.

That other way of analysing mental states which has been mentioned in the course of the foregoing discussion — that way of analysing the meaning which they possess in the logical or in the otherwise significant context of our mental life — does not concern the psychologist. The logician, the metaphysician, the moralist, and the student of æsthetics, are interested in the meaning of mental life. The psychologist is interested, first, in what is literally present to consciousness at any one moment; second, in the various series or successions of mental states that are discoverable; and third, in the laws which govern both these processes and the physical condition upon which they depend. For the psychologist, therefore, the complex meaning which every mental state undoubtedly possesses may indeed be infinite, but is not relevant.

---

§ 47. We have now considered the general characteristics of consciousness, and have also in the most general outlines indicated its relation to its external conditions, and cerebral accompaniments; and in the remainder of our discussion our task will fall into the following principal divisions : —

(1) We shall make a summary statement of the principal kinds of states of consciousness that occur within the range of our psychological experience ; and we shall consider these with especial relations to the sorts of physical conditions upon which they depend. Since states of consciousness take place from moment to moment in connection with the present state of the organism, and since in consequence all consciousness, at the moment when it takes place, may be regarded as an accompaniment of the responses of our sensitive organism to the world in which it exists, we may regard all this first division of our task as A STUDY OF SENSITIVENESS. This study will contain three subdivisions, the first dealing with our SENSORY EXPERIENCE, the

second with our IMAGES, the third with our FEEL-
INGS.

(2) Having become better acquainted, in this way,
with the contents of consciousness as it passes, we
shall next proceed in a series of chapters to a study of
the relations that bind the consciousness of any moment to previous experience. This division of our
discussion may be regarded as A STUDY OF DOCILITY.

(3) Since, as we saw before, our mental states not
only appear to be dependent upon our relations to
past experience, but also to depend upon factors that
make possible that kind of variation of our conduct,
and of our mental processes, which we sketched in one
section of our discussion of the signs of mental life, we
shall need to include under a third head a very summary chapter which we may entitle, THE CONDITIONS
OF MENTAL INITIATIVE.

CHAPTER V

SENSITIVENESS

A. SENSORY EXPERIENCE

§ 48. It is customary, in modern text-books of psychology, to introduce the study of all the higher forms of mental life by a statement of the results which experimental research has now reached regarding what are called the sensations. The term "sensation" is one employed, in its usual modern usage, in connection with that theory of the real existence of mental elements to which we have already devoted some attention. For the theory in question a sensation is an elementary mental state that is due, either to the direct excitement of some sense organ and of the corresponding brain centre, or to some central brain process that may be regarded as equivalent to a disturbance produced through a sense organ. It is essential to the concept of a sensation, from this point of view, that a sensation should be *an ideally simple state*. So far as the present state of our consciousness is directly due to the excitement of our organs of sense, *our consciousness* is considered, by the theory in question, as *a complex consisting of such elementary sensations*. In so far as our present consciousness consists of *images of objects that are not now physically present to us*, it is said by the theory in question *to be made up of elementary states which may be due to, or which perhaps must be due to, former sensations.* In any case, these elementary states, as they at present occur, — the elementary mental states, namely, of which our images of absent objects consist, or of which in general our "ideas" are said to be composed, — are regarded by many recent psychologists as *composed of elements which do not differ in any essential character from sensations.* They are said to be "faint sensations." Or again they are called "centrally aroused sensations," so that they are often regarded not merely as being due to former sensations, but as being even at present of the nature of sensations.

On the basis of such a theory, the concept of a sensation becomes one of the most fundamental importance for all descriptive psychology. The only other sorts of elementary mental states which such views commonly recognise are the elementary states called "feelings." Apart from the feelings, our present consciousness is regarded by such theories as entirely made up of the elements called sensations.

§ 49. Our own attitude toward theories of this type has already been indicated. In what sense consciousness can be said to be composed of any elementary states we have indicated, in so far as such indication is, in my opinion, possible. As we shall now have to see more in detail, all our present consciousness, of whatever type, is accompanied by central disturbances of the brain, which are either directly due to the excitements of our sense organs, or are of a type essentially similar to the disturbances which are due to the sense organs. In consequence, it is literally true for the psychologist that *all consciousness, when it occurs, and whatever else it implies or contains, is a manifestation of present sensitiveness,* that is of the fact that our organism is disturbed by external or internal stimulations, and of the fact that these disturbances reach the cortex of the brain. It is also unquestionably true that every present excitement of the brain consists of processes which can be more or less perfectly resolved by experimental analysis into elementary processes, such as can occur in relative isolation; and of these elementary processes there are a good many which, when excited in such relative isolation, are attended by relatively simple mental states. All this has been illustrated in the foregoing discussion, for example, by the case of musical chords and tones. But we cannot say that our consciousness in any literal sense consists of sensations, and still less that it consists of absolutely elementary sensations. Nor would the statement become true if we merely added the word "feeling" to the word "sensation." On the other hand, since our consciousness may thus be unquestionably described as an accompaniment of the sensitiveness of our organism, and since this sensitiveness of our organism is something very complex, and since its various modes can be more or less completely analysed, considerable light is thrown upon the relation of consciousness, both to its conditions and to our own habits of conscious analysis, when we examine as precisely as the modern experimental study of sensation does, *the various relatively simple states of mind that can be produced in response to relatively simple stimulations of our sense organs.*

§ 50. From our point of view, then, a sensation may be defined as *a relatively simple mental state, which we can by experiment more or less completely isolate, and which, when isolated, is found to be due to a relatively simple stimulation of brain centres*, either through the sense organs or through the revival of dispositions which previous sense disturbance has left in the brain centres. The relation of sensations to our actual consciousness, as it from moment to moment occurs, is the one formerly pointed out, namely, that to every present conscious state there may be made to correspond a mental state, or a collection of mental states which through training we have learned to analyse, and that, in these analysed mental states, elements, corresponding to what we have called sensations, will be found to be prominent. To discover this principle is to show how largely our conscious state at any moment, however lofty its dignity, or however unanalysable it then may seem, is actually due to conditions that accompany the excitement of our sense organs in determinate fashion.

§ 51. The general relations between our sense organs and the conscious present moments of our lives may be briefly summarised as follows : — In our normal waking life every conscious process, of whatever grade, may be said to be supported by sensory stimuli ; that is, our consciousness accompanies central nervous processes that depend upon the current stimulation of sense organs. On the other hand, every conscious process of normal waking life accompanies nervous processes that at least tend to produce more or less definite movements, and that, if not controlled through inhibitory processes, actually do so. A process of high intellectual level, such as writing, obviously illustrates this general principle. The conscious processes that occur when we write are in their most essential features inseparable from the sensory stimuli that we receive as we write, and from the movements that constitute the writing process itself. But the same holds true of mental activities that do not so obviously express themselves without in characteristic movements, and that are generally supposed to be mainly independent of our momentary relations to the outer world. The most absorbed meditation is affected by the sensory stimuli that we are receiving. This is shown by our well-known preference for certain places, surroundings, or objects, as aids to our meditations. One carries on a meditation of a given type best in his study, or again best in church, or again by preference during a walk in the fields. At such times one may not be at all directly conscious of how one's inner process is related to the sensory stimuli. Thus, in the fields, one may suppose that one is entirely oblivious of the natural facts about one, just because one is absorbed in some train of thought that bears on a scientific topic, or on a personal and practical problem. But none the less, the external objects are all the time sending in their sensory disturbances. These maintain certain current conditions of the brain. Were these conditions to change, the train of thought would change. And even where the connection between surrounding objects and the train of thought pursued is by no means one of which we are definitely conscious, the just mentioned preference for one sort of surrounding as against another, as the place for a given kind of meditation, illustrates how important this relation may be.

It is true that, for the purpose of supporting certain kinds of inner life, it is customary to cut off certain sensory stimuli. And while this is in obvious accordance with the principle here in question, it is also true that in certain cases the process may go so far as to make it appear as if the exclusion of sensation altogether, or as far as possible, is the device most useful for supporting some processes of meditation, or some

phases of what is often called the "interior life." Thus,
religious meditation has often been supported by devices which include solitude, going "into the closet and
shutting the door," and the effort to obtain silence in
one's surroundings.   Mystics and ascetics have carried
such processes of exclusion of external sensory disturbances very far; and have often supposed them to prove
that certain aspects of the higher life are dependent
upon the exclusion, rather than upon the support, of
any sensory stimuli.

But the psychologist is obliged to note that all such
processes of excluding certain sensory stimuli, are simply devices for the securing of the presence of other
sensory stimuli.   When the eyes are closed, we still
have a visual experience, that of the darkness of the
field of vision — an experience of a distinctly sensory
character, due to the remaining activities of the retina
of the eye.   If silence is obtained so far as external
sounds are concerned, one may all the more hear
sounds due to the circulation of the blood.   To suppress the disturbances of the usually more prominent
types, means all the more to emphasise those masses
of sensory disturbance which are due to our internal
organs.   The importance that instinct or habit may
give to these organic sense disturbances, when once
our consciousness comes to be very strongly coloured
through their presence, may be very great.   The literature of meditation is full of evidences of the promi-

nence that experiences thus determined have possessed in the life of those who often imagined themselves to be independent of the senses in precisely the highest of their mental processes. Thus fasting and wakefulness are productive of characteristic, although, in various people, of decidedly different sorts of sensory experience, due to the alterations of organic conditions. If an ascetic or a meditative person uses fasting or vigil as a means to support his meditation, he is quite as definitely dependent upon the excitement of certain sense organs as if he ate olives or played the violin. And it is perfectly true that certain of the organic sensations have a relation to the higher mental life which those who are devoted to the observation of things outside the organism often fail to discover.

But the connection between our mental and sensory life is not even thus exhausted. For, as we have just said, our sense disturbances, and the attendant central processes of whatever type, normally tend to get themselves expressed outwardly in motion. But *our movements, when they occur, are at every stage the source of new sensory experiences.* The contractions of muscles, the series of positions of a moving organ such as the hand or the leg, become reflected in our consciousness through sensory disturbances that *inform us of what takes place when we move.* These sensory disturbances are largely of the kind that, when isolated, give us the sensations known as the muscular sensations, the joint sensations, the sensations of strain, and in general *our motor experiences.* Visual experiences take part in this same process whereby we become aware of our movements. For at every moment, as we walk, we guide our steps by means of the eye; and most of the skilful activities of the hand are more or less supported in the same way. Experiences due to the sense of hearing guide us whenever we use the voice; so that deafness, even when acquired very late in life, tends to affect vocal skill. The weight of the experimental and pathological evidence is to the effect that *we are unaware of our own movements except in terms of the sensory experiences which thus accompany and result from their occurrence.* To the outgoing nervous current in the motor nerves, consciousness does not directly correspond. But all the more must our sensory experiences become important for the support of our voluntary as well as of our intellectual life, in view of the fact that our sensory experience is not only a constant accompaniment of the processes that determine our movements, but furnishes the basis for the only knowledge that we are able to possess of what our movements are.

The practical application of the foregoing considerations regarding the centrally important place which sensory experience occupies in our lives, is obvious, and is, for every one who has to guide minds, of the most critical importance. *The development and support of men-*

tal activities of every grade is dependent upon the constant and proper use of the sense organs. Every cultivation of even the highest inner life involves a cultivation of the sense organs. To use a very imperfect simile : the sense organs are related to the higher mental life somewhat as the keys and stops of the organ are related to the music. In vain is the organist's skill, if the keys and stops will not work. In vain is the composer's art, if the mechanism of the instrument is not also in working order.

The life of the senses does not constitute a sort of lower life, over against which the higher intellectual, emotional, and voluntary life stands, as a markedly contrasted region, relatively independent of the other, and ideally capable of a certain divorce from it. On the contrary, sensory experience plays its part, and its essential part, in the very highest of our spiritual existence. When we wish to cultivate processes of abstract thinking, our devices must therefore include a fitting plan for the cultivation of the senses, and must not seek to exclude sense experience as such, but only to select among sensory experiences those that will prove useful for a purpose.

In the attempt to cultivate and to support religious meditation of the higher type, the ritualist has consequently often appeared more psychological in his devices than did the Puritan of old, who endeavoured to support religious life by excluding what he regarded as a confusing or as a corrupting appeal to the senses. In so far as the devices of exclusion which so often characterise the Puritan forms of worship, were accompanied by an equal fear both of externally attractive sense experiences, and of many of the forms of worship which mystics have employed for the sake of arousing the fitting organic sensations, Puritanism, in some of its forms, seems to have tended inevitably to the impoverishment of religious experience. When it escaped this result, and passed through its times of awakening and of fervour, its success was due not to its mere exclusion of appeals to the senses, but to its encouragement of those forms of sensory experience which were connected with strenuous and dutiful activities, and with the motor processes accompanying earnest prayer. The mystics themselves, in waiting for "the voice of the spirit," were psychologically aided by the concentration of their attention upon certain types of organic sensation. In brief, whatever be the best form of religious training, *it ought deliberately to make use of a proper appeal to the senses.*

In general, then, higher mental training depends not upon avoiding sensory experience, but upon selecting the right kind of sense disturbance, and upon presenting sensory experiences in such order as to train fitting habits of movement.

§ 52. Any extended discussion of the various types of special sensations is impossible in this place. A full

K

account would demand, in the present state of experimental research, hundreds of pages. A mere catalogue of the distinguishable sorts of simple sensory experiences would prove uninstructive. For fuller accounts the reader must accordingly be referred to more special treatises. Our concern is here with some of the most general considerations as to the classification of our sensory experience.

One must distinguish, in the first place, between the sensory states that especially or principally *give us information concerning the movements and the internal changes of our organism,* and those which principally *give us information regarding stimuli which are external to the organism.*

The distinction here in question is indeed not altogether a sharp one. It cannot be sharp, simply because every external disturbance which affects our consciousness is also, in some degree, a disturbance of the whole organism. Moreover, when I move my hand, in order to grasp an object, I both see the outer object and also see my moving hand, so that, in this case, sensory experiences of the same general type give me information both concerning my own movements and concerning the external things. I use both these results of seeing as I guide my act of grasping. The same holds true when, in walking, I both see the inequalities of the path, and by means of my eyes am able in part to guide the movements whereby I adjust my feet to the ground;

or when, in conversing, I both hear my fellow's speech and am able, through my ear, to guide the modulations of my own voice. But there are indeed certain sorts of sensory experience, namely, the so-called " organic sensations," which are *principally* of use as informing me regarding the internal states of my organism; while such sensory experiences as those of sight are *most* indispensable to me when they are sources of knowledge about facts external to my organism. For while I can learn to carry out very complicated voluntary movements in the dark, and could learn such arts even if I were blind; on the other hand, if I were blind, I could never learn to distinguish between the presence and absence of light in the outer world.

§ 53. Beginning, then, with the sensory experiences which are predominantly *internal, i.e.* which especially inform one as to the states and the changes of one's own organism, we may name, first, the "organic sensations" themselves. Sensory experiences of this type form a vast, and in part a very vaguely complex realm; and the experimental production of analysed states of mind, such as enable us to study definite small groups of organic sensations in isolation, is extremely difficult. We are able, however, to name, as especially important amongst the organic sensory experiences: (1) those which inform us as to the *general position of our bodies*, and *as to the changes in the bodily equilibrium*. These experiences include certain sensory facts that enable us to judge of the direction of movement of the organism, especially of the head, whenever this direction is suddenly altered. (2) We have to name those organic sensory experiences by which we become aware of our *more special and differentiated movements*, in so far as these are known to us through sense disturbances directly due to *the contraction of muscles*, the *stretching of tendons*, the *contact of the internal surfaces of joints*, etc.   There are also (3) those experiences which take the form of more or less sharply localised internal *pains;* (4) those complexes of sensory experience which appear in *hunger*, *thirst*, and similar organic states; and (5) those which, when taken together with certain masses of feelings, give special character to our *emotional experiences* (as for instance the " choking in the throat" which accompanies anger, and many of the other sensory accompaniments of emotion). Of the importance of these organic sensations, as constituting a decidedly *fundamental sensory aspect of all our mental life*, we shall speak further in other connections.

Next to the organic sensations, both in their general character and in the kind of significance which they possess for our mental life, stand the sensory experiences due to the disturbances of the skin.   In case of a large number of our organic sensory experiences, the disturbances of the skin due to stretching, to wrinkling, to tickling, to perspiration, etc., join with the more internal organic conditions to determine what we notice as our own present bodily condition. The same is true of the sensations of pain, which a vast number of points on the skin can so freely give us.

In so far the "dermal sense," as it is sometimes called, is a part of the condition of our organic sensory experience. But the skin also contains a vast number of sense organs which are of constant use to us in learning about external objects. The sensory experiences here in question are those of *contact* and of *temperature*. They are due to the excitation of points on the skin which differ for the various special sorts of experiences in question. Experiment shows that certain points of the skin are especially sensitive to stimulations given by *cold* objects, while other points are sensitive to disturbances due to *hot* objects. Our ordinary sensory experience of warmth or of cold is due to a complex excitement of many points of both these types. Still other points on the skin, very wealthily interspersed amongst the others, give us, if excited in isolation, sensations of *contact* or of *pressure*. Complex sensory excitations, due to the disturbances of the skin, sometimes with and sometimes without, notable accompanying organic disturbances, give us our experiences of *hard* and *soft*, of *rough* and *smooth*, of *dry* and *moist* objects. Sensory experiences due to our own movements, made as we explore and handle objects, are seldom lacking as aspects

or portions of the experiences whereby we judge both
the foregoing, and many other of the qualities of the
bodies with which we come in contact.

§ 54. Next to the dermal sensations, in that series of
our sensory experiences which is now in question, come
experiences of the senses of taste and smell. These,
as they usually appear in our consciousness, are
very decidedly coloured by feelings, and are consequently closely associated in our mind with our
estimate of our own bodily state; but, on the other
hand, they are constantly used as indications of the
nature of external objects. The sensory experiences
of these two senses are very frequently aroused
together. This is the case with most articles of food.
Experimental analysis shows that, while the sense of
taste is comparatively simple in its experiences, there
being but four distinct qualities that can be referred to
the sense of taste alone, the sense of smell, on the other
hand, gives us experiences of an enormous variety, for
which no satisfactory classification has yet been found.
The four classes of taste experiences are those of the
qualities: sweet, acid, salt, and bitter. For the experiences of the sense of smell, language has a considerable,
but altogether inadequate collection of names, mostly
derived from the names of the objects to which the
odours belong. The more precise relations among these
odours are very little known either to common sense or
to psychologists.

The two highest among the senses are those of sight and hearing. Their experiences are of special importance to us in all our relations to the world outside the organism. Yet, as has already been pointed out, we also use the data of these senses in becoming aware of our own reactions to the environment. These senses then do indeed make us acquainted with our own bodily state, but their predominant value lies in the knowledge of outer objects that they furnish.

The sensory experiences of the sense of sight are of two great classes,— those possessed of the quality known as colour, and those possessed of the quality of colourless light. As to the precise relation of these two classes of experiences, it is impossible here further to speak. We can, however, point out that the sensory experiences of the sense of sight are capable of a decidedly exhaustive classification, and constitute one of the best-known regions of sensory experience. The experiences of the sense of hearing belong to the two great classes of the noises and of the musical tones. The musical tones have relationships whose æsthetic importance has made them extremely familiar. Nowhere better than in the case of the sense of hearing are we able to study the precise relations between our sensory experiences and their external physical causes; but the theory of the sense experiences of hearing forms again a specialty far too complex for the present discussion to enter upon.

As the senses of sight and of hearing are preëminent in their power to give us an acquaintance with the external world, so they are especially marked by the sorts of discriminating analysis which their sensory experiences awaken in the trained consciousness. The various sensory experiences of the sense of sight come to us, from moment to moment, with such an order and arrangement that we are able clearly to distinguish one visible object from another, and, with minute accuracy, to differentiate one part of the field of vision from another part. The experiences of the sense of hearing are such as to permit the training of a very high degree of power to analyse the constitution of sounds — a power of which we have already made mention in giving our examples of the general nature of analysed states of mind.

§ 55. Common to all the various types of sensory experiences which have been indicated in the foregoing discussion, is the presence of *two notable characters* which are sometimes called Attributes of Sensation. Every sensation possesses, namely, Quality and Intensity. Sensations differ in quality when the difference is of the sort whereby we distinguish two colours, or is of the sort whereby we distinguish hot and cold, or sweet and bitter. Two sensations differ in intensity when they differ as a loud tone at a given pitch differs from a softer tone at the same pitch, or as our experience of a notable pressure differs from our experience of a very light pressure. The characteristics of quality and of intensity can be most exactly attributed to single sensations in so far as the latter have been experimentally isolated. But the same characters are to be found also in the masses of sensory experience which characterise our naïve consciousness. *Ideally speaking, sensations or sensory experiences of any sort can be exactly compared in intensity only in so far as they very closely agree in quality.* Thus, it is impossible to say whether a given sensory experience of weight is more intense in its heaviness than a given sound is intense in its loudness. Yet, owing to the fact that entirely isolated sensations which are precisely the same in quality, but which differ only in intensity, are decidedly ideal objects of psychological conception, comparisons of the intensity of our experiences are generally more or less mingled with differences of quality. The variations in intensity of sensation are capable of being arranged in series corresponding, although not proportionate, to the physical magnitudes of the external sources of stimulation. To a stimulation that sufficiently exceeds another in magnitude, there will correspond, when comparisons in intensity are possible, a sensory experience of a noticeably greater intensity. But the correspondence in question must not be interpreted as implying that the intensities of sensations are themselves quantities in the same sense in which physical magnitudes are quantities. As to the relation between the intensities of sensations and the magnitudes of the stimuli, there has been very elaborate experimental investigation. The outcome of this investigation has been formulated in the so-called "psycho-physic law," which we shall briefly consider later under the head of Mental Docility.

The qualities of sensation have a much richer variety than the variations in intensity possess; for while the variations in the intensity of sensory experiences possessing the same quality form a simple series, the variations of quality of our sensory experiences can be arranged in no single series, but are presented to our attention, in so far as we have learned to discriminate them, in a very great complexity of series of facts. In our indication of the various general classes of sensations, we have already made some mention of certain characteristic and well-known qualities of sensory experience. The various senses are distinguished from one another in terms of sense qualities. Thus, the colours and the sounds differ from one another in quality. Here the difference of quality is associated with a very obvious difference of the sense organs. In other cases, where it requires decidedly careful experiments to detect any difference of the sense organs, the differences in quality first attract our attention. So it has been, for instance, in the case of the sense experience of the hot and cold points of the skin. It was long supposed that the temperature sense possessed a single type of sense organs, *all* of which gave us, according to the intensity of the stimulation, experiences of hot and cold qualities. It is now known that these qualities are due to the excitation of different sense organs. But within the field of any one sense, as for instance the sense of sight, we have variations of sense quality which correspond not only to differences of sense organ but also to differences in the way in which a single sense organ is stimulated by different external disturbances. No absolutely general rule can therefore be given as to the extent to which qualitative differences of sensory experiences imply the excitation of different sense organs. But, on the whole, *the qualities of sensation as they come to consciousness depend, in general, upon two types of facts, namely, first upon the different sense organs stimulated, and secondly upon the physically different characters of the external stimuli.*

§ 56. It remains to speak of still another attribute possessed by a great number of our sensory experiences, and especially by those of the dermal sense and of the sense of sight. This character is the one upon which our developed ideas of Space depend. It is a character noticeable in every instance of our sensory experiences of the types in question, however simple the experience may otherwise be. This character may be called Extensity. Thus, every disturbance of the sense of sight gives us an impression of

light which, even if it be of the character of the
simplest possible point of light, still possesses some
feature whereby the point of light is localised in the
field of vision, *i.e.* is related to our consciousness of
visual space. Our ordinary experiences of the sense
of sight are experiences of a disturbance which
extend over a considerable portion of the field of
vision. Precisely so, in the field of the experiences
of touch, we are normally affected by stimuli which
appear to us to be in contact with a considerable
surface of the skin. And, even in case of the most
nearly simple or punctual sensation of touch which
we can experience, there still remains about this experience a character which enables us to localise with
considerable accuracy the point touched.

While the accurate localisation of our sensory experiences of sight and touch unquestionably depends
upon habits and associations which are phenomena of
our docility, and not of our merely present sensory
experience, it is impossible to regard our present visual
and tactile experiences, even when taken apart from
habit, as wholly destitute of spatial characters. Whatever we see or touch has spatial magnitude as one of
its directly presented characters. How far extensity
belongs in any measure to the senses of smell and
taste when considered in themselves, apart from their
associations with other sensory experience, is a matter
of question. The experiences of the sense of hearing

seem to possess some measure of extensity; and this character is very markedly present in a considerable portion of our organic sensations, if not in all of them. So that there is much to say for the view that *all our sensory experience without exception possesses the primitive character upon which our developed notion of space is founded.*

To say, however, that this character belongs to our various sensory experiences, is not to say that the character in question is in all respects as ultimate and inexplicable as are the qualities of our sensations. Why the colours should possess their immediate quality, and the sounds their quality, it is of course impossible to attempt in any sense to explain. But why our sensory experiences possess a certain primitive extensity may be, not indeed entirely explained, but brought into relation with other facts, if we take account of certain phenomena which have important relations to our whole organic life. The researches of Loeb and others have called attention, in the recent literature of genetic psychology, *to the vast importance which is possessed, in all grades of animal life, by the types of reaction which have been called tropisms of Orientation.*[1] We earlier made mention of such reactions when we were speaking of the various tropisms which Loeb has experimentally examined, as they exist in lower organisms. The general character of such reactions is that

[1] Cf. Fritz Hartmann's monograph, *Die Orientirung*, Leipzig, 1902.

they determine, in an organism of a given type, *a certain characteristic normal position of the organism with reference to its environment*, and certain equally characteristic tendencies on the part of the organism *to recover its normal position when it is for any reason temporarily lost*, and to assume, in the presence of stimuli of certain types, *certain directions of movement and certain attitudes which may persist through a great variety of special activities*. The phenomena here in question are, in a sense, very familiar to us all. The animal laid upon its back may struggle back again to the normal position. Or again, the human being when engaged in normal activities either sits or stands erect. When the eyes are engaged in their normal activity, the head is held erect, or, if these normal attitudes are modified, as in reading or in writing, the modification occurs only within certain limits. To attempt to carry on the same activities when lying on one's back, leads to discomfort, and interferes with the normal special movement of the eyes. It is thus a familiar fact *that a certain orientation of body*, that is, *a certain general direction of the organism with reference to its environment and with reference to the most important kinds of stimulation which are falling upon it, is a condition prior to all special activities*. Hence *the reactions of orientation are amongst the most fundamental phenomena of healthy life*. Profound disturbances of orientation necessarily imply very considerable defects, and in most cases very gravely important defects, in central functions. Thus our responses to our environment are not only special deeds, such as grasping this object, or looking at that object, but include general attitudes, namely, such acts as sitting or standing erect or holding the head up in order that we may see. And *the special acts are always superposed upon the general acts,* in such wise that if the general tropisms of orientation are seriously disturbed, the special acts, however habitual, will be interfered with or will prove to be impossible.

Now, as has been pointed out in the foregoing, all our voluntary activities tend to be represented from moment to moment in our sensory experience. It follows therefore that *our sensory experience at any moment will stand partly for our more general activities of orientation, and partly for our more special reactions to individual objects.* Since, meanwhile, every disturbance produced in us by an external object will become a conscious disturbance only in so far as we tend to respond to the presence of this object in some way, *all our particular sensory experiences will be related, not only to our special acts, but to our general acts of orientation, and to those experiences which result from these acts.*

Now the acts of orientation — such acts as holding ourselves erect, balancing as we move, keeping the organism as a whole alert in its relations to the world — are attended by organic sensations of a massive but

usually unanalysed character. These include, for
instance, those organic sensations by means of which
our movements are so controlled that we keep our
equilibrium — the organic sensations, namely, which are
deranged when we are dizzy. It is well known how the
sensations of dizziness are generally associated with a
defect, and, if they are intense, with a profound failure,
of orientation. On the other hand, in normal conditions,
our sensations of equilibrium are of the utmost importance as a basis for guiding all our special acts.[1] Furthermore, the movements that we make as we keep our
equilibrium are represented in our consciousness by
numerous massive sensory experiences due to muscles,
joints, etc.

It follows that our sensory consciousness of the world
in which we are, and of our own response to this world,
will constantly be of a type such that *if we become conscious of any particular sensory experience, especially of
the senses of sight and of touch, we shall discriminate
this particular experience upon a background of sensory
experience which is made up of the general present contents due to our experiences of orientation.* The experiences of orientation will form a general basis for our
special sensory consciousness. Within the whole of experience that our experiences of orientation determine,
all our special sensory experiences will be found. This

---

[1] These sensory experiences are due to the organ of the so-called " static
sense," viz., to the semicircular canals of the internal ear.

will be especially true of the senses of sight and of touch, because of the very significant relations of these experiences to certain specific movements of the eyes and of the organs of locomotion. It will be to a less extent true of the experiences of sound, in so far as these are related to movements of the head. It will be to a still less degree true of the sensory experiences of smell and of taste, because the relation of these to specific voluntary movements is less constant, or is such as less to alter our relation to our external environment.

It appears, in consequence, that the character of extensity possessed by our individual sensations *is a character which has some intimate connection with the relation possessed by these experiences to the total complex of our experiences of orientation.* When our experiences of orientation come to us as a single undifferentiated whole, they appear to constitute *our primal experience of the character known as extensity.* Our organism, as something oriented in a particular way in reference to its environment, appears in consciousness as something large, and as something that possesses what we shall learn to call "directions," just as soon as we have begun to discriminate within the total experience. Our special sensory experiences of the types most concerned with our particular movements are such that they tend to appear *as facts differentiated within this whole of our total experience of organic orientation.* That this fact should occur, we do not indeed attempt here wholly to

L

explain.   But we point out that the conscious relationship here mentioned is parallel to, or correspondent
with, that relation between our general acts of orientation and our special acts which we have already indicated in the foregoing summary.   As the general
orientation of the organism is to its special acts and
sensory experiences, so is, in our consciousness, our
general organic sensory experience of the presence and
the total orientation of our organic activity, to the
special experiences which our differentiated acts give
us.   Whatever character a particular sensory experience possesses which enables us to localise this experience as coming at a certain point in the organism, and
whatever character a given movement possesses which
enables us to specify its particular direction and other
special characters, and, finally, whatever character a
complex visual or tactual experience possesses which
enables us to judge of the size of the object that we
see or touch, all such sensory experiences appear to
our consciousness *as facts existent within a certain
primitive whole*, which, apart from differentiation, is *our
experience of the general orientation of the entire organism*.   We know special facts about space, such as sizes,
particular directions, and distances, in terms of certain
acts of our own, which we either perform from moment
to moment, or imagine in consequence of habits already
formed.   *We know of the world as possessing spatial characters at all, because we experience our general relation to*

our environment in the form of our organic sensory experiences of orientation. The special facts of our spatial consciousness are related to our general experience of extensity, *because the single facts of sense, and the single movements which we make, are always related to, or, as one may say, are differentiations of, our general orientation.*[1]

---

[1] Compare the somewhat different but related view as to the basis of our consciousness of extensity in the monograph of Storch, " Muskelfunktion und Bewusstsein " in Number X of the *Grenzfragen des Nerven und Seelenlebens,* 1901.

CHAPTER VI

B. MENTAL IMAGERY

§ 57. The field of mental sensitiveness includes not merely those aspects of our mental life which are due to the present disturbance of sense organs. It includes also those processes whose mental aspects appear in the IMAGES which constantly accompany all our more complex conscious processes. *These images are in general the indirect results of previous sensory disturbances.* In so far the consideration of the conditions which determine their appearance belongs under the head of Mental Docility. On the other hand, *in so far as the images from moment to moment appear, they depend upon the present state of the brain.* They manifest a part of the present disturbance which is produced in us by our whole relation to the world about us. They are therefore in so far manifestations of our present sensitiveness to such disturbances. If we suppose, by way of a fiction, that there could exist a mental state consisting altogether of mental images, and involving no aspects of consciousness due to the present disturb-

ance of our organs of external or of organic sensation, this mental state would none the less accompany
a condition of brain which would itself be a part of
our organic response to the situation in which at any
time we find ourselves. Such a mental state would,
therefore, manifest our sensitiveness, in so far as our
organism thrills, or shows resonance, in consequence
of what is happening to us. For all our central conditions are affected by sensory disturbances, even
when the sensory disturbances in question are not
directly manifested in our conscious state in the form
of present and conscious sensory experience.

It is, therefore, natural that the partisans of the
usual view, which regards our consciousness as a
complex of mental elements, should consider our
images as complexes of what are often called "centrally aroused sensations," that is, sensations due not
to the disturbance of sense organs, but to disturbances
which reach given brain centres from other brain centres, and not directly from sensory nerves. This way
of stating the case calls proper attention to the fact
that our sensitiveness at any moment includes processes whose physical aspect is due to disturbances
that pass from one part of the brain to the other,
and that, therefore, may be referred to what we have
just called the resonance of our central organs. For
the environment of every portion of the brain includes not only the external world and the organism

outside the brain, but the rest of the brain, in so far as *what goes on at one point in the brain can be due to stimulations brought thither from other points of the brain.*

When special mental images come to our consciousness as a distinguishable part of our total mental state, they are of types that correspond to the various types of our sensory experience. Thus we have visual images, images of sound, of touch, and so on. These images differ from our current sense experiences, due to external stimulation, or to organic conditions outside the brain, in ways which may be generally characterised thus: The images are usually somewhat fainter, and in fact very much fainter, than our sensory experiences themselves. They are vague. They are not so clear or so definite in outline and in structure as are the sensory experiences due to the direct presence of external objects. They are commonly more evanescent and changeable than are the sensory experiences. It becomes more difficult to us to observe their minor differences when we compare them together, or when we endeavour to compare them with present sensory experience. A good illustration of this character of our mental images is the difficulty of trying to match the colour of some absent object, with the colour of some present object, when we have only the image of the absent object to guide our process of matching. There exist persons who in shopping can choose a ribbon that will precisely match a ribbon that they have left at home, although they carry no sample with them. But such success is comparatively rare. In consequence of such differences, images have normally no tendency to be mistaken for present sense experiences. Yet the boundary line is, in certain conditions of consciousness, by no means perfectly sharp. When we listen at night for an expected footstep, or in a silent place for the anticipated ringing of a distant bell, we may "seem to hear" the sound before it really takes place; and under such conditions images and sensory experiences tend to become confused. The relative vagueness of our images when compared with our normal sensory experiences comes to light as soon as we begin to cross-question ourselves with regard to what we can observe in the image. Thus we can form after a fashion a visual image of a printed page. But if we ask ourselves what is the third word in the fourth line, we find in most cases that the image is unable to tell us.

Notwithstanding these usual characteristics of our images, closer examination shows that mental imagery varies very widely from mind to mind, and probably, if we were able to compare directly the processes of various minds, we should find a diversity even wider than our present means of comparison make clear.

§ 58. The modern study of the types of mental

imagery was begun by Mr. Francis Galton, who published his first results in the book called *Inquiries into Human Faculty and its Development*. Galton used the method of the so-called "questionaire" — a method since widely used in other psychological researches. He sent, namely, a circular to a large number of people, asking them to state in some detail the way in which they formed mental pictures of objects. His circular related to the so-called visual imagination, that is, to the power of seeing absent objects "with the mind's eye," or of forming images of objects that, when present, had been perceived through the sense of sight. He studied, in particular, the visual images of familiar objects. His results have since been supplemented by a large number of similar inquiries, many of which have been extended so as to cover the images belonging to other senses than that of sight. Certain pathological facts, presented by the cases of persons whose normal mental imagery had been affected by brain disease, called attention, a few years after the publication of Galton's study, to the importance of comparing the prominence which the imagery of one sense had in a life of any given person, with the importance possessed by the imagery of other senses.

The general results of these researches have been to show that the imagery of any one sense, in particular that of sight, has very great normal varia-

tion from person to person. While in general the
rule holds that normal mental imagery differs in a
very marked fashion from the experiences produced
through the direct excitation of sense organs, it
is still possible [to find people in whom the visual
images seem decidedly comparable in clearness,
in vividness, and in detail to the original sense perception. In many such persons it is possible to see
"in the mind's eye" more of a given familiar scene,
such as the interior of a room, than could be seen
from any one point of view in actual perception. It
is as if various images coalesced to form a mental
whole, which could not be attained in any one act
of perception. On the other hand, a very large number of persons have visual imagery which they themselves describe as very much less clear and definite
than the original object; and the test of asking such
persons questions about how much of the detail of a
visualised object they can report, if the test be
further controlled by comparing the report with the
original object, shows very decided limitations as to
the minuteness and the accuracy of the images that
are in question. A familiar test takes the form of
asking a person to visualise the face of his own
watch, and then to answer questions about the figures
on the watch face, and the position of the dial of the
second-hand with reference to these figures. Such
tests may be multiplied indefinitely. They show that

a large number of persons who have but a moderate
vividness and clearness of visual imagination are
conscious of images which are decidedly defective (1)
as to the scope of the field which they can get
before them in imagination, (2) as to the brightness
of the light and the precise shade of colour in this
field, and (3) as to the minuteness of detail which is
represented in the image. The last feature, namely,
the minuteness of detail, has a lower limit that, in
such cases, is very decidedly low when it is compared
with the normal precision of actual visual perceptions.
In many cases of a poorer visual imagination, *i.e.* in
the lower grades of the scale of visual imagination
which Galton originally set up, the individual objects,
when presented to the visual imagination, appear in
a blurred and fragmentary way, so that only parts
of them can be seen at once. Thus, for example, a
decidedly poor visualiser may be able to picture at
one time only the bowl of a silver spoon, or again
only a part of its handle, but never the whole spoon
at once. There remain a considerable number of
persons, often of a high degree of intelligence and
mental training, who have almost no visual images
at all, and whose mental imagery is made up entirely
of material belonging to other senses.

It is difficult to get sufficiently exact returns from
untrained people to estimate precisely the distribution
of these various classes of persons in the community

at large. On the whole, it appears that children, and young people generally, possess a better and richer visual imagination than the same people are likely to possess in middle life. It also appears that women possess a better visual imagination than men. The students of American institutions of learning appear on the whole to be better visualisers than the English men of science, of whose experiences Galton gives some account in his original study. How far the visual imagination can be trained, or prevented through training from fading away in middle life, is not yet known. There is some evidence that training has less effect upon the type of one's visual memory than some sanguine teachers are accustomed to suppose. At all events, there is considerable unlikelihood that a naturally poor visualiser can be turned into a very good one through training.

The visual imagery is predominant over the imagery of the other senses in a very great number of people, and this fact accounts for a great deal of the usage of language when the imagination is in question. Those who prefer the visual images, seem, so to speak, to have had possession of the language; so that the word "image," derived from visual experiences, is the only one at our disposal in the description of this type of mental processes; while the expressions concerning " mental vision," "clearness of insight," and the rest, which are so common in popular language in describing mental imagery, show that the experiences of the visualisers have come to be treated as if they were the only characteristic types of mental imagery. But, as a fact, there exist images belonging to the sense of sound, and to the types of sensory experience, muscular, organic, etc., in terms of which we recall our movements. Images of the sense of smell have been declared by some psychologists to be very rare; but there are indications in the reports of some collectors of facts which seem to point in the contrary direction, although it is obvious that such images are usually very subordinate. Images of taste appear most markedly in association with present sense perception, as when the sight of an apple known to be sour, or of vinegar, arouses the image of the sour taste. Yet in this case the taste image is probably much mingled with other forms of sensory experience.

Two types of persons have come to be especially noted in the literature of the subject as those in whom some other form of sense imagery is more prominent than the visual imagery. These two types are (1) the auditory type, in whom images of sounds predominate; and (2) the motor type, perhaps better to be called the verbal-motor type, in whom the predominant imagery takes the form of images of movement, together with images partly motor in type, but partly also auditory, of words. The third of these types seems to be, at least under modern conditions of training, and in middle life, decidedly common, although also decidedly inferior in number to the more or less skilful visualisers whose visual imagery predominates in their own experience. The motor type image their world especially in terms either of the movements that they themselves tend to make in the presence of things, or, in particular, in terms of the words which they use in naming and in describing things.   Much less skilful than the good visualisers in seizing upon, and retaining the visible details of objects, they may be more skilful than some fairly good visualisers in forming precise ideas of the space relations of objects.   In consequence, they are often skilful in noting those various more abstractly definable characters of things which can either be interpreted in terms of motor experience or fittingly described in words.

§ 59. The relation of our mental imagery to the higher mental processes must be indicated in passing, even before we reach the study of mental docility.   All our higher mental processes, in so far as they occur at any present moment, and in so far as they do not consist merely of sensory experiences and of feelings, must involve mental imagery.   Whatever the mental significance of a thought, however far-reaching its scope, however vast its meaning, it must, as a present thought, be embodied in a consciousness either of objects present to the senses or of objects present as images.   The sensory experience and the imagery, of any moment, when taken together with the state of feeling of that moment, constitute the mental material of the moment; and that, too, whether we are thinking of the loftiest or of the most trivial matters. The cultivation of the right mental imagery consequently constitutes a very important aspect of mental training.

It is to be noted, however, that our current mental imagery is normally by no means independent, either of our sense perceptions, or of our motor reactions. When we are engaged in the ordinary processes of external perception, the sensory experiences and the images of the moment are usually very intimately associated, so as to appear closely welded together. So it is when the sight of an edged tool is associated with the images of a possible cut to be received from it, or when the perception of a tennis-racket arouses the motor images which have their origin in the movements made when one used it. Even those trains of images which the reading of a story arouses have a similar connection with the sense impressions made by the printed page as one reads; and the trains of imagery which seem most independent of present sense perceptions (as in case of revery, when one stares into the fire or is in the dark) are still connected with the sense impressions produced by the firelight, or by the disturbances of the retinal field in the dark, or by organic sensory experiences. It follows that *the training of the imagination cannot normally occur apart from a fitting training of the senses*. For

not only are our imaginations, in general, due to re-
vivals of the effects left by former sensory experiences,
but the revival itself has relations to present sensory
experience which we shall later mention in connection
with mental docility.   The lesson of these obvious considerations has been neglected by those who have endeavoured to cultivate certain forms of abstract thought,
or of religious imagination, or, in general, of meditation,
apart from a due attention to the connection between
normal images and normal present sense experiences.

Less frequently noticed is *the connection between sensory images and our motor response to our environment.*
This connection appears, with special evidence, in the
case of our *motor images themselves.*   When in presence of familiar objects, such as our pen, our watch,
our knife, our dictionary, or our bunch of keys, we
examine the images that these objects awaken in us
as we observe them, we may often find images of a
more or less obviously motor type — images which take
the form of tendencies to conceive to ourselves certain
familiar acts which these objects call up in our minds.
Thus the pen may arouse the image of grasping the
pen for the purpose of writing, the knife may suggest
cutting, and so on.   Especially common is the presence
of a word-image at the moment when we observe an
object whose name we for any reason find it at all convenient to recall.   Such an image stands for the fact
that we actually begin the motor reaction of naming

the object. It is not, however, necessary that the images recalled in the presence of an object should be explicit motor images in order that they should be nevertheless related to the acts which the objects tend to arouse in us. At the sight of a steamboat that plies upon a lake or river known to me, I at once may begin to image, perhaps in visual form, scenes and other experiences that I have had as a tourist on that boat. But these images themselves very likely stand for a tendency now present in my consciousness to become again a voyager on the boat, and if I am at leisure, such images may erelong give place to the actual motor process of buying a ticket and going on board the boat. Furthermore, a vast number of images, visual as well as motor, relate to our anticipations of future events. But these *anticipations generally go along with tendencies to prepare for the future events by one or another sort of action.* In brief, *the whole normal life of our imagination has a most intimate connection to our conduct*, and should not be studied apart from conduct. The central processes which our images accompany form themselves a part of our reaction to our environment, and our more organised series of mental images actually form part of our conduct. This aspect of the matter is one which many psychological studies of our mental imagery lead us altogether too much to neglect. And many teachers suppose that to train the imagination of children involves something quite different from training their motor processes. But the normal imagination of healthy children is likely to get a rich expression in the form of their plays, of their dramatic impersonations, of their story-telling, and of their questions about things. And *the most wholesome training of the imagination is properly to be carried out in connection with the training of conduct.*

As is seen from the foregoing, the term "imagination" is most conveniently used as a name for the sum total of the mental processes that express themselves in our mental imagery. When used psychologically, the word "imagination" conveys no implication that the mental imagery in question stands for unreal or for merely fantastic objects. All mental imagery results from former sensory experience. Why images arise in the order in which they do arise is a question whose answer belongs under the head of our Mental Docility. As a consequence of the general character of all our mental imagery, our images tend to be decidedly imperfect representatives of real objects, and may be very highly fantastic. But the estimate of the value of our images is an estimate founded very much more on the consideration of the sort of conduct which results from their presence, than from any direct estimate of their value as pictures of objects. Good imagery is that which leads us to correct opinions and to useful conduct, as well as to harmlessly agreeable and satisfactory states of consciousness in general.

M

In training the imagination, a decided respect has to be paid to the varieties of types of mental images which have now been mentioned. The teacher who endeavours to train all pupils as if they were alike good visualisers, will indeed, in view of the fact that the good visualizers are numerous, obtain many successes. But he will be likely to regard as stupid those pupils who perhaps are defective only in the peculiar type of mental imagery which he asks them to use. There are some branches of early education, especially spelling, whose successful acquisition must to a considerable extent depend upon the choice, on the pupil's part, of the right sort of mental imagery for the retaining of the desired facts. What the right sort is, will depend upon whether such a pupil is rather of the visual, of the auditory, or of the motor type. For this will determine whether he most readily learns to spell by eye, by ear, or by means of the use of his tongue. In cases where the pupil himself finds difficulty in choosing the right imagery, the teacher may do well to take pains to discover something of what his type of imagination is, and direct his attention accordingly.

CHAPTER VII

Sensitiveness

C. THE FEELINGS

§ 60. We now come to that aspect of our mental sensitiveness which is the one most immediately interesting to ourselves, and also the one that, psychologically speaking, still remains the most obscure. This is the aspect which is sometimes known by the name of the FEELINGS. Owing to the ambiguous way in which the word "feeling" is used in popular language, some psychologists have preferred to speak of the "affective aspect" of our mental life. The term "affection," used in a technical sense, has also been employed for this aspect of our mental life. In speaking, in our introduction, of the signs of mental life, we have already called attention to the aspect of consciousness which is here in question. It is the aspect which becomes extremely prominent in case of very notable pleasures or pains due to our sense experience. It is the aspect also very marked in all our emotional life. It is also the aspect upon which our immediate sense of the present worth or value of our conscious states as they appear to ourselves must always rest.

It is plain that this aspect of our consciousness has
a very close relation to our activities, since both the
attainment of pleasant or of satisfactory feelings, and
the avoidance of painful states, constitute important
factors in the determination of our conduct.   Those
who divide mental life, in the well-known traditional
way, into the life of cognition, the life of feeling, and
the life of will, are accustomed to assign to the feelings
a stage intermediate between the life of cognition and
the life of will.   From this point of view our cognitive
consciousness first furnishes to us *facts*.   In terns of
our feelings we estimate the *values* of these facts for
us.   In view of these values our *acts* are determined.
That this traditional view has a real significance cannot be questioned.   But in the present exposition of
the structure and laws of consciousness we are not at all
closely following the lines of the traditional exposition.

From our present point of view *all consciousness
without exception may be considered as accompanying
our acts, or at all events as taking place side by side
with the tendencies to action*, which are at any moment
aroused within our organism.   And thus *all consciousness without exception might be considered as an expression of the will*, since that of which we are aware is
always related, in our own minds, to some tendency
on our part to act thus or thus.   Furthermore, in so
far as our consciousness is an expression of our sensitiveness to the disturbances which the environment pro-

duces, *our whole consciousness has a cognitive aspect.* And since our consciousness is related, as we shall later see, not only to the present state, but to the acquired habits of our organism, or in other words is a result of our docility, *our consciousness has no voluntary aspect that is not also in some respects a cognitive aspect.* Since *the feelings form a part of a consciousness which is thus always more or less obviously both cognitive and volitional,* the feelings can hardly be regarded as a link binding together two relatively distinct phases of consciousness, namely, the cognitive and the voluntary. For us, in this discussion, *the feelings,* in so far as they are present, *are phases of our present mental sensitiveness.* In what sense they have a cognitive significance we can better see in a later portion of our discussion. Their volitional significance will also come to light more clearly in later connections. We are concerned with them at present in so far as they stand side by side with our sensory experiences, as an aspect of our present conscious response to the situation in which at any moment we find ourselves.

§ 61. In view of our attitude toward the doctrine of mental elements, it is no part of our present task to look for elementary feelings, and to give a catalogue of these before showing how they, in connection with other elements, enter into our more complex conscious life. While some of the feelings can be more or less definitely isolated by means of psychological experiment, the motives that make a catalogue of the sensations a convenient preliminary to the study of the sensory side of our present consciousness do not exist, in the present state of experimental psychology, in nearly the same degree, in case of the affective aspect of consciousness. For the isolated feelings that can be produced,—not, indeed, in absolute isolation, but in connection with certain simple sense experiences, such as odours, tastes, and sounds, — for the purposes of experimental observation, form but a small portion of our affective life, and do not, as in case of the sensations, furnish to us anywhere nearly an exhaustive list of the qualities of feelings which our ordinary experience seems to furnish. On the whole we are therefore still forced to accept, in the case of the feelings, accounts and analyses which are but very imperfectly subjected to experimental control.

Our ordinary consciousness very frequently distinguishes within its own unity, between the facts of which we are aware, and *the present value that these facts seem to us to possess*. This present value, for instance, — the pleasurable or painful character of a sound, or of a sensory experience of touch, — we learn to refer, in our ordinary life, *to the relation of the object to ourselves*. My suffering does not belong to the character of the object that touches or burns my skin; but as I am accustomed to say to myself, "It is my suffering, it exists alone in me." Thus my sensory experiences, as such, tend to be referred to objects, the things of the world which cause them, while my feelings appear to me to be my own. This aspect of the distinction between feelings and other experiences can be fully justified and described only on the basis of a theory of what I mean by myself. And such a theory cannot be assumed at the outset of psychology as a means of furnishing a sufficient account of the true nature of feeling. Yet it is an important feature of the feelings that, when we have once developed our notion of the difference between the self and the world, we refer feelings especially to the *self* rather than to the *world without the self*. This "subjective" character of feeling is used by many psychologists as a means of defining its essential nature.

§ 62. If we look for a simpler criterion of what we mean by feeling, it seems worth while to point out that *by feeling, we mean simply our present sensitiveness to the values of things* in so far as these values are directly present to consciousness. My feelings do not assure me of what the ethical, or the scientific, or the otherwise remote value of an object may be. But as they pass, my feelings tell me what is *the seeming present value of this state of consciousness*, or of this complex of states of consciousness, as the contents of consciousness pass before me. The question, *What aspects of feelings, or of what kinds of feelings exist?* therefore reduces itself to the question, *In what way do our states of consciousness seem to us, as they pass, to possess a present and immediate value?* The *usual answer* to this question in the psychological text-books is, that the present values of our conscious states, the present kinds of feelings, can be reduced *to two opposed kinds*, either one of which may predominate, or be alone present, as the one immediate value of a passing state, at any present moment. The two types of feeling in question are often called PLEASURE AND PAIN, or again the Agreeable and the Disagreeable, or again Pleasure and Displeasure, or the Pleasant and the Unpleasant. It is often said that only feelings of these two kinds exist. The further question whether there exist, under each of these kinds, subordinate types (for example whether there exist pleasures of various kinds which cannot be reduced one to another), is a question about which great difference of opinion has existed. The well-known theory thus defined denies, however, in any case, the existence of any other essentially different kinds of feelings except those of pleasure and of displeasure.

This theory seems at first to meet with a very obvious obstacle, so soon as an effort is made to apply it to the case of our more highly complicated affective states, such as our moods, our emotions, and our passions. But here, in many modern text-books, the already considered theory that our consciousness is composed of mental elements, in connection with a certain result of

the habits of introspective analysis which experimental
psychology has trained, comes to the aid of the partisan
of the pleasure-pain theory of the feelings.   Our emotions, viz., when carefully studied, prove to be, in large
measure, sensory experiences.   By analysis we become
more or less able to substitute for a complex emotional
condition an analysed mental state, or a series of such
states, wherein we take note of the sensory elements
that, as the usual theory insists, are present in our
ordinary and unanalysed emotions.   For such a view,
an emotion consists of elements due to organic sensations,
these elements being joined very closely with a vast com-
plex of elements of the pleasure-pain type.   Thus, in case
of anger we have complexes of sensations due to the
organic excitement which accompanies the emotion —
sensations of choking in the throat, sensations of the
violent beating of the heart, sensations due to the active movements which express anger, etc.   It is said
that, if we abstract from our ideas of the object which
arouses our anger, and from these various masses of
organic sensory experience, there remains in the emotions, as the aspect constituting our present sense of the
value of our state, only the pleasure-pain aspect.   Anger
is very generally a painful emotion.   Some stages of it,
however, may be relatively pleasant.   Similar analyses,
it is asserted, will hold true of such emotions as fear,
love, joy, or of the relatively placid moods such as accompany our unexcited mental condition.   Thus there

would remain, as the essential kinds of feeling, pleasure and pain.

In order to complete the general statement of the analysis of feeling thus attempted, it remains only to note the fact that the word "pain," as used in ordinary language, is somewhat ambiguous. It is very often used to name certain *sensations*, which have already been mentioned in our catalogue of the elementary sensory experiences. It is also used to name the painful, *i.e.* the unpleasant or disagreeable *feelings*. Now in many of our more ideal sorrows, and in many of the feelings associated even with our direct sensory experiences, there is no kind of *sensation* of pain. On the other hand, the sufferings due to an intestinal disorder, or to a burn, have a close connection with sensations of pain, or with sensory experiences, that, from the point of view of the usual theory, are complexes of such sensations. When a disagreeable combination of colours, or an otherwise offensive object of decorative art, gives us displeasure, the sensations present, or the sensory experiences, are of a totally different character from those present when we are aware of a burn or of an intestinal suffering. There are no sensations of pain amongst the purely visual experiences. But the intestinal suffering and the burn agree with the disagreeable æsthetic experience in so far as painful, *i.e.* unpleasant *feeling* enters into both, *i.e.* in so far as both are more or less intolerable to us. In the same way an ideal sorrow is disagreeable, but it is not necessarily accompanied with any sensations of pain. If once the ambiguity in the use of the word "pain" is detected, and the word is used as the name for unpleasant *feelings*, not as the name for painful sensory experiences, the theory here in question receives a statement which avoids all unnecessary misunderstanding.

As regards that aspect of the theory thus stated which involves the doctrine that consciousness is composed of simple elements, we of course need here make no new comments. For our present purpose the issue is, *whether the aspects which give our consciousness its present and passing value are sufficiently described by classifying them into two kinds*, and whether these two kinds are sufficiently characterised by the names Pleasure and Pain, or by the somewhat less ambiguous names, Agreeable and Disagreeable, or Pleasant and Unpleasant.

§ 63. It will be noticed in any case that the feelings, as thus characterised, *are divided into two antagonistic groups*. Whether we can *at once* be conscious of the presence of *agreeable and disagreeable* objects, *i.e.* whether we can at once enjoy and suffer, or find our present state agreeable and disagreeable (as Juliet seems to do when she calls parting "such sweet sorrow"), this is a question concerning which opinions somewhat differ. But nobody can doubt that there is a distinct *opposition* between our sense of the agreeable and our sense of the disagreeable, so that, in so far as we tend to find something disagreeable, we at least tend to exclude finding it then and there agreeable.   In other words, pleasure and pain, as antagonistic values, *tend to exclude each the other.*   The feelings thus have a character which does not to any similar extent belong to the sensory experiences.   Colours are not antagonistic to sounds.   And both are consistent with experiences of touch and of movement.   But pleasures war with pains, and where one conquers the other is abolished.

And now according to the theory here in question, the same also holds true as to *the relation of the feelings to our voluntary actions.   Pleasure*, it is said, *necessarily attracts us*, so that we tend to get more of it.   *Painful feeling repels us*, so that we tend, in so far as possible, to remove its cause from consciousness or from existence, so that the pain may cease.   The two sorts of antagonistic feelings are thus *connected with antagonistic tendencies of action.*   And as there are only two kinds of feeling, so there are also only two antagonistic sorts of action, — the sort of action by which we seek to approach, to retain, to get more of an object, and the sort of action by which we seek to get away from an object, or to destroy it.   In brief, we desire the pleasurable, we show aversion toward the painful.

And finally, as this theory insists, pleasurable and painful states of consciousness are respectively associated with antagonistic organic conditions.   Where pleasurable feeling is found, the organism shows various signs of present heightened vitality. There is an expansiveness and a vigour about the whole life which is absent in case of painful emotion. On the other hand, in painful emotion, the organism tends to contract in various ways, to "shrink," and, in the long run, shows signs of lowered vitality. Thus facts relating to our actions, as well as those relating to our organic conditions, tend to support the dual theory of the life of the feelings.

§ 64. Nevertheless, after all this has been said, it remains true that there is a great deal about the complex life of the feelings which seems to render doubtful the sufficiency of the foregoing dual theory. For one thing, we are frequently conscious of an attitude toward objects which seems to give them at once more than one kind of value, and which determines value in other than pleasure-pain terms. Thus, we may find a situation painful, and yet be in a state of feeling which renders us decidedly averse to altering what is essential to the situation, even for the sake of escaping the pain. For instance, the sulky child, although suffering the pangs of its mood, may decline to accept comfort, apparently because it finds the pain somehow fascinating. On a far higher level, the mourner may refuse a proffered and comforting distraction, because he finds his sorrow for some reason preferable to a cheer that he all the while knows to be possible. The athlete, the military, and the moral hero may all of them agree in *choosing a situation which involves suffering*, although they dislike the suffering. For they find this very suffering itself in some wise also fascinating.

In order to explain such cases of complex feeling, the dual theory of the two antagonistic types of feeling finds it necessary, either to suppose that pleasure and pain are mixed at the same moment, and that the pleasurableness of the experience which attracts us, despite its painfulness, predominates over the painfulness itself; or else to assert that pleasurable and painful aspects of a situation, or of an object, are alternately presented to our consciousness, in such wise that we sometimes find agreeable what at other moments we find disagreeable; while, in case of the fascinating sorrows, the pleasurable feelings that we obtain prove to be more effective in directing our action or our attention than the intervening sufferings.

But to both these ways of explaining the so-called mixed feelings some objection naturally arises. That the pleasurable and painful aspects of the fascinating but miserable experience merely alternate in consciousness seems hardly to be verified by introspection. For here the whole weight of the evidence furnished by the literature of sorrow, by the poets, the autobiographers, and the other confessors of human experience, who have brooded over such conditions as these, and have reported them, seems to be in favour of the view *that the mixed feelings offer instances of actual conflict, within the conscious field, between opposed feelings.* Such conflict is reported by the most various observers, even in cases where those who report find the conflict inexplicable, and think that it ought not to exist. On the other hand, granting that various conflicting feelings *can* at once be found present in the same consciousness, it seems somewhat difficult to accept the view that the only antagonism present is that between the pleasurable and the painful aspects of the object of consciousness. For the one who reports such conflict is likely to say that what he finds attractive, he also finds painful, or that what he delights in, that he also in some fashion, and at the same time, abhors and despises. But that the one aspect is in such wise opposed to the other, that the one simply tends to annul the other, is often not reported. One is very conscious of being pulled in various ways at once, rather than of the fact that his conscious account has, so to speak, two opposed sides that tend to balance each other. For the rest, we should expect pleasure and pain, if present together in equal intensity, to come to consciousness as values opposed in such wise that the sum of the two equal and opposite values would be nothing at all. But the report generally is that the opposing values present are so to speak incommensurate, so that the sense in which the experience is pleasurable is simply not the sense in which it is at the same time abhorrent. The account consequently suggests that the terms "pleasure" and

" pain " may be made by the theory now in question to cover tendencies of feeling which are really not of two kinds only, but of more than two.

§ 65. In decidedly recent psychology, the great experimental psychologist and philosopher, Wundt, has been led, not indeed upon the basis of such general considerations as this, but upon the basis of experimental investigations (pursued in his own laboratory), to a theory of the types of feeling which he still advances in a somewhat tentative fashion, but which promises to throw a very considerable light upon the complex facts of feeling. *According to Wundt*, the feelings, which he views, in accordance with the theory of mental elements, as consisting of a vast number of different elementary states, *form a complex whose facts vary in three different " directions."* One feeling may differ from another according to its place in a series whose members differ according to any one of these "directions," or according to all three at once. The three directions are those : first, of the pleasure-pain or pleasant-unpleasant series ; second, of a series which Wundt calls the " excitement-depression series," and third, of the " tension-relief series." There are some feelings whose place is in a single one of these series almost wholly. Thus there are feelings of pleasure and pain purely, which have no place in the other series. Again, there are feelings of excitement and of depression which are neither pleasurable nor painful.

Finally, there are feelings of tension and relief which have hardly any trace of the two other characters. But many feelings, even very elementary ones, have, according to Wundt, two or all three of these characters at once.

In view of the facts which constitute Wundt's admittedly still incomplete evidence for his three " directions " of feelings, and in view of the really very large body of inexact but impressive evidence on the subject which the literature of the emotions seems to contain, I am disposed to regard it as *decidedly improbable that the dual theory of the feelings gives an adequate account of the phenomena.* On the other hand, there can be no doubt of the great difficulty which exists in distinguishing, in introspective analysis, between the aspects of sensory experience which any complex state of feeling accompanies, and this state of feeling itself; so that we have indeed to admit that almost any account of the feelings which seeks to differentiate them from the sensory experiences is at present open to the objection that it confuses these two aspects of our mental life whenever it goes beyond the dual theory in its account of the feelings.

§ 66. Nevertheless, it seems worth while to attempt, in the present connection, *a tentative view of the nature of the feelings* — a view which shall try to be just to the classes of facts that the literature of the emotions, and the experiments of Wundt seem, in very different

N

ways, to emphasise. I venture, then, to advance the hypothesis that our feelings differ from one another *in at least two decidedly distinct and relatively independent ways*, while I am uncertain whether Wundt's *three* dimensions, or some still more complex account, may not prove in the end to be more acceptable. I limit my hypothesis to *two* relatively independent "dimensions" of feeling, only because *at least so much* variation seems very probable, while more "dimensions" seem less probable. In each of these two ways in which feelings can differ, I find mutually opposed kinds, or antagonistic characters of feeling. *First*, then, *feelings differ as to their pleasantness and unpleasantness*. In so far we have *the pleasure-pain dimension*, as it might be called, of the variation of the feelings. At the same time the feelings differ *as being more or less either feelings of restlessness or feelings of quiescence*. By *restlessness* and *quiescence* I mean a sort of antagonism introspectively easy to observe, but on the other hand rather easily confounded (as I readily admit) with those aspects of sensory experience which guides us in knowing what movements we are making. By a feeling of restlessness I mean, however, *not* the sensory experience of movements that we are actually carrying out, but *the feeling of that value of our experience which makes it an object of momentary discontent*. By a feeling of quiescence, on the other hand, I do not mean exclusively such a feeling as is associated

with the word "contentment" when that word is opposed to the word "discontent," because by the word
"contentment" language has come to mean a feeling of
quiescence which is *also* one of pleasure; while feelings of quiescence, as I shall point out in a moment,
may be relatively painful. The word "quiescence"
does, however, fairly express my meaning. I shall now
illustrate the ways in which, as I maintain, feelings *can
vary in either one of these two dimensions, or types of
variation, in such fashion that instead of two, there will
be at least four principal kinds of mixed feeling present
in various states of consciousness*, as well as two pairs
of mutually antagonistic, unmixed forms of feeling
possible.

§ 67. First, then, to call attention afresh to Pleasure
and Displeasure. *Pleasures* are feelings that seem to
accompany states in which the organism is being, so
to speak, *built up*, or *prevailingly refreshed*, so that *its
vitality is for the moment heightened*. *Pain* or *displeasure*, on the other hand, is such feeling as is predominant at moments when the organism *is breaking
down, or is being lowered in vitality*. In so far, pleasure and displeasure tend to reflect a condition of the
organism as a whole, although at any moment they
may, in my opinion, be more or less mixed, just because the processes that have to do with increase and
decrease of vitality are so complex, and are so imperfectly represented in consciousness. Meanwhile,

pleasure and displeasure, when they appear, are *aspects or qualities of conscious states in so far as they are now present, and not in so far as our consciousness emphasises the changes which are constantly going on in the conscious field.*

On the other hand, *restlessness and quiescence are sorts of feeling that have to do with our consciousness, not of any particular movements, but of the general tendency to a change in the motor processes present in our organism.* In consciousness itself these feelings therefore have to do with *the changing or temporal aspects of our conscious states.*[1] We tend on the whole to regard with restlessness whatever tendency involves our interest in immediately future changes. The emotions of expectation, of curiosity, of fear, of hope, of suspense, are accordingly especially coloured by restless feelings. On the other hand, the feelings of quiescence predominate when no change is notably interesting to us, or when no conscious stress is laid upon the changes that are occurring. In consequence, we regard the past, when we look back to it, with a quiescence which we do not generally adopt toward the future. The complex mood called "fatalism" is one in which all happenings, both past and future, are regarded with a predominance of those

---

[1] A similar reference of the feelings of excitement and depression, and of tension and relief, to the temporal aspect of consciousness, appears in Wundt's theory.

quiescent feelings that usually predominate when we think of the past. Hence the fatalist views the future as having the same value for his feelings that the irrevocable past already has. Again, quiescent feelings predominate both when we approach sleep, and when we suffer from marked and long-continued physical depression. On the other hand, restless feelings predominate when we are wide awake, or when the stored energies of the organism are in a condition which disposes them to rapid and vigorous discharge. What is commonly called active attention, as when we listen intently for a faint sound, is characterised by feelings of restlessness. On the other hand, the so-called passive states of one who helplessly observes a present object is characterised by a predominance of quiescent feelings.

The restless and the quiescent feelings may, and in general do, *colour particular sensory experiences*. That is, we may be prominently conscious of the sensory experience, and of what it means, and may, at the same time, be aware of its value as one which arouses us to restless activity, or which leaves us quiescent. On the other hand, it seems to me an inadequate statement to identify our feeling of restlessness with the sensory experience that informs us of what movement we are making at a moment when we are active. *We are restless in so far as we are actively dissatisfied with a present experience, and are so disposed to change the experience.* The *result* of this dissatisfaction will in general be a consciousness of movement. While the movement is going on, every stage of it will be somewhat unsatisfactory, and our consciousness will be one of restlessness. *But our consciousness that we are moving is a sensory experience. Our consciousness that we all the while feel restless, or disposed to move,* constitutes the feeling here in question. This feeling makes us aware of the value of our present state, which in case of restlessness is a value that we desire momentarily to change.

§ 68. And now for the relation between the pleasure-pain dimension of the feelings and the second dimension, that of restlessness and quiescence. It is true that, as the customary view says, we never wholly "acquiesce" in presence of pain or of the disagreeable. On the other hand, there are sufferings which leave us relatively quiescent, while there are sufferings which are accompanied with vigorous restlessness. When a physical pain begins, we are restless, and our feelings include those usually called rebellious. After hours of suffering, we may remain still as clearly conscious of the pain as ever, and quite as ready as ever to call it intolerable. That is, our unpleasant feeling is as notable as ever. But we may find ourselves very much less disposed to any present tendency to change our situation. We then fall into the state of passive suffering. We even feel that we *could not* do anything, that we have no tendency to strive against the pain. In this case, we combine suffering with quiescence of feeling. The emotion called "despair" is a classic instance of such an union of unpleasant feeling with predominantly quiescent feeling. Various classes of nervous sufferers confess such an union of pain and quiescence as something which they themselves find puzzling. The apathetic stages of nervous exhaustion may furnish instances of what the patient describes as great suffering, but as misery against which he has no conscious tendency to contend.

On the other hand, pleasure may be of the restless type. In this case, *although we like what we have, we are dissatisfied with the situation, and restlessly seek for more.* In active temperaments and states of mind this character of pleasant feelings becomes very prominent; hence those observations of the *dissatisfying character of the pleasures* which are found so richly scattered through the writings of poets and moralists. They rest, I think, upon the basis of a sound introspection. But the ordinary dual theory of the feelings offers no sufficient account of their significance. Goethe's Faust makes a wager with the Devil which is substantially to the effect that Faust is ready to give up his soul to the adversary, whenever the latter can furnish to him a *satisfying pleasure, i.e.* a pleasure that he desires to keep at the very moment when he has it. The signal that this result has been reached is to be furnished, according to the terms of the wager, whenever **Faust** is ready to say to the present moment: —

"O moment, stay, thou art so fair."

As a fact, the Devil leads Faust through the entire round of sense pleasures and worldly felicities, without being able to get this report from the hero, until a situation is reached, in the closing scene of Faust's life, which does not here concern us.

But from the psychological point of view, it is indeed possible that *pleasure should be associatèd with a* relatively, although never absolutely, perfect *feeling of quiescence. In this case the pleasure is of the kind that satisfies.* The conscious attitude is then one, *not* of seeking for more pleasure, but *of desiring nothing more*, and nothing other than what we have. The attainment of this state is indeed never complete, but constitutes an ideal limit of our conscious search for pleasure.

§ 69. The relation of pleasure and displeasure, and of restlessness and quiescence, to consciousness in general, is somewhat different. The painful is capable of coming very prominently and very intensely to consciousness. Seldom does pleasure compare in its intensity with the degree of consciousness which the unpleasant often attains. On the other hand, there is nothing in the nature of pleasure which forbids our being decidedly and intensely conscious of its presence. Restlessness, however, is distinctly more capable of becoming intense in consciousness than is quiescence. The feeling of quiescence, or the tendency in our feelings which I intend to characterise by the word, can indeed be present to consciousness; but, on the whole, quiescence never becomes entirely complete so long as consciousness persists.   It might be objected to my whole account that quiescence means rather the absence of disquiet, or of restlessness, than the presence of any positive character of feeling.   But while I admit that restlessness is a much more positive experience than is any extreme form of quiescence, there still seems to me ground for regarding quiescence as a positive state of feeling.   But that restlessness is decidedly distinct from painfulness or from unpleasantness seems to me to be illustrated by the foregoing instances; while the positive character of the experience of quiescence seems to me to be at least probable, and to be distinct from the character which we associate with the name Pleasurable.

§ 70. From the point of view now advanced there would therefore be at least possible four distinct kinds of mixed feelings, due to the union of the two pairs of characters, or of the two dimensions of feelings now defined. These four kinds would be: First, *the pleasures that are quiescent*.   These would be illustrated, especially, by instances of what is usually called contentment, as opposed to discontent.   The quiescent pleasures would again be *the most distinctly satisfactory sorts of feeling that we possess,* so far as the judgment of the present moment is concerned. On the other hand, the tendency of quiescence to be associated with a diminution of conscious intensity is responsible for the fact that the pleasures which tend to content us are in general not very prominent or intense experiences, and are therefore regarded with a certain restless contempt by active-minded people, who do not often possess such experiences, and who, viewing them from without, find them indeed morally unsatisfactory, or tame, as Goethe and his Faust do find them.

Second, we find the *dissatisfying pleasures.* These have the present character of being pleasant. On the other hand they are distinctly unsatisfactory. As we have already pointed out, the dual theory of the feelings finds it very difficult to assign to them a definite place. If pleasure is the state of feeling that we desire, and if we have it, why are we not satisfied with it? But such discontent is the well-known, and in fact the normal, experience of human nature with regard to *most* pleasures. As Faust says : —

> " So in desire I hasten to enjoyment,
> And in enjoyment pine to feel desire."

From our point of view such mixed states become natural enough. The *pleasurably restless* feeling involves, in any case, dissatisfaction with the pleasure so far as that is merely present. Our desires in such cases, when defined in terms of ideas (that is, when our consciousness is not merely of our feelings but of our thoughts and our objects), may be either desires for other pleasures of a different kind, or desires for more of the same kind of pleasure, or may sometimes involve a discontent which prefers even painful experiences to the present pleasures, simply because the painful experiences will give an opportunity for the exertion of those activities which our restless feelings demand. Wagner's Tannhäuser, at the point where he is about to attempt escape from the Venusberg, experiences such an union of restlessness with pleasure. Browning's hero, who expresses —

"The need of a world of men for me,"

is similarly dissatisfied with the enjoyments whose presence he still experiences.

The biological importance of this union of pleasure and dissatisfaction is very great. The normal animal, engaged in successful activity, experiences many states of consciousness that accompany heightened vitality and that are accordingly pleasurable. But since its relations to its environment need constantly fresh readjustment, such an animal must feel not merely the pleasure, but the incompleteness of its present state, in order that it may constantly desire such readjustment.

Third, we find in many feelings the *union of the painful and the restless*. Our experience is painful in so far as it accompanies a certain present diminution of the energy at the disposal of the organism, or in so far as the present situation is more or less injurious to the organism. Such pain is, in so far, very naturally accompanied with dissatisfaction. But since dissatisfaction can accompany pleasure without thereby necessarily involving the distinctly painful feeling, we must indeed *distinguish between the restlessness that accompanies suffering and the suffering itself.* If the organic injury to which the suffering is due is present, but is not very severe, the restlessness may predominate over the suffering. *In all such cases,* according to our account, *the feeling present has two distinct aspects,* namely, our sense of the present pain, and our feeling of the restless tendency to change our situation. The dual theory of the feelings regards this connection between pain and restlessness as an inevitable one; and distinguishes the one from the other only by calling the pain a quality of the present state, and the restlessness, perhaps, a sensory experience of the movements that we make in order to escape from the pain. Our own theory regards the restlessness and the pain as distinguishable aspects, *both* of which belong to the world of the feelings, and *neither* of which is wholly dependent upon the other.

Fourth, we may have, in certain feelings, *the union of suffering and quiescence.* As already admitted, this quiescence is never an absolute indisposition to make any change whatever. On the other hand, the quiescent aspect of consciousness seems to me to have a positive character, which is distinctly illustrated by all those experiences to which Wundt gives the names Feelings of Depression and Feelings of Relief. That feelings of the relatively quiescent sort can be associated even with great suffering seems to be illustrated by the emotion of despair, and by our passive acceptance of the hopeless sorrow, or of the overwhelming physical pain. Very great and long-continued pain inevitably tends to bring about a state in which feelings of quiescence are prominent.

§ 71. If the foregoing are the four kinds of possible mixtures of the two types of feelings, it may be indeed also pointed out that we have feelings in which *one of the two types of variation here in question may so predominate that the other of the dimensions of feeling almost wholly vanishes.* Such feelings, in so far as pleasures and pains are concerned, have been especially noted in experimental work in the laboratory. Disagreeable tastes, experimentally and unexpectedly produced by stimuli put into the mouth of a passive subject, may be for a moment almost purely disagreeable; pleasant tastes may be almost purely agreeable; and in both cases there may be comparatively little prominence given to the other dimension of feeling. Yet, on the whole, such experiences of the unpleasant, if not very intense, will be in general associated rather with feelings of quiescence than with those of restlessness, just in so far as the subject remains passive. On the other hand, feelings of restlessness and of quiescence can be obtained in various degrees with little mixture of pleasantness and unpleasantness. *This especially occurs in case of the phenomena of what are called active and passive attention to indifferent objects.* By the phrase "indifferent objects," the customary dual theory of the feelings distinguishes those objects that seem to us at any moment neither pleasurable nor painful. Such, it is usually said, are the vast number of objects of our colder "intellectual" concern. Such, in general, are all very familiar objects, of whose presence we may take note, while their character as pleasant or unpleasant is almost if not altogether absent. But we may, and constantly do, attend to such objects. If we attend to them in what is called the passive way, they become clear and prominent in our consciousness without any effort of our own. If we attend to them with some effort, they become prominent, but not without thereby obtaining some sort of present and relatively active interest to us. *From our point of view, attention to such "indifferent objects," whether it be active or passive attention, involves processes into which feeling enters. The feeling is one of quiescence in passive attention, of restlessness in active attention.* The moods of intellectual interest, the feelings which accompany our questions and determine our curiosity, are feelings in which restlessness is prominent, and in which we are therefore dissatisfied with the imperfect knowledge that we get so long as our insight is incomplete. But feelings of pleasantness and unpleasantness may be, in such cases, almost wholly absent however active our attention is.

It is notable that, as the ordinary theory admits, *our active attention may also be awakened, either by pleasant or by unpleasant objects.* The fact that *both* pleasantness and unpleasantness may thus agree in constituting stimuli for our active attention, while nevertheless the difference between attention and inattention seems to be one that is largely determined by feeling — this fact involves a problem which the ordinary dual theory of the feelings leaves unexplained. If *both* pleasure and displeasure tend to make us actively attend, what kind of feeling is it that makes us inattentive? From our point of view, the explanation lies in the fact that active attention involves feelings of restlessness, while feelings of quiescence tend to the cessation of active attention. Thus, both pleasurable and painful objects may awaken our active attention, because both may arouse feelings of restlessness. In case active attention succeeds in bringing the state of knowledge which we desire, the result is a feeling of quiescence which once more leads to the cessation of active attention, and consequently to that which, apart from passive attention, would constitute the state of inattention.

§ 72. We have now considered those aspects of our consciousness which are especially concerned in the sensitiveness to its present surroundings that the mind manifests at any moment. In considering the stream of consciousness, we already saw one of the principal characteristics of what is called our present Attention to a portion of the states of consciousness that at any moment float before us. In the narrow field of the present passing moment, some states are emphasised, or are clear, while the rest of the passing states constitute what is often called the background of consciousness. The states present, whether they are in the background or not, are of *three* principal kinds, Sensory Experiences, Images, Feelings. These states are not a mere collection of separate facts. Still less are they, when they ordinarily occur, composed of the elements that analysis can discover in those analysed mental states which, as a result of special training and of experiment, can be substituted for the states of our naïve consciousness. On the contrary, consciousness as it passes always involves Unity, and within this unity finds a certain Variety then and there distinguished. The unity and the variety are inseparable aspects of the conscious life of any moment. Neither can be resolved into the other. And at each moment there exist only such unity and such variety as is then and there observed. When we consider the conditions upon which the consciousness of the instant depends, we are able to refer one aspect of all our conscious life to the present activities of our sense organs. And this aspect we have called our present sensory experience. A similar study of the conditions of consciousness enables us to distinguish our images from our more direct sensory experiences. Finally, our feelings are distinguished from our other experiences by the direct consciousness of the moment; but their classification is rendered difficult, because of their evanescent character, and of the variety of the ways in which they appear at different present moments of consciousness. The classification that we have offered is merely an effort to be just to the complexity of the facts. It follows in some respects Wundt's account, but simplifies the latter.

Yet now the question may still arise as to whether the account thus far given of our passing consciousness is exhaustive. For is there not, one may ask, still another kind of consciousness present, namely, that which constitutes what is usually called the Will, as it is manifested at any moment? Is not this other kind of consciousness that which is sometimes also called Conation?

§ 73. To this question we answer by a few further words concerning the place which the Will ought to occupy in a psychological study. All consciousness without exception accompanies the reaction of the

o

organism to its environment.   There is no sensitiveness
without at least a tendency to the outward expression of
this sensitiveness.   While the manifold inhibitions of
which we have earlier spoken may suppress the outward appearance of the movements which we tend to
make, inhibition itself is, on the physical side, an essentially motor process; and there is therefore no exception to the rule that *all consciousness accompanies
responses of the organism to stimulation.*   As these
responses, in so far as we are aware of them, not only
are from the objective point of view adjustments to our
situation, but in general are viewed by ourselves as expressions of our desire, there is a general sense in which
*we can speak of all consciousness as an inner interpreta-
tion of our own attitude toward our world.*   Of whatever
I may be conscious, I am always aware of how something is consciously estimated with reference to my
needs and desires.   There is, therefore, a good general
ground for declaring that *the whole of our consciousness
involves will, that is, a collection of attitudes which we
feel to be more or less responsive to our world.*

But, as a fact, this our conscious response to our
world takes the form *of being aware of objects, of being
aware of what we are doing about the objects, and of feeling pleasure and pain, restlessness and quiescence, in the
presence of these objects and of our own acts.*   The questions as to why we act as we do, and why we feel as we
do, involve inquiries that can only be answered in the

light of considerations which will concern us later under the head of Docility or of Mental Initiative. But in our consciousness of our present action, and of our present attitude toward the world, in other words, *in the consciousness of our present will*, there are involved no other present features than those already described, namely, *the sensory experiences, the images, and the feelings*, as they are present at any time in the unity of consciousness. The words "desire," "longing," "choice," and the rest of the terms which are very properly used for the elementary attitudes of the will, are names for conscious processes in which the aspects of sensory experience, of images, and of feelings can be readily distinguished. But besides these aspects, no essentially new ones are to be found, except in so far as we take account of the conditions upon which desire, choices, and the rest, depend. Of these conditions we shall later speak. But so far as present consciousness is concerned, *to desire an object is to feel pain at its absence, or else is to be restless in the presence of our mere images of the object*. To strive after an object is to combine such a feeling of restlessness with the sense of strain due to our organic sensory experience of the actions whereby we pursue the object. To make a choice, is to assume an attitude toward certain objects which involves special instances of attention, accompanied with certain shades of feeling wherein various restless feelings gradually or suddenly give place to certain characteristic feelings of quiescence.

In brief, while we are far from denying the presence of will in consciousness, our own view is that, in one aspect, *the whole consciousness of any moment is an expression of the will of that moment*, in so far as that will is concerned with these sensory experiences, and with these objects, in view of the present values which our feelings give to the objects in question. *The term "will" itself is one which is derived rather from a consideration of the significance of our conscious life*, when ethically estimated, or when viewed with reference to the outward acts which express it, or with regard to the inward results which flow from it, than a term of psychological description. The understanding of the phenomena of the will from a psychological point of view cannot result from a study of present consciousness alone, but must involve the considerations which concern us in later sections. We conclude, then, that the term "conation" stands for no aspect of present consciousness which has not been already, in general, characterised.

Herewith our study of mental sensitiveness is completed. We turn from the examination of our present consciousness to a consideration of the relation of this consciousness to our former experiences, and to the acquired habits of our organism.

CHAPTER VIII

The General Laws of Docility

§ 74. Our whole method of treatment in this sketch forbids us to separate the study of the intellectual life from the study of the life that gets expressed in our conduct. Accordingly, in our account of mental docility, *we are equally concerned with the question as to how we acquire knowledge, and with the question as to how our habits of action become moulded by our environment*, in such wise that these habits get represented in our consciousness. Externally viewed, the organism shows docility by its power to exhibit, in the activities of any moment, the results of former experiences, that is, of what has happened to the organism in the past. From the point of view of consciousness, our docility shows itself in the fact that our consciousness at any moment not only involves a response to the present situation, but shows signs of the way in which present experience is related to former experience. Since the consciousness of any moment is concerned both with the objects which we know, and with the acts which we perform or tend to perform in the presence of these objects, as well as with the feeling that the objects arouse in us, our docility is equally shown: (1) by the fact that our present knowledge of things shows traces of the influence of former experience; (2) by the fact that our present consciousness of our acts shows signs of being influenced by a consciousness that we have possessed of former acts, at the time when they occurred, and (3) by the fact that our present feelings show signs of being influenced in their character by our former feelings. Since all these evidences of docility constantly coexist in consciousness, there is no reason, except convenience, for treating them at all separately. The general laws that govern docility in the one case apply to all three cases. Our course of treatment of the phenomena of docility will therefore begin by pointing out the most general laws which govern the process, and by then illustrating the applications of this law to various special cases.

§ 75. In speaking of the functions of the brain, we already laid stress upon the principle that determines all our docility, in so far as that docility depends upon physical conditions. *Any function of the brain tends, within limits, to be performed with the more facility the more frequently it has been performed before.* This is the law of Habit. Its interpretation in terms of consciousness is, that *any conscious process which is of a type that has occurred before, tends to recur more readily*, up to the point where the limit of training has been reached, and to displace rival conscious processes, according as its type has frequently occurred. We speak a foreign language the more readily the oftener we have already spoken it. We repeat a poem more easily the oftener we have already repeated it. A frequently recurring emotion is of a type such that we readily fall into that emotional condition. The only qualification needed in making this assertion depends upon the fact that our training may reach a limit, beyond which we do not increase in facility.

The chief consideration that needs carefully to be borne in mind, in even the most general application of the cerebral law of habit to the phenomena of consciousness, is expressed by calling attention to the fact that we can only speak of the recurrence of a certain *type* or sort of consciousness, never of the recurrence or repetition of a given conscious state itself. There are reasons why, without danger of serious error, we can speak of the *same* cerebral function as recurring. But it is not proper to speak of the same state of consciousness, or of the same experience, as being repeated. For into the stream of consciousness no one can twice step and find it the same. No state of consciousness ever recurs. We can only speak of the repetition at different times of the same type or kind of conscious condition. The sorrows, the ideas, the sights, all the experiences of last year, of yesterday, or of ten minutes ago, have vanished, and will never recur in the world known to the psychologist. But the sorrow or sight or thought of this moment may *resemble*, in type, experiences of former consciousness. And in so far as the same brain function recurs, the similar state of consciousness will occur also, and will repeat the type of its predecessor, which on the former occasion accompanied that function. It is with this restriction that the law of habit may be translated from cerebral terms into the terms that apply to consciousness.

§ 76. The first result of the law of habit is that any complex cerebral function, which in the course of our experience gets established, is likely to have a history which includes events of the following sort. The function first comes to be established, in general, through the results of external disturbance, transmitted through sense organs to the brain. Let the disturbance involve the sensory elements A, B, C, D. Let the cerebral function which these disturbances at first determine involve certain corresponding processes a, b, c, d. What these corresponding reactions of the brain are, will depend upon the inherited structure of the brain, and upon the habits that it has acquired up to the time of the occurrence of the disturbances in question. In general, if the disturbances are novel, the brain will exhibit a certain inertia, or a certain slowness of definite response to the new stimuli. This inertia will be a symptom of the fact that the stimulation is new. Let the disturbances, however, often recur, and let the functions a, b, c, d, be often repeated. Then, in general, these functions will become quicker, and more definite, and will recur more readily. In a large number of cases the functions will appear to be not only quickened, but simplified, as the process often recurs. At the first, the response of the brain to the new disturbances may be decidedly diffuse, and may contain elements that are not useful to the organism. As a result of frequent stimulation, the useless elements may tend to be removed from the response, which may therefore become less diffuse and more simple, as well as more definite. Witness the way in which, when we acquire a new habit of a skilful sort, we gradually eliminate, even quite apart from any conscious selection, many useless movements of the type of " overflow," many awkwardnesses and redundancies which accompany our first efforts. The question why these redundancies disappear is a complex one, which involves physiological problems relating to the whole process of adaptation. But we all know that early movements of any sort are likely to be hesitant and redundant ; and that the sign of acquired habit is the presence at once of swiftness and of useful simplification.

But still a further modification of the brain function results from the law of habit. The elementary processes which constitute the cerebral response may become so united together that, when the habit becomes well established, *only a portion of the original stimuli*

may suffice to produce the whole of the habitual response.
Thus, in time, A may suffice as a stimulus to release
the entire system of now closely knit elementary processes of which the response *a, b, c, d,* is made up. *In-*
creasing swiftness, useful simplification, definiteness,
and a *close welding together of elementary processes*
in such wise that the stimulus which arouses one
suffices to arouse all — these are the familiar phenomena of cerebral habits as these become settled.
Such phenomena may be illustrated without limit in
case of what happens with all our trained movements,
with all our skilful arts.

It will be noticed that the welding together of
various elementary functions, which is so important
a factor in the acquisition of complex habits, may
appear either in the simultaneous or in the successive
functions of the brain. Thus if, when we acquire any
skill, the various fingers of one hand, or of both hands,
have been led, through the appropriate stimulations,
to coöperate in the same movement, as in sewing, or
in knitting, or in playing a musical instrument, the
brain functions which direct them in this activity may
become so welded together that *a single stimulation,*
or at all events a very simple one, *may suffice to release*
at once all the simultaneous motor disturbances which
are needed to carry out the function in question. Thus,
when one learns music, the various fingers have at first
to be guided by different stimulations into the acts

that are necessary for the playing of chords; but, for the trained musician, a glance at the printed music may suffice to put at once all the fingers needed into the simultaneous positions which secure his striking the chord. *The same holds true in successive functions;* that is, one whom any stimulus starts in the motor processes that lead to a given series of acts may find these acts so welded together by habit that *the accomplishment of each act in the habitual process furnishes of itself the sufficient sensory stimulus for the accomplishment of the next stage in the same process*, so that no new guidance is needed for carrying out the whole series of acts, beyond the first stimulation, and the resulting series of motor, sensory, and central processes.

§ 77. Interpreted with reference to consciousness, *the law of habit appears as the* LAW OF ASSOCIATION. The conscious states that accompany any process which becomes habitual are such that, within certain limits, they are similar in any particular instance to the states that accompany any other repetition of the same process. In so far as they are similar, they directly illustrate the law of habit. If to the cerebral functions a, b, c, d, at the time when they were first performed, there corresponded the conscious states 1, 2, 3, 4, then when the function recurs, a sequence of conscious states $1'$, $2'$, $3'$, $4'$, may be observable, similar to the former ones. Or if the functions a, b, c, d, involve elements that are simultaneous, and if in the same way the conscious facts 1, 2, 3, 4, are a simultaneous variety within the same unity of consciousness, upon the recurrence of the function, a similar simultaneous variety of conscious states will tend to be observable. In consequence, there will appear in the conscious states the law that *conscious processes which have been either simultaneously or successively associated will have such a relationship established that frequently, when states similar to one or to more of these associated states occur, states similar to the others will tend to associate themselves with these new states*, so that, for instance, when the states 1' and 2', similar to the former states 1 and 2 are found in consciousness, states 3' and 4', similar to the states 3 and 4 will tend to take place. Just as there will be a law of the tendency of various functions of the brain to become welded together either simultaneously or successfully, precisely so *the laws of mental association will involve both simultaneous and successive associations*. The existence of such instances of mental association, and their relations to the laws of cerebral habit, appear very readily in any case where we learn by heart a series of words, and so illustrate, as we repeat our lesson, the principle of *successive association*. Such connections also appear, on the other hand, when for instance we put a key into a lock. Here, however, we have *simultaneously associated ideas*, corresponding

both to the keyhole and to the shape and position of
the key.   But it is indeed the case that the facts of
mental association tend, in one respect, to lose their
parallelism to the facts of cerebral habit when we take
account of the easily verifiable principle that, *when our
acts become very rapid, or our simultaneous motor functions become very complex or very closely welded, our conscious states no longer possess a wealth at all correspondent
to the complexity of the functions*.   To the rapidly performed act, only a single conscious state may correspond.
To the complex collection of simultaneous functions
there may correspond only a single idea.   Thus, acquiring a skilful habit, such as is involved in writing
our own names, we may almost entirely lose consciousness of how we form the single letters.   The musician,
in striking the chord, may be aware only of how he
intends the chord to sound, and may no longer have
any mental process corresponding to the conscious
states which were in his mind when first he learned
simultaneously to adjust his fingers to the act.

§ 78. In consequence of this failure of our conscious
processes to correspond in their wealth to our habits,
many further psychological complications result.   For
instance, we may learn a song.   The function involves
cerebral processes having to do both with the words and
with the tune.   These processes are perhaps developed
somewhat in isolation, but, in any case, become welded
together when we acquire the power to sing the song.

Because of the welding together of the functions, and because the tune and the words are represented also in our consciousness, we come to have a mental association of the words with the tune. In so far, the mental association very correctly represents the cerebral facts, although it is never adequate to their wealth. It may now happen that, in some entirely different context, we hear a tune which, while not identical with the former tune, resembles the latter in some of its strains, or in the chords of its harmony, or sometimes merely in extremely subtle features, such for instance as the character of its rhythm, or the way in which it is sung. In such a case music, which is *remotely similar to the original tune*, may arouse in our minds a memory of the former tune and of the associated words. Such "associations by similarity" may occur in cases where the connection seems still more remote. Thus an expression on a stranger's face may remind us of something that was said at home yesterday. Upon examination we may discover that this expression resembled one which frequently appears on the face of some inmate of our home, and that it was this inmate who uttered the words in question. In all such instances the associative process, as it is represented in consciousness, *seems to bring together facts that have never before been represented by similar conscious facts that occurred together*. And hence, in such cases, the conscious association may at first seem to be following other lines than those which the laws of habit suggest.

But *if we pass to the conditions of the conscious state*, in so far as these conditions are cerebral functions, we are able to reduce the explanation to the law of habit. The new experience that arouses what is called an "association by similarity," awakens functions that are not only habitual, but that involve elementary functions which had *also* taken part in other habits. Because, in these other habits, these elements had become welded with yet other simultaneous or successive functions, they have tended to arouse those *other* habitual functions into which they had entered. But these other functions, when once aroused, *are accompanied by conscious processes whose similarity to the conscious processes that reminded us of them we can only detect after the association has taken place.* Thus the music now heard involves a harmony or a cadence whose cerebral accompaniment has occurred before in my life. And this elementary cerebral function, when it has occurred before, has been a part of the very process that I went through when I learned a certain familiar tune with which certain words were associated. The elementary function once having awakened the rest of the habit of which it was formerly a part, I proceed to recall words which are associated with a music only remotely similar to the music now heard. A similar explanation holds in the other case cited. Hence my habits may so work as to bring together conscious facts such as were never together before.

§ 79. The partisans of the theory of mental elements, and in particular the school of Wundt, are nowadays accustomed to summarise all such processes as are here in question by saying that *associations are formed not principally amongst our various total states of consciousness, but amongst the elements of which these states consist, so that the elements which enter into one mental state may recall through simultaneous or through successive association elements which make up other mental states.* In this way total states of consciousness, such as have never been habitually together in consciousness, may, upon occasion, appear to become associated through the association existing amongst their elements.

If we substitute for the fictitious mental " elements " *the elementary cerebral functions* which take place as the accompaniment and condition of our mental processes, the application of the law of cerebral habit seems to be always possible; and then our account is freed from the entanglements of the theory of mental elements. From this point of view *every elementary cerebral function, a, may become habitually united with various other cerebral functions in various complex habits.* Whenever a state of consciousness, I, occurs, which accompanies this elementary function, *a*, then, if the conditions favour the awakening of some other

cerebral habit into which the elementary cerebral function enters, the other habit, if once awakened, will be
accompanied with *another* mental process which will
hereupon appear to be associated with the conscious
process that we have called 1. *In consequence, the
associative connections amongst our various conscious
states will generally be much more subtle than the gross
application of the law of habit will at once suggest.*

On the other hand, when we learn to substitute for
our naïve states of consciousness those analysed states
which we have before described, and which the theory
of mental elements regards as such important guides,
we tend more and more to detect, *in these analysed
states of consciousness*, relatively simple states which
now correspond to the elementary cerebral functions,
and which enable our account of the associations to
be stated more in terms of the habitual connections
amongst the mental processes whose types we now
have consciously before us. Thus we are able to say
that the expression of the stranger's face now appears
as that *factor* in the present consciousness whose similarity to the expression of the face of the inmate of our
own family has directly suggested, by habitual connection, the word spoken yesterday. And this is the
empirical truth that lies at the basis of Wundt's theory
of the association of mental elements.

§ 80. In ordinary mental experience we most readily
observe associative connections in two forms, which

P

tradition has long since called by the names, Association by Contiguity and Association by Similarity. Association by contiguity is illustrated by any case where, for instance, a saddle reminds us of a horse, or a man reminds us of some other man with whom he has often been seen. Association by similarity has already been illustrated. It takes place, also, in case a portrait reminds us of a living man. The older accounts of the associative process sometimes mentioned other associative connections than these. Thus one spoke of association by contrast, as when a wedding reminds us of a funeral, or when a good man reminds us of a vicious man, whose characteristics are strongly opposed to his own. But such association can easily be viewed as association either by contiguity or by similarity. Association by cause and effect used sometimes to be mentioned, and illustrated by cases such as those wherein the surgical instrument reminds us of an operation, or when the gathering clouds before a thunder-storm remind us of the rain. But here again association by contiguity is obviously prominent. From what has been said it is now evident that all these forms of association are instances of the same fundamental process, viz., the law of habit.

§ 81. It is manifest that the general law of association, as thus far stated, concerns itself only with tendencies constantly present; but in no wise exhaustively describes the conditions that determine any individual sequence, or simultaneous union, of our conscious states. For, at any moment, our present consciousness accompanies cerebral functions that have been in the past connected with very different other processes. Which one of these connections shall determine the actual process which hereupon becomes prominent in the life of the brain or in our outward conduct, is not thus determined. Thus, for instance, the speaking of any word of our language involves a cerebral function, which has in the past been connected with great numbers of other functions, since we have spoken this word in the most various contexts, and have connected the speaking of the word with very different other functions. In consequence, the general law of habit insures indeed that the word, if familiar, shall arouse certain functions which are inseparably associated with it. But the general law of habit does *not* determine *what* other functions, for instance what other words, or what other cerebral processes of a nature such that mental images accompany them, shall be aroused immediately after we have heard or have spoken a given word. In consequence, our mental associations with the word may, upon different occasions, vary very widely, and yet all be due to the general law of association. Thus, for instance, let the question be asked, Of what other word does the word "curfew" remind me? In case I have begun to repeat Gray's *Elegy*, the word "curfew" will at once by habit arouse the

sequence of words, "tolls the knell of parting day."
In case a familiar modern bit of verse comes to mind,
the word "curfew" will be associated with the phrase
"shall not ring to-night." And thus the associations
may vary indefinitely.

What particular cerebral habit triumphs in case of
a given present experience, the general statement of
the law of habit enables us to predict, only in so far as
it lays stress upon the fact that, all other things being
equal, the most frequently exercised habit tends in any
given case to be most readily aroused. As a fact, the
word "curfew" is certain to have some inevitable, or
as some call it "inseparable," association in the mind
of any one who is familiar with the word. This association will be determined by the frequency of the repetition of the habit in the past. But beyond this most
general rule, the law of habit cannot lead us, unless
it is supplemented by other considerations.

§ 82. One of the most familiar of these supplemen-
tary considerations is the one expressed by saying that
*vividly experienced and connected mental contents tend
to be favoured by the associative process.* Interpreted
in terms of cerebral habit, this means that functions
which have involved decidedly vigorous alterations of
our central condition tend to persist, and to be re-
aroused more readily because of the deep impression
made. Or, in other words, habitual tendencies become
more potent not only by virtue of frequency of repeti-

tion, but also by virtue of the vigour of the central impressions made when the habit is established. Thus, a single occurrence of a connection that makes a very deep impression may suffice to fix a habit which is expressed to consciousness in an inseparable association. Yet this principle of the associative potency of the vividness of our experience is insufficient to supplement the principle of frequency sufficiently to explain our actual associations. A further principle of considerable guiding value is furnished by the fact that habitual functions which have *recently* been aroused, tend to affect the direction which present functions take. When we have been for some time speaking in a foreign tongue, the present act of speech is accomplished more readily than it is when we first begin, after a long pause, to speak the foreign language. Here our present associations are in part determined by the character of the immediately preceding associations. Every kind of activity tends to run more smoothly after it has been carried on for a little time. If we miss our way in repeating a well-known recitation, the prompter may fail to guide us successfully if he gives us but a single word. But if he repeats several words of the forgotten passage, the combined associative effect of these words enables us to go further. Thus, in general, *the present course of association is determined by the associative influence, not merely of mental states now present to consciousness, but of mental states which have re-*

cently been present to consciousness. The interpretation of this fact in terms of the nature of our cerebral function is not difficult. Every function, when once exercised, tends to prepare the way not only for the immediately succeeding functions, but for functions which follow at any time within a considerable interval. And consequently, amongst the associations that might occur at any moment, that one most likely triumphs which is most helped out by recent associations.

§ 83. But the course of our associations is also determined by still more complex processes. Some of these are dimly represented by the whole state of our feelings at any moment. In one mood we think of one kind of series of objects; or in other words, one set of associations then triumphs over all others. Change the mood, and the direction of our associations changes. James instances in this connection the influence which an emotional disturbance, such as that which accompanies sea-sickness, may seem to exert upon the sequence of our associations. Yet the emotions themselves are inadequate to indicate the way in which the general conditions of our brains at any moment determine the selection of one rather than another series of habits as the triumphant tendency.

We earlier spoke of what we called the "set" of the brain at any time. As, in a great railway station, with a system of interlocking switches, one group of tracks may be simultaneously set so that they are open to traffic, while other tracks are closed, so, only with infinitely greater complexity, the brain at any time is in a condition of preparedness for one rather than for another collection of interrelated and interwoven functions. Associations that correspond to some other connection of functions may be entirely excluded by this present "set" of the brain. Thus, during a lecture, the lecturer is forced to one series of associations, which the various incidents of the lecture room may modify, but which nothing but an entire interruption of the lecture can alter during the hour. The lecture over, his brain soon assumes another "set," and he may be even unable to recall sequences of ideas that during the lecture appeared perfectly obvious and necessary. Now our current mood, or emotional condition, often represents with considerable accuracy such a general condition of preparedness on the part of the brain. In consequence, we may know that, in a given mood, we can think successfully on certain kinds of subjects, but not upon certain others. But there are indeed changes and conditions of "set" of brain which are not adequately represented by our moods and changes of mood. In such cases we have very imperfect conscious warning as to what course our associations will take, and are obliged to find out what connections are then paramount merely by observing the result.

Social influences especially affect the "set" of the brain. In one kind of company we find ourselves prepared for one type of association, while in another company the same objects or ideas when presented arouse wholly different conscious consequences. In the phenomena which occur in great crowds of people, under exciting conditions (the so-called "phenomena of the mob"), the alteration of associative processes from those which occur under ordinary conditions may be very impressive. Thus, at a public foot-ball game, a woman, usually pitiful and tender-hearted, and accustomed to associate the sight of physical injury only with kindly acts, or with expressions of sympathy or of horror, may show, in the excitement of the moment, extravagant signs of joyous fury at the sight of an injury to a player on the side to which she is opposed, and may for the time be reminded by this sight of nothing so much as the wish that this opponent should be rendered wholly incapable of playing further. The popular excitements of the French Revolution were largely made up, so far as concerns the psychical processes involved, of anomalous associations of ideas, and of deeds due to such changes in brain habits as were occasioned by the extraordinary social situations of the time. Such phenomena tend greatly to veil the regularity of the general laws of association, and come to be explained only when we observe that the habits aroused at such moments have a sufficient basis in cerebral tendencies established far back in the childhood of the persons concerned, or in activities that their normal life keeps in the background.

Amongst the general brain conditions which most modify the types of associative processes that can occur, the conditions of acute fatigue, and those chronic conditions which are in many respects equivalent to those of acute fatigue, are prominent. The German psychologist and psychiatrist Kraepelin has experimentally investigated such processes in his laboratory. In acute fatigue the associations tend to acquire a character of incoherence, somewhat similar to that which is observable in the deliriums that accompany exceedingly exhausting nervous disorders. In the field of verbal associations, rhyming and punning associations often tend in such states of fatigue to take the place of more rational and useful sorts of association. The habits upon which the power to add figures depends come to work loosely at such times, and frequent errors result. The phenomena are in a measure known to us in ordinary life. Laboratory experiment emphasises them, and shows them to be present in cases where they would escape ordinary observation. The psychological continuity between the phenomena of fatigue and those of the incoherent forms of delirium is thus suggested.

CHAPTER IX

Docility

A. PERCEPTION AND ACTION

§ 84. The general law of habit is manifested throughout the whole range of our docility. But its results
appear in a large number of different types of mental
phenomena, whose relations to the general law may
now be illustrated. In case of all these types of experience, we have phenomena illustrating the way in which
what has happened to our organism in the past modifies
both the present state of our consciousness and the
present tendencies of our actions. We shall endeavour
as far as possible to develop *both* these aspects side by
side, not sundering the intellectual life, which has to do
with our consciousness of objects, from our voluntary
life, which has to do with our consciousness of acts,
except in so far as mere convenience of exposition renders it advisable to do so.

§ 85. When external physical objects affect our sense
organs, they produce complex disturbances both of these
and of the corresponding centres of the brain. These
disturbances in general tend to pass over into motor
tracts, and to produce certain movements which, at first,

are determined by the hereditary tendencies of the brain, *i.e.* by what is called our instincts; while, in the long run, these instincts, modified as well as aroused through our various and repeated sensory stimulation, take the form of *acquired habits of action. The accompanying consciousness, in so far as it is simple, and is determined by our habits of direct adjustment to objects that are repeatedly present,* constitutes what we call our *perception* of these objects.

Thus, to take a comparatively simple instance, a child in the first year of life, who has already reached the " grasping " age, sees a bright-coloured object, grasps at it, seizes it, and carries it to his mouth. The act is determined by complex sensory stimulations, visual and tactual. The act itself consists of a series of movements. These involve focusing the eyes upon the object, by movements which include the accommodation of each eye to the function of clear vision, and the convergence of the eyes through a coöperation of the muscles of both. That the eyes thus act together as a single organ, has resulted from a very early training of inherited tendencies. The movements concerned also include the act of grasping. This is a complex motor process, which depends upon a modification of instinctive tendencies that slowly grow up during the early months of life. When the sight of the object is followed by the seizing of the object, one set of sense impressions leads, through a series of movements, to the

obtaining of another set of sense impressions, viz., those
of touch. The child's effort to get at the object, in
order to seize it, suggests to us that, before he grasps
the object, he has mental images which, in connection
with certain feelings of restless eagerness, constitute a
certain anticipation of how the object will feel when it
is touched. These images are similar to former experiences of touch which the child has already obtained
when, on former occasions, he grasped something. The
successful seizure of the object leads over, through a
series of feelings, and perhaps of images, to the consciousness that the child obtains when he gets the object
into his mouth.

We have here, in the outward manifestations of mind,
*a sequence of movements which are manifestations of hab-
its*, the habits being due to the effect of former experience upon inherited instinct. Within the child's mind
we may very naturally suppose *a sequence of conscious
states, which is determined partly by sense impressions,
and partly by associations*. When he sees the bright
object, he simultaneously associates with this object certain images and feelings; and these images and feelings
resemble his former experiences in cases where he has
seen and grasped objects. The child's consciousness, as
it proceeds from this first simultaneous association to
the later stages of his grasping of the object, constitutes what we should call *a series of perceptions* of the
object which he successively sees, touches, and tastes.

But when he sees the object, he already, by means of simultaneously associated images of touch, and of his own muscular movements, and possibly of taste, anticipates and perhaps eagerly desires what later becomes a present fact of his consciousness.   In other words, the sight of the object becomes to him a sign of its attractiveness and of its character as an object of touch and of taste.   And in similar ways the object, when touched or when tasted, becomes to him, through association, a sign of yet other experiences than those that are present to him.   For he continues to experiment upon it until he drops the play and passes over to some other object.

The process thus hypothetically analysed from our point of view, is of a type that we are likely to conceive as present to the child's mind, just because the child, when awake and lively, may show, for a while, such a strong interest in studying the objects of sense.

§ 86. In our own perceptive consciousness, as we ordinarily possess it, there is usually less of emotional concern and of varied sensory examination than the child shows us.   Hence our own perceptions often seem to us to be purely intellectual facts directly present to consciousness when our sense organs are stimulated, and not to be so mingled with a consciousness of our feelings and of our motor processes as the child's consciousness would seem to be.   But we have only to consider the origin of our present perceptions in order to become convinced that *what at present our sense organs show us with regard to the object, not only constitutes but a small portion of what we know or may know about the object, but also has acquired its whole present meaning for us through processes that, in the past, have been as complex as those of the grasping child, or perhaps much more complex than his have yet become.* Our present conscious perception of any object which impresses our sense organs is a sort *of brief abstract and epitome of our previous experience in connection with such objects.* Because we have so often grasped such objects or approached them, or considered them, from various points of view, because they have so often excited the movements of our sense organs, or have incited us to get this or that control over them, because they have so often aroused our feelings of restlessness or of quiescence, of pleasure or of pain, because so often we have discovered by experience the results which follow upon our movements in the presence of these objects — because of all this, I say, do our present sense experiences come to mean to us what they do at the moment when we perceive anything. We may perceive a remote object, which we have never grasped, such as the moon or as yonder mountain. But this object has in the past aroused us to great numbers of acts whose results we have experienced. Or, if the object is new to us, similar objects have aroused our movements.   These movements have been attended with feelings, and have led to definite results. *The total result of all such experiences is epitomised in the present instantaneous perception of this object.*

At the very least, then, when we perceive, our consciousness involves whatever our sense experience, due to the object, now forces upon our attention.   Our consciousness also includes, as a general rule, something corresponding to those complicated tendencies to movement which the object arouses within us.   For perception accompanies some adjustment of our sense organs.   And this adjustment is reflected in our consciousness, in however faint or unanalysed a form. And the perceived object, if dwelt upon, very frequently, reminds us in a more or less vague fashion of *various sorts of action* that in the past we have performed in the presence of such objects, in addition to these adjustments of our sense organs.

Look long at a knife, and you are likely to think of cutting.   Dwell long on your perceptions of a dog or of a horse, and you will find yourself tending to fondle or perhaps to avoid him.   To perceive the curbstone just before you, as you walk, is to adjust your movement to the object.   To hear the bell ring at the close of the school hour, or of a lecture, is to be aware of something now to be done.   And meanwhile, as you dwell upon your perception of the object, you are likely to image what *would be* the result of doing this

or that with the object.   When you perceive the sharp-
edged knife, you may be reminded not only of the
act of cutting, but of the possible experience of being
cut.   When you see the heavy object, you may find
yourself anticipating the effort that you would feel in
lifting it.   When you observe the bottle of medicine,
you may remember the unpleasant taste of the dose.

§ 87. Meanwhile, whatever your other memories,
*the perceived object is pretty certain, if you dwell upon
it, to arouse at least a shade of feeling.*   If it is a familiar object, it feels familiar.   The *"feeling of familiarity"* has been a good deal discussed by some recent
psychologists.   It normally accompanies the perception of well-known objects.   It is, on the whole, of the
type of the feelings of quiescence.   It is slightly pleasurable in so far as other characters of the object do
not unite with it painful feelings.   Its persistent
absence makes us long, when in a foreign land, for the
sight of something homelike.   Its marked presence
when we return makes the most indifferent aspects of
the home land seem decidedly pleasurable, so long as
the joy of return lasts.   In very faint form this feeling
colours a great number of perceived objects, when
other features of the perceptive consciousness are almost wholly obscured.   The feeling may be present
even when we are quite unable to recall upon what
former occasion we have observed a given object.   The
occurrence of the feeling under relatively abnormal

conditions, that is, when we are sure that the object to which the feeling attaches itself is not really familiar, leads to that uncanny sense of having "experienced this before," which some people find a frequent and puzzling incident in their experience. In such cases the incident is due to conditions which remain still obscure, but which seem to be of central origin, and of a slight significance as signs of weariness or of a certain diminution of nervous tone. And in such cases the feeling of familiarity leads at once to contrasting and to often disagreeable feelings of restlessness and perplexity.

Now the feeling of familiarity seems to be a normal accompaniment of the excitement of established cerebral habits, and seems to have to do with the ease with which they are carried out. And thus this aspect of the conscious process of perception has its obvious relation to our cerebral habits.

§ 88. What we mean by the perception of an object is a cerebral process involving features of the foregoing kinds. The substance of the matter is that *the present sense disturbance is at once associated with a consciousness due to already established motor habits, which have been trained in the presence of objects similar to the one now present.* These habits may be of the most various kinds, and the consciousness excited by the object may have the most various relations to the habits themselves. They were slowly acquired, by

Q

means of acts that took a considerable time, and that were associated with the varied and complex consciousness. The perception is relatively instantaneous. *It is a case of simultaneous association.* It is relatively simple. *None the less, it is what it could not have become except for the previous habits of movement in the presence of such objects.* When dwelt upon, a perception tends to pass over into a more explicit consciousness of what some of these motor habits are. It also tends to develop, in such cases, some of these habits themselves; since, as we watch an object, we are likely to approach it, to grasp it, to point at it, to name it, and otherwise to indicate that *our perception is but a fragment of a possible consciousness involving a whole system of feeling and of conduct in the presence of such an object.*

The practical application of all this is obvious. If you are to train the powers of perception, *you must train the conduct of the person who is to learn how to perceive.* Nobody sees more than his activities have prepared him to see in the world. We can observe nothing to which we have not already learned to respond. The training of perception is as much a practical training as is the learning of a trade. And it is this principle upon which the value of all arts, such as those of drawing, of experimenting, and of workmanship, depends, in so far as such arts are used, as in all modern training is constantly done, for the sake of developing the power to perceive. It is because he has played music that the musician so well perceives music. It is because of his habits of workmanship that the skilled artisan or engineer can so well observe the things connected with his trade. It is because they do not know what to do that the untrained travellers in a foreign land often see so little, and find what they had hoped to be a wealth of new experience a dreary and profitless series of perplexities.

The ordinary tourist who goes out in a "personally conducted party" to see the beauties of nature, or to marvel at the wonders of art, first looks to his guide-book or to the conductor of his party to find out what he should do or say or remember in the presence of the wonders when he meets them. His device is in so far psychological enough. But since the guide-book and the conductor only teach him to repeat formulas, such as the number of feet contained in the height of the pyramid or the precipice, or such as the phrases of admiration that it is customary to use in certain cases, the tourist, unacquainted with other modes of familiar reaction in the presence of the great objects which he is to observe, gains from the trip little but the memory that he has been in certain places, and has gone through the fitting postures and the conventional speeches. Such a traveller brings back what he carries with him. And so indeed must all of us do, only it is a pity that the habits to which such perceptive processes appeal are so barren. It is the leisurely traveller who finds time to cultivate new habits, and thus gradually to see the wonders as they are.

CHAPTER X

DOCILITY

B. ASSIMILATION

§ 89. All our higher intellectual and voluntary processes depend upon the general laws of habit in ways which still need a further characterisation. This characterisation must consider *three aspects* of the ways in which our habits become organised, and of the external and internal conditions which determine such organisation. The first of these aspects may be expressed in the following formula : *New habits tend to become assimilated to older habits.* The result is that *all new events in the conscious realm tend,* in consequence of the workings of the associative process, *to be assimilated in type to the conscious events which have already occurred.* The more special results of this tendency are seen in the fact that our intellectual life is an interpretation of new data in terms of already formulated ideas. A parallel consequence appears in the fact that our new fashions of behaviour tend to superpose themselves upon our former habits in such wise as to produce a minimum of change in these latter. All forms of conservatism, both in the life of the individual and in the life of society, illustrate this principle.

The second general aspect of our higher intellectual and voluntary life is expressed by the principle : *In the course of mental development our conduct tends from simplicity and uniformity toward a constant differentiation* — a differentiation which is not opposed to, but which runs parallel with the processes of assimilation just characterised.   At the same time, and for the same reason, *our consciousness, as it develops, tends to that substitution of more highly analysed and more definitely varied states of mind* which we have already illustrated when we spoke of the way in which the psychologist tends, as he studies mental life, to substitute analysed for unanalysed states and processes of consciousness.   The existence of psychology itself is consequently an extreme instance of this tendency to differentiation in the course of the development of consciousness.   Yet it is not alone the psychologist whose mental life tends in the course of its development from the simple and uniform to the complex, analysed, and differentiated.   All higher development illustrates the process.   It is true that this process is always opposed and limited in its development by tendencies which we have already illustrated when we spoke of the general physical laws of habit.   For functions which have become habitual do indeed tend, by virtue of that welding together of elementary pro-

cesses of which we before spoke, to become so swift
that our consciousness no longer follows their complexity.   But in so far as our functions remain conscious,
our consciousness tends to a constant differentiation.

Third, we have an aspect of the higher conscious
processes which no mere outline of psychology can
pretend to treat adequately, but which even such an
outline cannot venture wholly to ignore.   The habits of
the human being and his accompanying consciousness
are on all their higher levels principally determined by
social influences.   His acts are either imitations of the
acts of his fellows, or else are acts determined by a
spirit of opposition to them.   In consequence, we may
formulate the principle here in question as follows:
*All our more significant activities and states of con-
sciousness occur under social conditions*, are responses
to socially significant stimuli, and lead to the organisation of a socially effective personality.   The general
significance of this principle will soon be made more
manifest.

I propose briefly to treat these three principles in
their order, and to show how they influence the higher
grades of mental life.   The first, Assimilation, shall
form the topic of the present chapter, the others of
the immediately subsequent chapters.

§ 90. In stating the general law of habit, we supposed the ideal case of a brain subjected to the influence
of certain new stimuli A, B, C, and D.   We supposed

the response of this brain to these stimuli to take the form of the corresponding cerebral adjustments a, b, c, d. We then pointed out how these functions, a, b, c, d, would hereupon tend to become associated together, so that further occurrences of even a portion of the former stimuli might be sufficient to arouse to activity this whole collection of functions, whether they were simultaneous or successive functions. But as a fact, when the already highly developed brain is impressed by new stimuli, or by new combinations of stimuli, the resulting cerebral functions are sure to be functions that already have habitual connections with still other cerebral functions, which the law of habit has already woven into closely related total processes. Thus the function a, which the new experience tends to arouse in connection with the functions b, c, d, is already connected by habit with functions a', a'', etc. In similar fashion b is connected with functions b', b'', etc. And the same holds true of the other functions concerned in that new connection which the disturbance A, B, C, D, tends to bring to pass. It follows that the new connection a, b, c, d, cannot be formed, through the influence of the new external disturbance, without the attendant awakening of former connections amongst cerebral functions. But these older connections may, and generally will, be antagonistic to the formation of the new habit. For the connection of the function a with a' may by itself tend to lead to an act very different from that in which the functions *a*, *b*, *c*, *d*, express themselves when they are free to be carried out.

To illustrate: Let the new stimuli be the sounds of certain words heard in this connection for the first time. The new habit, which this series of words would by itself tend to establish, would take the form of a power to repeat just that series of words. But now each one of these words may already have other habitual associations. If any one of these associations is so strong that it tends at the moment to get expressed in acts, these acts, so far as they become realised, will prove antagonistic to the formation of the new habit. In general, if familiar objects are already known to me in certain connections, it may be for that reason all the harder to learn to remember them in new connections. Or again, suppose that I am required to repeat some familiar act or series of acts, in a novel order, as for example to repeat the alphabet backwards. The new habit will meet at every step with a certain opposition due to the persistence of the old habit. A complex case of the difficulties in question is furnished by the perplexities of a countryman who first comes to live in a city, or by the vexations of a traveller in a foreign country. For, in all such instances, many of the new impressions tend to revive old habits, and consequently tend to hinder the acquisition of those new habits, which are needed in order to adjust the stranger to his novel surroundings.

In consequence of this inevitable relation of new habits to old ones, what is most likely to occur in consequence of the influence of new disturbances upon an already highly trained organism, tends to involve *a sort of compromise between new impressions and former habits.* Because the new impressions are vivid, they will tend of themselves very strongly to the formation of new habits and adjustments. But because the older habits are persistent, either they will constantly tend, by their interference, to prevent the new habits from becoming fixed, or, in case such fixation occurs, the old habits will gradually assert their influence by adding to the new functions older ways of behaviour, or by eliminating some of the characteristic features of the newer modes of conduct, or in general *by assimilating the newly acquired functions to functions already present.*

§ 91. The resulting effects upon our consciousness is very profound. *New ideas are likely to be acquired only in case they become in a considerable measure assimilated to ideas such as we already possess.* New fashions of thinking tend, as we form them, to lose something of their novelty by assimilation with older ways of thinking. Our whole life both of conduct and of intellect, both of volition and of comprehension, is therefore pervaded by interpretations of new facts in terms of old facts, by reduction of new practices to the form of old practices, and by a stubborn resistance, which increases with our age and training, to the formation of novel customs, or to the acceptance of novel opinions.

This bearing of *the law of the conservatism of cerebral habits upon the constitution of our conscious life*, is of the sort that we already in general characterised when we spoke of the law of association. While our consciousness does not in general correspond in its complexity to the wealth of our habitual cerebral processes, there are no connections amongst our conscious states which are not also represented by connections amongst our cerebral processes. Hence, the tendency of new habits to be assimilated to old ones is represented by the tendencies of relatively novel mental states and connections to resemble in type those to which we are already used.

§ 92. The illustrations of the law of assimilation in our conscious life are multitudinous, and are of great practical importance to the teacher. It may be well to enumerate a few of them : —

First, *novel objects*, that are otherwise indifferent, and that are presented to the senses, *tend to awaken our attention, and to become objects of definite consciousness, at the moment when we are able in some respect to recognise them.* Apart from some decided importance which a novel object possesses for our feelings, *the new in our experience, in so far as it is unassimilable, tends to escape our notice.* This has already been illustrated in case of our perceptions.

The way for new experiences that are to be assimilated must be carefully prepared. If a pupil is to be made to understand novel objects, they must be made, as far as possible, to seem relatively familiar to him at each step of the process, as well as relatively novel. Otherwise he may simply fail to notice them. Sense in vain presents what organised experience is not prepared to assimilate. The exceptions to this rule occur, as just pointed out, only in case either of very intense experiences or of experiences that appeal pretty strongly to the feelings. Since experiences of this latter sort play too small a part in the practical work of teaching, the law of assimilation must be especially and consciously considered by the teacher. *We see in our world, in general, what we come prepared to see.*

The psychologists of the Herbartian school are accustomed to call this process of the acquisition of knowledge through the assimilation of new data to former experience by the name of Apperception. The insistence that all learning is a process of apperception, and that perception without apperception is impossible, is one of the principal practical services of the Herbartian psychologists in their efforts to apply psychology to education.

§ 93. But the principle here in question is not confined in its application to the phenomena of direct perception. *The tendency of the old to assimilate the new influences the formation of all our customary mental imagery.* We have but a very inadequate tendency to image the details of our past experience, in so far as these details are unique, and are not repetitions of customary facts. Hence it is that *our memory of our past lives takes the form of a memory of typical fashions of behaviour, of experience, and of feeling,* rather than the form of a precise and detailed recall of the exact order of individual events. How far this holds true, popular psychology is disposed to ignore. For since it is indeed true that we do often recall, with more or less accuracy, a large number of detailed events in our own past lives, it becomes customary to suppose that such recall of details is the regular manifestation of a normal memory. As a fact, however, the individual events in our past experience which we accurately remember, and which we are able to bring before us in the form of precise and adequate images, are but an extremely small portion of our actual past lives. Let the reader try to write down how many of the events that occurred in a single month of last year he can remember or image, as they occurred in his experience, and in their true order, and he will quickly be able to verify how small a proportion of the facts of which his life has consisted he is able to recall in the way in which they occurred. One reason why we commonly fail to take note of these defects of our memory for the details of experience lies in

the fact that those events which we most easily do recall are likely to have been so often gone over and
over in our memory that, in the case of such events,
we have formed certain fixed habits of narrating them,
or of presenting to our consciousness detailed series
of images by means of which we depict them. But
in all such instances a generalised habit has been in
large measure substituted for the live memory of the
individual event itself. And so we indeed recall this
or that scene of childhood or of last year very clearly;
but we cannot recall how often we have recalled that
event. For, as a fact, the memory of the individual
event, as it now is in mind, is the result of gradually
acquired habits of depicting the event in this or in
that way. These habits, as they have been formed,
have been subject to the law of assimilation. Repeated
efforts to recall interesting past events have taken
place, in accordance with our tendency to repeat over
and over certain fashions of action, and to assimilate
new processes with old processes. *The result is that
most of our memories of long-past events are systemati-
cally, although very unequally, falsified by habit.* We
remember a way of recounting, or of imaging our
own past, rather than this past itself. The result very
clearly appears when one is able to compare the reminiscences of pioneers, military heroes, and similar reporters of their own experience, with contemporary
records and monuments.

§ 94. What we do remember with the greatest accuracy regarding our past life is *the repeated occurrence of some type of experience*. Thus, you remember what kind of person your brother is, and what it means to meet with him or to converse with him. But you do not remember upon how many and what individual occasions you have seen your brother. If some such occasions do indeed stand out with a relatively individual character in your experience, that is because, through the assimilation of new events to former fashions of memory and of behaviour, you have formed certain fixed habits of repeating over and over in the same way your images or your narratives relating to those individual occasions. Or again, you remember the way home; but you do not remember how many times you have passed over that way.

A classic instance, both of the defects of our memory and of its general subjection to the law of assimilation, is furnished by the well-known accounts which older people are accustomed to give of what they frequently describe as the "old-fashioned winters" of their childhood. "The winters," so such a person may say "are no longer such as they used to be when I was a boy. At that time the snow began to fall in November, and lay almost steadily until March. We had sleighing nearly all the time, and especially at Christmas. The harbour used to freeze over. The skating was almost steadily good. But nowadays the winters are full of

unsteady weather: there are frequent thaws; the sleighing and skating are in no wise trustworthy; the harbour
almost never freezes; in fine, the climate has changed."

That such reports are in general not confirmed by
meteorological records, may and usually does seem of
little importance to the reporters of such reminiscences.
His memory is his own. Facts are facts; and meteorological science, he tells you, is notoriously uncertain.
He prefers to trust his memory, which is perfectly
clear on the subject. Now what most persons fail to
notice is that the "old-fashioned winter" of such reminiscences is, on its very face, a psychological and not a
meteorological phenomenon. The human memory is
essentially incapable of retaining a series of accurate
reports of phenomena so variable and inconstant as
those of the weather. In such a field only general
characteristics can be remembered, especially after
many years. How good an account can you now give,
from memory, of the precise weather changes of even
the past month? But even general characteristics are
themselves not accurately recorded by memory, in case
of the weather, as they were presented in fact; since we
have no cerebral habits that are capable accurately
of representing either mean temperatures, or amounts
of snow fall, so long as precise records of these phenomena were not kept at the time. On the contrary,
what we can retain in mind, especially from our early
youth, *are the memories of the more interesting and*

*significant habits that winter weather formerly developed
in us.*   In our memories the images that survive are,
for the most part, assimilated by those which, when we
recall the past, are directly connected with our more
vividly recalled habits.   As the youth formed his most
important winter habits in connection with great snow-
storms and decidedly cold weather, and as such phenomena occurred sometimes early and sometimes late
in winter, and were of especial importance to him in
holiday season, his memories were formed accordingly.
What the old man recalls is therefore a general collection of interesting winter habits, and of images clustered
about them.   These habits define for his consciousness
a certain typical object, the "old-fashioned winter,"
which presumably never existed as he remembers it.
The dreary individual detail of the actual winters of his
boyhood has happily escaped his memory.   But since
lately, say in the present winter, he has such dreary
details forced upon his present attention by uncom-
fortable experiences, he does indeed recognise that
there is a present state of facts which he cannot assimilate to his memories of the "old-fashioned winter" in
question.   He consequently concludes that the climate
is changing or has changed.   Similar processes occur
in all cases where the "good old times," the "young
people as once they were," and the other facts of the
past, are praised on the basis of established memory
habits.

R

§ 95. Notwithstanding the prevalence of assimilative processes of this kind, it indeed remains true that *we are able, by persistent activities, aroused in us by our environment, to establish new habits which do stand in strong contrast to the habits formerly acquired.* The assimilative tendency is merely one aspect, although indeed an enormously important aspect, of the brain's functions. And even the very fact mentioned already in connection with the general laws of association — the fact, namely, that at any stage of our development *a great number* of habits have already been developed in the brain, and that these older habits *themselves tend to conflict with one another* — gives us a means for finding room for decidedly new tendencies. For if a new tendency, namely, is to be formed, if there is also a predisposition to assimilate this new tendency to a previous cerebral tendency "*a*," and if in addition, there is a predisposition to assimilate the same new function to still another former tendency "*b*"; but if meanwhile the functions "*a*" and "*b*" are *inconsistent with each other,* and so tend to inhibit each other mutually, then there is, relatively speaking, more room for a new function to get established, much as it might have been established, in a brain not already burdened by the former habits "*a*" and "*b*." Thus assimilation, which is usually a foe to novelty, may indirectly become a supporter of novelty, if only there are conflicting tendencies to various assimilations which in some respects inhibit one another, while nevertheless enough of our former habits remain positively effective to prepare us in a sufficient measure for the new coming habits.

Thus, to illustrate: the untrained traveller sees at first little that is important in the foreign country, because he assimilates what he sees, in so far as it interests him, to the things which he already understands, while what he does not assimilate he despises. On the other hand, let a traveller who has already seen various countries, for instance, countries in Europe and countries in North America and in Asia, visit another new country, such as one in South America, or in Africa. Such a traveller learns, of course, by assimilation, like any one else. But he also learns more in the same time than does the inexpert traveller; and, while he assimilates, he rapidly acquires new insight. Why? In part, because what he sees tends at once to remind him of the conditions present in various formerly observed countries. But any two sets of recognitions, in such cases, stand as rivals one of the other. If both reach his clearer consciousness, the resulting contrast is helpful. If each inhibits the other altogether, the traveller is all the more prepared to be impressed by the new facts. In brief, if I observe C, and tend to assimilate C both to A and to B, while A and B are themselves so different from one another that each assimilation tends to inhibit the other, then through

this very conflict, I may become more aware of the
novel features of *C*. My assimilation is then no longer
an unobstructed process in which the new is apper-
ceived merely in so far as it at once "blends" with
the old; but becomes an obstructed process in connection with which I have the maximum of opportunity
to acquire decidedly new habits and images.

It will thus be seen that *the assimilative process is
by itself never the whole of the process of acquiring
knowledge*, or of organising either our perceptions or
our memories. The novel object that is *merely* assimilated is perceived indeed, but not as to its essentially
novel features. In order that new habits and ideas
should be acquired, *i.e.* in order that knowledge
should grow, it is *in general necessary that our assimilative processes should be obstructed as well as potent,
and that there should be conflict amongst our former
habits as well as support of new habits by them.*
In brief, just as the perception of similarity is supported by the perception of difference in all our consciousness, just so the acquisition of knowledge never
occurs by means of mere assimilation. Assimilation
must always be supported by the presence of disturbances which arouse us to attempt the expression of our
habits, and consequently must always involve such
activities as tend in some measure to the modification
of former habits by virtue of the influence of the new
disturbances.

§ 96. Our assimilations have not merely to do with the processes of perception and of memory : they appear on the highest level of the intellectual life. *All our thinking involves assimilation.* When a novel object puzzles us, or when a problem baffles us, that is because we have not yet learned to assimilate the new experience to our former fashions of conduct. But when our puzzle is thoughtfully satisfied, this occurs because *we have learned to assimilate the new facts to the old principles, i.e.* to adjust our former methods of conduct, with a minimum of change, to the new situation. When the problem is solved, that is because what baffled us about a question which was asked, but to which we could not respond, disappears, because we have assimilated the matter at issue by remembering from our former experience an answer that serves the purpose. To be sure, such assimilation may be accompanied with alterations of habits that will need to be considered later under the head of Mental Initiative. *But every thoughtful process is, in at least one aspect, a process of assimilation.* The same consideration occurs to us when we take note of what is meant by the process so characteristic of all the workings of thought, viz., of the process called, in ordinary language, the " explanation " of facts. To "explain" a particular fact, is to mention a principle under which that fact falls. But if this principle is to explain the fact, it must be an already known principle. An already known principle

exists for our consciousness, because we have formed
certain habits of conduct and of memory which this principle expresses in a brief formula. Before we discover
how to explain the fact, it affects us as any sensory disturbance does, arousing reactions, but not as yet estab-
lishing in us any sufficiently definite reaction. When
we find the principle that explains the fact, we assimilate
our mode of treating the fact to the already established
habits of behaviour which the principle exemplifies.

The reasoning process, as it usually occurs in consciousness, also involves, psychologically, a form of
assimilation. We reason in so far as we discover that a
result is true because of its relation to previous results.
The "conclusion" of a process of reasoning follows
from the "premises," because we already believe the
premises, and observe that, if they are true, we are committed, in advance, to the conclusion. The psychological processes that go on when we reason involve the
assimilation of the act which our conclusion expresses
to the habits of action expressed by the premises. The
psychologist is indeed not concerned with the logical
question as to why the conclusion necessarily follows
from the premises. But he is interested to observe that
what goes on in the mind when we reason is of the
nature of an assimilation of relatively new modes of
conduct, such as the conclusion expresses, to already
established modes of conduct which the premises put
into words. That no such assimilation is complete, that

every new mode of conduct differs in some respects from every former mode of conduct, even from those which it most resembles, has already been pointed out. In a later chapter we shall study certain higher aspects of the reasoning process. What here concerns us is that while reasoning is decidedly more than mere assimilation, it always involves assimilation.

Thus, *on the highest and on the lowest levels of consciousness the assimilative process appears* — never as the whole of what happens, since whenever we assimilate anything new to anything old, we also establish new associative connections; but always as an aspect of what happens, since the trained organism can never do anything entirely new, and since relatively new habits inevitably involve modifications of already existing habits.

CHAPTER XI

DOCILITY

C. DIFFERENTIATION

§ 97. In speaking of the unity of consciousness we pointed out that there is in it always a variety, which is itself inseparable from some sort of unity. We also pointed out that this variety appears in two ways; namely, as simultaneous variety; (as, for instance, when we see at once several letters on the page before us) and successive variety (for instance, when we hear in the psychological present moment a brief series of sounds, such as drum-taps, or such as the successive tickings of a watch). We further saw that, as our consciousness develops, we may come to possess more and more highly analysed mental states, such as the musician possesses when he analyses the chord that, to the unmusical man, is a single, although rich sound, whose variety is but faintly observable. It is important to notice that this *increase* in analytic power occurs especially in case of our analysis of the *simultaneous variety* present in consciousness. If the tones of the chord are struck separately and successively, even the unmusical man notes their variety, in case the succession is sufficiently rapid, and is not too rapid. The musician observes the variety when it is simultaneous. It is, indeed, true that, in different states of our consciousness, we are, indeed, differently disposed to observe successive varieties; and by habit we do greatly increase our skill in observing the successions that occur in the world. Nevertheless, *the increase in our power to perceive simultaneous variety and to bring it into relation to successive variety, especially marks mental growth*. To the untrained man a collection of presented facts is likely to seem a confused unity. *To the trained mind collections of facts which are presented simultaneously are more clearly differentiated*. To be sure, our power to distinguish simultaneously presented facts, is always very sharply limited by the narrowness of our conscious field. Only a very few (three or four) distinct facts can be discriminated in any single act of observation of simultaneous varieties. But within the limits of consciousness *we can learn to discriminate what is not successive*. And doing this, even in our own narrow way, *again and again*, gives our consciousness its character as a sustained process of distinguishing between the facts present to us. In general, nearly every instance of such power, as it appears in the adult consciousness, seems to involve acquired skill. It is this skill to which we refer when we speak of the differentiation of consciousness. The result of such skill is that, at every moment, the simultaneous and the successive varieties of consciousness come to be intimately interwoven and connected.

§ 98. How the world appears to the wholly untrained consciousness we can only conjecture. But we certainly get no evidence that, at the outset of life, the infant clearly distinguishes between various present facts. It is also certain that, as the case of the musical chord shows, the significant discriminations made farther on in life are, in general, the results of training. Of what nature is this training? As pointed out by Professor James, and as very generally emphasised by modern psychological work, *our discriminations of simultaneous facts seem, in general, to be derived from previous discrimination of successive facts*. It is not possible to say that this law is absolute, or that *no* discriminations of the simultaneous can occur apart from previous experience of the successive. But on the whole, the influence of the discriminations that we actually make between successive facts upon our later discriminations of simultaneous facts is obvious, and is of very great importance. Thus, when the notes of the chord have been heard in quick succession, it then becomes much easier to distinguish them when they are sounded simultaneously in the chord. When one has first observed in succession a number of various tones of red, and has then observed in succession a number of cases of red that differ only in saturation, *i.e.* in the degree in which they resemble colourless light, it then becomes possible to distinguish between the colour and the saturation of a given presented instance of red. When one has become acquainted separately and at different times with two persons who look very much alike (as for instance, twins), it becomes much easier to observe the difference between them when they are together. Whoever wishes to compare very carefully two objects that are nearly alike, examines them in succession, first one, and then the other. Then, as he sets them side by side, their difference becomes more obvious. The general result of such familiar facts is the proof that, on the whole, *we learn about the differences of things as these differences appear in succession, and that hereby we acquire, or at any rate very greatly increase, our power to observe simultaneous differences.*

The process in question goes on through life. Successive variety is continually used as a means of interpreting simultaneous variety. The series of conscious facts that follow one after another are constantly used as a means of interpreting the coëxistent varieties of the world without us. This tendency *to interpret the simultaneous in terms of the successive*, is one of the most deeply rooted tendencies in our nature. It *has to do with that connection between consciousness and movement upon which we have all along been insisting*. Our acts come first to our consciousness as successive experiences

which present to us differences as they pass.   As a
result of these successively observed differences we become able, even when we cease some particular act, to
become aware, even in our simultaneous experiences, of
varieties which correspond to those that the act presented to us successively.   In consequence, our world
comes to seem to us differentiated into various coëxistent and contemporaneous facts.   Yet we first learn of
these very facts through our consciousness of the successive stages of our deeds.   Our whole idea of the
world of coëxistent facts seems thus to be derived, just
so far as it is an articulate idea, from our perception of
successive facts.   At least, if this is not wholly the case,
the matter is in the main thus to be expressed.

§ 99. The first great example of the way in which
the world of coëxistence becomes differentiated as a
consequence of what we have learned through successive acts, is furnished to us by *the properties which we
ascribe to the physical world in space*.   In space before
me I see two objects which I regard as coëxistent, and
which I more or less clearly observe as simultaneously
present. Yet I learn to discriminate just such objects,
to compare their places, to know whatever I know about
their spatial relations, through successive acts by which
I first fix my eyes upon one, and then focus them upon
another of these objects, or by which I first touch one
and then the other.   In other words, I continually explore space through countless successive acts of sight

and of touch, and through countless movements which I also accomplish successively. But I also constantly reap the harvest of these numberless successive acts in the form of my power to discriminate simultaneously present spatial phenomena, and to set them in definite relations as coëxistent. The process, despite its complexity, reduces to the general type already described, viz., I perceive the difference between *a* and *b* as simultaneous facts, because I constantly study afresh the successive differences of the type of a transition from *a* to *b*.

This process of exploring space by successive movements never comes to an end throughout our waking life. Our restlessly moving eyes, our constantly changing attitudes, as we observe spatial relations, show that we are all the while interpreting spatial relations afresh in terms of our experiences of succession. But what here most interests us is that *we constantly make use of the successive discriminations for the sake of interpreting coëxistent and simultaneous facts*. The physical world without us contains coëxistences. These we wish to interpret as they are. But we must first give these coëxistences, so to speak, a *dramatic* expression, in terms of our acts, in order that we shall be able to appreciate their very coëxistence. How numerous and how fine the acts of successive discrimination are which we thus employ in our observations of the space world, modern experimental psychology renders constantly more obvious. Every picture that we ob-

serve is explored by the eyes in ways which determine our whole judgment of the relations of the
various parts of the coëxistent picture. Every carefully observed object about us has its contour explored
by successive focussing of the eyes on one part and
another of its outline.

§ 100. Another important instance of the bearing of
succession upon simultaneity in the acquiring of new
powers to discriminate, appears in *the whole process of
education*.   To learn about a new subject-matter that
involves complex relationships of any sort includes, in
the first place, *long series of successive acts properly
arranged*, — acts of sensory observation, of recalling
images, of repeating words, of drawing diagrams, of
performing experiments, and so on indefinitely.   Then
we acquire gradually the power to "survey at a glance"
the results slowly brought to consciousness through
these successive acts.   This process of surveying at a
glance involves a high degree of differentiation of our
simultaneous conscious states.   *This differentiation of
the simultaneous slowly results from the repeated acts,
and from the powers of discrimination which have been
cultivated in connection with them*.   The more successful we have been in the successive acts, the more skilful we shall be in the perception of relationships
between simultaneous facts.   The results of our deeds
may thus be surveyed by us as if from above, as the
traveller who has reached a height looks back with

appreciation on the country through which he has wandered, while unless he had wandered through it, or through similar country, the view from above would mean little to him.   Narrow as our field of consciousness always remains, *what power we have to survey the simultaneous bearings of its facts is thus due to our power to find in the instant, in some sense, an epitome of the history of our own deeds.*

An important practical result follows as to the meaning of the *prominence that the dramatic element has in all instruction.*   Narrative more readily appeals to us than does description, because the latter calls upon us rather more for the formation of distinct but simultaneous groups of images, while the latter plainly appeals to our power to repeat, in the form of images, successive acts with whose types we are already familiar. Although, in case of both narrative and description, as they appeal to a somewhat mature consciousness, both simultaneous and successive images are presented to consciousness, still *narrative has the advantage of fixing our attention more upon the kind of discrimination which we find easiest, namely, the discrimination of successive facts.*

§ 101. A very notable further instance of our tendency to interpret simultaneously presented objects, images, and relationships, in terms of successive acts, *is furnished by our whole process of judgment, and in consequence by the entire work of our thought.*   If a rose

is before me, and I proceed to judge that this rose possesses colour, odour, and various other properties, the
properties are simultaneously present in the rose; and
I wish to make clear to myself and to others this simultaneous complex structure of the rose. But I do this
through a series of acts of successive attention, which
differentiate to my mind first one and then another of
the properties of the rose. *Having thus distinguished
the properties through successive acts of attention, I am
able to recognise them again as present simultaneously in
my object.* That they coëxist is something that I
appreciate and express by successive deeds. Only at
the conclusion of these deeds do I again appreciate, at
a glance, the variety in unity of the rose. Our judgments thus always involve two aspects of the conscious
process, — aspects which are often called Analysis and
Synthesis. The analysis, — here the naming and
attentive dwelling upon each of the various characters
of the rose, is accomplished through a succession of
deeds, whereby I bring to my mind names, and other
associates of the various properties which I distinguish.
The so-called synthesis, in so far as it is a simultaneous
synthesis, I accomplish at the instant when I am able to
be aware of these properties not merely as successive
facts, but as coëxisting in the rose. The synthesis
results from the analysis. But the judgment is not
complete until both processes are accomplished. The
mere analysis gives me a succession of states of mind,

which are in so far not perceived as aspects of the one
rose. To obtain this latter knowledge I must possess
the synthesis. Yet the synthesis could not be unless I
analysed. All our processes of judgment involve such
reconstructions in terms of successive acts, — reconstructions of that unity of things which we conceive as also
possessing a simultaneous character. One may also
call our judgments *Imitative Processes*, whereby *we
reconstruct our views of objects by putting together successive ideas of our own.* But such imitations do not
get their complete meaning for us until we have recognised that they express, in our own terms, what we find
in the object that our imitative reconstruction is analysing. And this is what we have called *the recognition
that, in our object, those characters are brought into
simultaneous synthesis, which our judgment has interpreted through a succession of deeds.* Whenever, again,
we study the nature of an object by drawing a picture
of it, *our successive processes make us conscious of what
is simultaneously present in the object*, in the same way
in which our processes of judgment accomplish a similar
end.

§ 102. The differentiation of consciousness occurs
then in the main through these dramatic processes. It
is in this very way that the psychologist himself learns
to substitute analysed states of consciousness for the
relatively unanalysed states of our naïve consciousness.
It is in this way too that all the simultaneous relations

s

of things become clear to us. It is in this way that comparison and scientific synthesis and our conception of the whole of things grows up in our minds. For the trainer of minds the general resulting advice is: *Undertake to systematise this differentiation of consciousness through fitting series of successive deeds.* Remember that *without such successive deeds there is no noteworthy intellectual understanding of simultaneous facts. The whole process of education is therefore a dramatic process, an interpretation of truth through conduct,* a learning to appreciate the universe by successively responding to various parts of it, *a reaching of unity through variety, an attainment of synthesis by means of analysis.*

§ 103. The process of differentiation is accompanied by a series of phenomena of which we already made mention in our opening account of the unity of consciousness (§ 34). The consideration of this series of phenomena brings to light a most important relation between our current feelings and our docility. To this series of phenomena we give the name: The Process of Attention.

As we saw in our opening statement, our developed consciousness has a foreground and a background, or, again, has two or three or four mental states that at any moment possess a certain "relief" as they "float on the stream," while "the body of the stream consists of contents that can no longer be sharply sundered from one another."

It is needful here to speak of the process by which our momentary mental states get this clearness or the "relief." In so far as we consciously profit by the relation between our present and our former states, our mental states are the expressions of docility. But in so far as we are directly satisfied or dissatisfied with our passing mental states they are the objects of our feelings. And now as it happens, we often find present in ourselves feelings of satisfaction and dissatisfaction *in the very fact that given present states have some sort of relation to former states* (*e.g.* are novel or familiar, are puzzling or comprehensible, have obvious relation to our past habits, or need new adjustments, etc.). But thus our experiences come to have a new and important relation to our feelings. An experience may be said to possess intellectual value in so far as it tends to mould our conscious habits. This value it possesses over and above the value for passing feeling of what, as a momentary mental state, it contains (as, for example, pleasure or pain). But as a fact *we are able to have feelings which express an immediate, a passing, and, of course, often a mistaken, estimate of this intellectual value itself*. Such feelings are called our current "feelings of interest." They have, in the main, the character of feelings of restlessness and of quiescence, — of restlessness so far as we question, seek, or expect information, of quiescence so far as we get our interests satisfied.

They have, however, a curious and invariable character, which often brings them into sharp conflict with our other feelings of the same moment. A pain or an agonisingly perplexing problem, although we hate it keenly, may interest us intensely, *because we want to dwell upon it until we have understood its cause or nature.* When such interests are those of predominant satisfaction they may lead us to dwell on the experience for its own sake, as a familiar or comprehended fact. Thus a young child may love to have its known stories told over and over, or to find picture after picture of familiar objects (*e.g.* men), and to say triumphantly " Man," " Man," on viewing each picture. Here the mere familiarity of the experience is itself what satisfies. But even if the predominant interest in the experience is one of dissatisfaction (as when one is pained or puzzled), still, the only way to satisfy the current intellectual interest in the pain or puzzle (*i.e.* to reduce the dissatisfaction) is again to dwell on the experience until its relation to the past has been altered (*e.g.* until it has become familiar or has been "made out"). So it is peculiar to the feelings of interest, or to the "intellectual feelings," that, whether they are cases of satisfaction or of dissatisfaction, the only way to hold the satisfaction or to diminish the dissatisfaction is, in any case, *to dwell for the time on the experience as an experience.* For, as we have here defined our term,

the interest is not a feeling of satisfaction or of dissatisfaction with what the mental state in itself alone
chances to contain (*e.g.* with its pleasurable or painful
tone as such), *but with its relation to other states or
to one's habits.* Hence in states of intellectual interest, one questions, analyses, compares — does whatever
tends to relate this object to other objects. One is
seeking to know "what to do with it," or is rejoicing
in the fact that one does know what to do with it.

Now, *attention is a process that involves states of
mind and physical activities which tend to satisfy such
an intellectual interest* or, in other words, *attention is
the process of furthering our current interest in an
experience when viewed just as an experience.* When
I attend to a thing I either try to recognise or to
understand it, or I take contentment in an already
existent recognition or understanding of it, and dwell
upon it accordingly. Attention is called "active" in so
far as the feelings of restlessness which accompany our
trying to recognise or to understand, predominate, or
are at any rate prominent, amongst the feelings present at the moment of attention. But when the other
phenomena of attention are present, while the predominant feelings are those of quiescence, the attention is called "passive."

If our attention succeeds in any case — *i.e.* if our
passing feeling of current interest is furthered — the
object of this interest *grows clearer in our minds;*

that is, it grows more definite and gets a better "relief" upon its background. This is the one sure result of the furthering of the temporary and passing intellectual interest, as this interest has here been defined. What we attend to may, as a mental state, be faint in content, but as an experience it grows important. It is differentiated better from whatever goes along with it, is more effective in arousing associations, is recognised more readily, if already somewhat familiar, and tends to be more effective in modifying our already existent habits. Attention involves, of course, by definition, feelings. But these feelings from their nature have, even as feelings, their intellectual value. And attention is the *conditio sine qua non* of all important intellectual processes.

The less artificial and adventitious are our passing interests, the easier and more effective is their satisfaction. Accordingly, it is difficult to attend long to anything merely because we abstractly think that we ought to attend. We must have our interest pretty spontaneously, or we can never hope to satisfy it. What already attracts us in itself is therefore, in general, the more readily attended to in regard to its interest as an experience. The relatively familiar is also more closely attended to than the incomprehensibly strange, unless the latter, by its painful or its portentous aspect, or by its sensuous or other direct charm, arouses our longing to comprehend its significance. Children often wholly neglect whatever is not yet comprehensible to them in their lessons, although some uncomprehended things, such as fairyland, or the doings of their elders, may arouse their keen interest by appealing to their love of beauty, or by awakening their imitative instincts. Interest in objects because of their familiarity or their comprehensibility has been called "derived" interest, and its furthering "derived attention"; but, as a fact, all current interests are, as already shown, more or less secondary feelings. In general, active attention to any one object is highly unsteady and fluctuating in its character. Sustained active attention, just because of the restlessness involved, is possible only in case our objects, or our own relations to them, are constantly undergoing change.

The physiological accompaniments of attention seem to be of three sorts : (1) Adjustments, of a motor type, whereby our sense organs are brought into better relations with the object of our interest, or are brought into positions that habit has associated with clear attention, while our organisms are also rendered otherwise more impressible. Certain characteristic attitudes, gestures, and alterations of breathing and of circulation, belong to this type. (2) The assumption of a "set" of brain that tends especially to favour those cerebral habits which are of most use to use in our efforts to comprehend objects of the kind wherein we are interested. The control which the attention appears to possess over our trains of association is due to this type of cerebral accompaniments of the process. (3) In close connection with (2), the assumption of a "set" of brain which tends to inhibit all movements and habits such as would interfere with the satisfaction of the ruling interest. Hence the stillness, the "absorption" of the attentive person. Active attention is always a highly inhibitory function. Herein lies another reason for its fluctuating character in children, and in many of our states of weakness.

§ 104. The presence of discrimination in our trained consciousness is subject, even on the highest levels, to decidedly obvious limitations. If we are carrying a heavy weight, and some one adds to that weight a very small additional burden, we do not feel the difference. If the sun is shining through the window and somebody lights a gas-jet, we notice very little, if at all, the difference. In brief, decidedly slight differences in the intensity of our sensory experiences escape us. This is a matter of common knowledge. But the very mention of these facts calls also attention to another and closely associated consideration, — one which has acquired great notoriety through the close examination which modern experimental psychology has given to the whole subject. If we estimate the character of our mental experiences merely in terms of the characters which we know to belong to their stimuli, we are disposed at first to expect that, if we are observing a bright light, and if some one adds a new light (namely that of the gas-jet) to the light already present, we shall observe the difference, if the additional stimulus is great enough. But from this point of view we should expect that the lighting of the additional gas-jet would make the same difference to our internal experience, whatever might be the brightness of the light before the new gas-jet was added. Or to take another illustration, if I have an experience corresponding to the attempt to lift an object that weighs a pound, and if this experience normally corresponds to that object, then I should be disposed to expect that in case I were carrying ten pounds and some one added a pound to my burden, the addition would make the same difference to me as it would make if I were carrying a hundred pounds, and the pound were then added to my burden. But a moment's reflection shows us that we are unable thus to make our mental experiences precisely correspond, in all respects, to what we know about the objects which are the stimuli of these experiences. For the addition of the pound will be noticed if it be added to the burden of ten pounds. It may altogether escape attention if it is added to the very much heavier burden. The lighting of the gas-jet will make a very great difference if the gas-jet is lighted when the room is nearly dark. But the lighting of this same gas-jet will make very little difference to our experience if the room is already bright, that is if the sun is shining. A stimulus may thus be such that, if it acted alone, the corresponding experience would be very important or very intense. Yet if this stimulus be added to another which is of considerable magnitude, and which has already produced an experience of great intensity, the additional stimulus may go wholly unnoticed. That the principle here concerned has some very deep relations to our experience becomes fairly evident, even apart from experiment, if we consider certain other very familiar facts. When we are reading print on a page before us, we are constantly guided in our reading by the fact that we discriminate between the brightness of the white page and the lesser brightness of the portion of the page where the printer's ink lies. Our power clearly to see the letters depends upon this difference of brightness. But if the light fades, it may fade very considerably before we notice that the letters have begun to grow dim. Yet when the light is faint the actual difference in brightness between the white page and the black letters will be very much less than the difference between the two when they are seen in a bright light. Not only does this hold true of objects such as letters printed on a page. It holds true, within limits, of the finer markings in an etching or a drawing. The light may diminish considerably and yet we may see as much and as fine detail in the drawing as we saw in the brighter light. Thus even ordinary experience forces upon us the fact *that our judgments of differences are in some measure relative.* One of the earliest fields of research in modern experimental psychology was the one opened up, in the effort to understand such facts, by Weber, and by the distinguished psychologist and philosopher Fechner. Experimental research soon showed that our discrimination of small differences, in the case of weights and in case of a considerable number of other types of experience, conforms to a rule which these common-sense observations already suggested. The rule was stated in one form by Weber and in another by Fechner, and appears in modern text-books as the so-called "psycho-physic law." This law has been subjected in later years to an elaborate variety of experimental tests. In a very considerable region of our sensory experiences it has been found to remain approximately valid. In certain regions of our sensory experience it cannot be verified. In case of decidedly faint or of decidedly intense sensory experiences of any sense it appears not to hold. Where it is approximately valid it is so for sensory experiences of medium intensity.

The law is that *in order that differences of sensory experience should have,* in two different cases of comparison, *the same value for our reacting consciousness, or should appear to be equal differences, the stimuli that are compared in the two different cases must differ from one another, not by the same absolute physical difference in their magnitude, but by the same relative difference.* Thus, if we suppose that, in a given region of sensation, a stimulus having a physical magnitude 21 appear to have a just perceivable difference from a stimulus possessing the magnitude 20, then, in order that a stimulus of the same type, and appealing to the same sense, but having the magnitude 42, should appear just appreciably greater than another stimulus, this other stimulus would have to have the magnitude 40. While if, again, a stimulus having a magnitude 84 was to appear just less than another stimulus, this other stimulus would have to have a magnitude 80; and so on. Or if, in case of the same series of sensations, stimuli of the magnitudes 10 and 20 appear to consciousness as possessing a certain difference, then two stimuli, possessing, other things being equal, the magnitudes 20 and 40, would produce in consciousness sensory experiences having appreciably as much difference, or the same difference, as the foregoing pair of stimuli. Thus *one pair of stimuli have the same difference for consciousness as another pair of stimuli, in case the members of the two pairs have the same proportionate magnitude when compared together.*

§ 105. With the range of validity of this law, and with its apparent exceptions, we have here no space to deal. That it stands for a very important relation between our conscious discriminations of stimuli and the physical facts seems unquestionable. What it is important for us to note however in this connection is that the psycho-physic law, whatever else it is, *is a law relating to our Mental Docility*, i.e., *to our power to acquire skill in discriminating between the facts of our sensory experience.* The psycho-physic law is treated in some discussions as a law directly relating to our sensations. It is often said, that like differences in intensity of sensation correspond to like proportional differences in the stimulations. But as a fact the experiments upon which the psycho-physic law is based are not and cannot be experiments upon the pure sensory experiences as they exist in themselves, still less upon the absolutely pure and isolated sensations. For the first, we never have any purely sensory experiences which are not woven into complexes that have value for our whole present unity of consciousness. For the rest, *to compare two sensory experiences, and to judge them as different, is to perform a specific reaction in the presence of this pair of experiences*, that is, it is to pronounce the judgment "Different," or it is to make some other reaction which shows that the difference has value for consciousness. *The difference is perceived when the reaction is accomplished. It is not perceived unless some such reaction is present, at least as a tendency.* Now most experiments upon the psycho-physic law are carried on under conditions of concentrated attention, the attention being directed to the comparison of the stimuli in question. In so far as the common-sense experiences before mentioned throw light upon the tendency which the law represents, or in so far as the laboratory experiments are made to approximate to the conditions of the naïve consciousness, it still holds true that *the perception of the difference between two experiences takes the form of some specific reaction to this difference.*

Now in the present chapter we have been setting forth the conditions under which sensory discriminations are learned. We have seen that these conditions favour the sensory discrimination of successive differences, although we can acquire the power to discriminate simultaneous differences. We have also seen that the power to discriminate successive differences, for example, the power to observe the difference between two weights by lifting first one and then immediately the other, or the power to distinguish between two tones by hearing first one and then the other, is a power that can indeed be cultivated by attention, and by training various kinds of reaction in the presence of the objects. The psycho-physic law appears now to formulate *a certain limit to which the Docility of the organism in responding to finer differences in stimulation is subject.*

It has often been disputed whether the psycho-physic

law is a physiological one, having to do with what happens in the organs of sensation before the centres are reached, or whether it is a psychological law, having to do with the way in which our conscious process represents what goes on in the world. From our present point of view the psycho-physic law may well be both physiological and psychical. It certainly has a physical or physiological aspect. If I am affected by two stimuli *A* and *B*, in proper relations of succession, *I am able to discriminate between them in case I am able to perform some act of which I am conscious, an act due to the difference between them, or an act such that I respond to A in a way different from the way in which I respond to B. If I cannot perform the act, I cannot make the conscious discrimination.* The limitation of my conscious discrimination must run parallel to the limitation of my power to act.

Now what the phenomena summed up under the psycho-physic law indicate is, that if you ask a man to react in the form of a judgment of difference, or in any other exactly definable form, which is subject to test, and if you ask him to perform this act in the presence of stimulations, then if the stimulations *A* and *B* are sufficient to produce an act indicating discrimination, stimulations having physical magnitudes other than those of *A* and *B*, must have the same proportional difference in order to produce the same result. What the facts teach is therefore that both the organism and the conscious process tend to adjust themselves *to relative and not to absolute differences of stimuli*. The tendency is so strong that 'no degree of closeness of attention and no degree of docility at our disposal enables us to overcome it. The law therefore stands for a limitation of our docility. It also stands for an obviously convenient relation between the organism and the external world. As many physical stimuli are subject, in case of variations in light or in other physical conditions of our surroundings, to proportional variations in physical intensity, while these variations do not affect the relative importance of the objects that produce these stimuli when considered in their bearing upon the organism, it is of course important that the kind of reaction which the organism makes should not be affected by these unessential variations in our environment. In other cases a similar teleological relation of the facts to our behaviour in their presence can readily be traced. It is important, however, to remember that *the psycho-physic law is not a law directly relating to our sensations, but is rather a law of our reactions*. It is substantially the law that *we make, within limits, the same reaction to the same relative variation in the magnitude of stimuli*. The relation of the law to consciousness is simply due to the fact that we are conscious of a response that we actually tend to make, and of differences among facts, only in so far as we respond to these differences. If it be remembered that the conscious process accompanies not merely our external sensory experiences, but our total organic reactions to these experiences, the mystery which has sometimes been made about the pyscho-physic law appears less significant.

T

CHAPTER XII

DOCILITY

D. THE SOCIAL ASPECT OF THE HIGHER FORMS OF DOCILITY [1]

§ 106. Man's response to his environment is not merely a reaction to things, but is, and in fact predominantly, is, *a reaction to persons*. There is no opportunity, in the present connection, to trace with any detail the rise and growth of our consciousness of the human personalities with whom we are accustomed to deal. The laws of habit and of association are unquestionably of importance as throwing light upon the way in which we come to regard certain objects in our environment not merely as physical things possessing size, movement, etc., but as objects endowed with an experience like our own, and possessing a consciousness that, inaccessible as it may be to us, is still, in so far as we get its expressions, essentially intelligible and profoundly interesting to us. It is necessary in the present connection, without undertaking in the least the task of a specific social

[1] Cf. on the present topic the author's papers on "Self-consciousness, Social Consciousness and Nature" and on the "Anomalies of Self-consciousness" in *Studies of Good and Evil* (New York, 1898).

psychology, to give some indication of *the way in which all our higher intellectual and voluntary habits are affected by this our conscious interpretation of the inner life of our fellows.*

§ 107. The foundation for our whole social consciousness seems to lie in certain instincts which characterise us as social beings, and which begin to assume considerable prominence toward the end of the first year of an infant's life. These instincts express themselves first in reactions of general interest in the faces, in the presence, and in the doings, of our social fellow beings. Among these reactions some show great pleasure and fascination. Some, the reactions of bashfulness, show fear. This fear is an instinctive character, and in some cases may display itself in reactions of violent terror in the presence of strangers. But on the whole, more prominent, in the life of a normally tended infant, is pleasurable reaction at the sight of people. It is unquestionable that, from the very first, these instincts are subject to the regular processes that everywhere determine our docility. Our social environment is a constant source of numerous sensory pleasures, and by association becomes interesting to us accordingly. But, in addition to the pleasures of sense which are due to our human companions, there are, no doubt, from the first, deep instinctive and hereditary sources of interest in the activities of human beings. On the basis of the general social interests, there appear more special instincts, amongst which the most prominent is the complex of instincts suggested by the name IMITA-TION.[1] It is by imitation that the child learns its language. It is by imitation that it acquires all the social tendencies that make it a tolerable member of society. Its imitativeness is the source of an eager and restless activity which the child pursues for years under circumstances of great difficulty, and even when the processes involved seem to be more painful than pleasurable. Imitativeness remains with us through life. It attracts less of our conscious attention in our adult years, but is present in ways that the psychologist is able to observe even in case of people who suppose themselves not to be imitative.

This human imitativeness assumes very notable forms in excited crowds of people, in what the recent psychologists have called in general "the mob." A mob, in the technical sense, is any company of persons whose present set of brain involves the abandonment of such habits as have most determined their customary individual choices, and the assumption, for the moment, merely of certain generalised modes of reaction which are of an emotional, a socially plastic, and a decidedly imitative type. Under the influence of such social conditions, the members of the mob

[1] Cf. Professor Baldwin's *Mental Development in the Child and in the Race*, especially the second volume of that work.

may perform acts of the type before referred to, acts which seem to the casual observer quite out of character in view of the training and of the ordinary opinions of the people concerned. Outside of the mob, the imitative reactions appear in all the phenomena of fashion and of transitory custom, such as any popular craze of the day, or the success of any favourite song, opera, or novel, may daily illustrate. The most of people's political opinions, the most of their religious creeds, the most of their social judgments, are very highly imitative in their origin.

§ 108. Side by side with the social processes of the imitative type appear another group of reactions practically inseparable from the former, but in character decidedly contrasted with them. These are the phenomena of SOCIAL OPPOSITION and of the love *for contrasting one's self with one's fellows in behaviour, in opinion, or in power.* These phenomena of social contrast and opposition have an unquestionably instinctive basis. They appear very early in childhood. They last in most people throughout life. They may take extremely hostile and formidable shapes. In their normal expression they constitute one of the most valuable features of any healthy social activity. This fact may be illustrated by any lively conversation or discussion.

As a rule, the acts that express this fondness for social contrast, and for opposing one's self to the social environment are, in their origin, secondary to the imitative acts. It is true that the instinctive basis for them appears quite as early as do the manifestations of the imitative instincts. And since this fondness for opposition is in part based upon the elemental emotions of the type expressed in anger, obstinacy, and unwillingness to be interfered with, the instinctive basis for the type of action here in question may be said to be manifest even earlier in infancy than is the case with the imitative reactions. But while the instinctive basis of opposition is primitive, the social acts that can express such instincts must be acquired. And in order to contrast one's self with one's social environment it is necessary, in general, first to learn how to do something that has social significance. I cannot oppose you by my speech unless I already know how to talk. I cannot rival you as a musician unless I already understand music. I cannot endeavour to get the better of a political rival unless I already understand politics. But speech and music and politics have to be learned by imitation. Hence the social reactions which express the fondness for contrast and opposition must on the whole follow in their development the social reactions dependent upon imitation. This accounts for that close weaving together of the two types of functions, of which we have already spoken. The playful child already seizes whatever little arts he has acquired by imitation to express his wilfulness, or to develop his own devices, or to display himself to his environment. And, on the other hand, a form of wilfulness, or of obstinacy, in an already highly intelligent being, may lead to a deliberately painstaking process of imitation, such as happens whenever an ambitious artist devotes himself long to training in order that thereby he may get the better of his rivals. In brief, the preservation of a happy balance between the imitative functions and those that emphasise social contrasts and oppositions forms the basis for every higher type of mental activity. *And the entire process of conscious education involves the deliberate appeal to the docility of these two types of social instincts.* For whatever else we teach to a social being we teach him to imitate. And whatever use we teach him to make of his social imitations in his relations with other men, we are obliged at the same time to teach him to assert himself, in some sort of way, in contrast with his fellows, and by virtue of the arts which he possesses.

The full consideration of the social value of imitativeness and of the love of social contrast and opposition, would carry us wholly beyond our present limits. What we are concerned to notice, in this elementary study of psychology, is that *the nature of these functions profoundly affects the structure and the development of the processes known as thought and reasoning.* We are also concerned merely to mention a fact into whose adequate consideration we cannot hope to enter, the fact, namely, that *all the functions which constitute self-consciousness show themselves outwardly in social re-*

actions, that is, in dealings with other real or ideal personages, and are, in our own minds, profoundly related to and inseparable from our social consciousness.

§ 109. To specify more exactly the matters to which reference has thus been made : *what is called thought consists* (as has already been pointed out) *of a series of mental processes that unquestionably tend to express themselves in characteristic motor reactions.* Many of these reactions notoriously take the form of using, of applying, and of combining words. Now the reasons why our thinking process should so largely depend upon using words have often been discussed by psychologists, but at first sight they may appear to the elementary student of psychology somewhat puzzling. The general solution of the problem lies in the fact that *words are the expressions of certain reactions that we have acquired when we were in social relations to our fellows.* If we once understand how these social relations determine that character of our consciousness which essentially belongs to all thinking, we become able to see why verbal associations and habits should be so prominent in connection with all the thinking processes. We shall also be able to see what is frequently neglected by psychologists, namely, the possibility that *processes of thought should on occasion appear dissociated from verbal expression, although never dissociated from tendencies to action which have a social origin* essentially similar to that of language.

Our words are first learned as part of our social intercourse with our fellows. As recent students of the psychology of the language of childhood have pointed out, words cannot be said at the outset to express to a child any exact abstract ideas. They are at first, as Wundt and his school have well insisted, rather the expressions of feelings than the embodiments of thought.[1] The whole vocal life of infancy is primarily an expression of feeling. In social relationships it later becomes to a child associated with his socially fascinating feelings, with the sense of companionship, with his joy in the power to make sounds which others admire, and to imitate sounds which he hears others make. But now, in time, these expressions of the child's feelings become associated not only with social situations and delights, but with objects and deeds observed. The social utility of taking advantage of these associations, is emphasised, in the child's training, by the behaviour, and by the deliberate efforts at instruction in language, which he meets with in his elders. At length a stage comes when language is the expression of the child's wish, at once to characterise objects present in his experience, and to appeal intelligibly to the minds of his fellows. Now these two aspects of the language processes are never to be separated from one another, either in the life of childhood or in our much later rational development. A

[1] See Wundt's *Volkerpsychologie*, Vol. I, " Die Sprache."

word, a phrase, a discourse, is always at once a response to certain facts in the outer or inner world which we attempt to characterise, and an appeal to the consciousness of our fellow. It is the latter aspect which gives language its primary practical importance. Language is not a direct adjustment to the facts apart from the purpose of communication. It is the purpose of communication that alone makes language essentially significant as a part of our mental equipment. But in view of this fact it is obvious that *language acquires its value as a means of characterising facts through processes which appear, in the mind of one who learns language, in the form of a long-continued, a laborious, and generally a fascinating process of comparing his own way of using words with the ways employed by other people.* From the time when a child plays at imitating his nurse's words, or at hearing his own babble imitated, to the time when, perhaps, as a lawyer, he adjusts his arguments to the requirements of judges and juries, and to the criticisms of an opponent, he constantly adjusts his reactions, as he speaks, to the reactions of other people, by comparing his own way of behaviour with the behaviour of others. Such comparison involves inevitably *both* of the two great social motives before emphasised. That is, it involves both the motives of imitation, pure and simple, and that love of social contrast which has before been emphasised.

But now what is the inevitable result of all such

activities? It is that the one who makes such social comparison becomes *very highly conscious of the details of his own acts*, and of the criticisms that other people are making upon these acts, and of the feelings which these acts arouse both in himself and in others. But now it is at the same time the case that the acts of which one becomes conscious are also acts which one is also seeking to adjust to objects as well as to social judgments. The result of this twofold adjustment is precisely *the kind of consciousness which constitutes thinking*. For thinking differs from naïve action chiefly in this: When we act in naïve fashion, we are especially conscious of the objects to which we adjust ourselves, and of the feelings of success or of failure, that is, of satisfaction or of restlessness, of pleasure or of pain, that accompany these acts. Of the details of our acts we are not in such cases conscious, although our consciousness of our objects is unquestionably dependent upon the performance of our acts. Thus, one who seeks food is very imperfectly aware of how he moves his legs or his arms in walking or in grasping; but he is aware of his images of the food, and of his relatively satisfactory or unsatisfactory efforts to obtain it. The reason why the details of our acts do not come in such cases clearly to consciousness is dependent upon the fact that our sensory experiences of the objects in question are prominent, while our sensory experiences of our acts, just in so far as the acts have become habitual, tend to be too swift for consciousness to follow; while only our feelings remain, amongst our internal experiences, as the prominent accompaniments of the act. But, on the other hand, *one who thinks makes it part of his ideal to be conscious of how he behaves in the presence of things.* And this he does because the social comparison of his acts with the acts of other people not only controls the formation of his acts, but has made his observation of his own acts an ideal. For so far as he is imitating others, he is fascinated by the adjustment of his behaviour to the behaviour of others. So far as he is dwelling upon social conflicts and contrasts he is displaying his own acts to the other people; and so he is conscious that they are observing him, and is desirous that they should do so. *In consequence, the social conditions, under which language is acquired produce the thinking process, just because it is of the essence of the thinking process that we should become aware of how our acts are adjusted to our objects.*

The acts in which we express our thinking are not, however, exclusively confined to the process of using words or of combining them. The drawing of a scientific diagram, the construction of a work of art, the performance of an experiment, the adjustment of the playing of one's musical instrument to the criticisms of one's musical rival, or to the guidance of the conductor of an orchestra — all these are activities which involve thinking processes. They do so because they are social adjustments of the type now in question, that is, *social adjustments, involving imitations and social contrasts, and including the consciousness of how one performs the act, and so of how it is adjusted to the ideal.*

§ 110. Such, then, is the general character of thought, namely, that it is *our consciousness of an act or of a series of acts adjusted to an object, in such wise as fittingly to represent that object, or to portray it, or to characterise it, and in such wise that the one who thinks is conscious of the nature of his act.* Hence it will follow that, all the special processes of thinking, such as those usually discriminated as conception, judgment, and reasoning, exemplify this general character of the thinking process, and *result from the effects of social stimulations.* The process of contrasting my own acts with my fellow's acts, and in consequence of contrasting my own views with what I regard as the ideas of my fellow, this is the process which is responsible for that kind of consciousness which appears in all of our thoughtful activities.

Let us exemplify these considerations by a few words about each of the thinking processes which have just been mentioned. The process called Conception, or the formation of Abstract General Ideas, is rightly regarded as essential to the thinking process. General ideas are the ideas which we associate with those words that have an application to any one of many individual

cases or situations. The word "man" or "horse" is a
word of general application. The knowledge of what
this word means involves a possession of a general idea
of men or of horses. Now of what mental material
does such an idea consist? When it is a lively, or a
highly conscious idea, it unquestionably involves, in all
cases, and in one aspect, some kind of mental imagery.
This imagery may, in visualising people, take predominantly the form of mental pictures of representative
men or of representative horses. It may in some minds
take the form of vague mental pictures corresponding
to what one might call "composite photographs," such
as the mind would seem to have formed from retaining
in imagination the characters common to many individual horses or men, while forgetting the characters
wherein various individuals differ from one another.
But it is, nevertheless, possible for one who is not a
visualiser to have as clear an idea of what he means by
"man" or "horse" as the visualising man possesses.
And our more developed abstract ideas, such as mathematical abstractions, or such as our conception of jus-
tice, involve mental processes to whose portrayal visual
imagery is extremely inadequate. One comes nearer to
dwelling upon the essential characteristics which the abstract ideas of a horse or of a man must possess when
one observes that *whoever knows what a horse or man in
general is, knows of some kind of act which it is fitting
to perform in the presence of any object of the class in*

question.   This act is of such a nature as either directly portrays the characters of the object, or else in some fashion tends, if expressed outwardly, to convey to another the idea of man or of horse that one possesses. The name " man " or " horse," the word-image associated with any such object, is itself a part of a well-known act by which one may react in the presence of an object of the class in question.   For *naming objects* is *one way of responding to their presence.*   And the name has value for consciousness, not merely because it happens to be associated with the object, but because it is associated with the object as my fitting and proper way of treating the object or of reacting to its presence, especially in case I wish to inform another of the fact that I have seen man or horse.   But, in addition to the use of the name, the one who possesses the correct general idea of the objects is able to perform numerous other fitting acts in presence of any object of the class in question.   At the moment when he brings to clearer consciousness his general idea of man or horse, he *either* remembers some such act — some act by which he could fittingly characterise his own usual relations to man or horse, — or some act by means of which he could imitate or portray (much as, in the gesture language, any one portrays an object by an imitative sign) an aspect of the nature of man or of horse; *or else*, if he performs no such act at the moment, he has *a feeling of confidence that he could perform*

such an act, that he could tell himself, if he chose, more
clearly what he means by man or by horse. Such a
feeling of confidence is a feeling similar to those feelings of familiarity earlier described. It is a feeling of
the relatively quiescent type. Such a feeling frequently
takes the place in our minds of any more explicit effort
consciously to understand what we mean by a familiar
word; so that often what we call the understanding of
a word is simply the hearing of the word, attended by a
feeling of familiarity, and of confidence that we could,
if necessary, proceed to give further accounts or portrayals of the nature of the object whereof the word is
the general name. But as soon as we proceed from
such feelings to the more concrete act of conception,
our general ideas, if they become explicit, *must take the
form of further tendencies to conduct, of tendencies to portray or to describe or to depict the nature of the object by
a fitting series of reactions*, such as would be suitable, on
our part, in the presence of any object of the class
in question, and such as would be suitable to portray to
another our general ideas.

§ 111. *Our general ideas, whether exact or inexact,
stand therefore for certain mental attitudes* assumed
toward any object of the class of which we have the
general idea. Any such mental attitude is accompanied by imagery, and the mental imagery may be
so prominent that certain people, especially visualisers,
suppose that they sufficiently describe their conscious

states when they characterise their general ideas as images, more or less vague, of typical objects of the class in question. But, as we pointed out in discussing our mental imagery, *our mental images of outer objects are never to be divorced from our reactions*. When we have lively images, we tend to express our whole attitude toward their objects in fitting behaviour, as the child, when playing with imaginary comrades, or telling stories, illustrates. Moreover, *whoever has a general idea of a class of things, is able to show you that he has a correct general idea only in so far as this idea expresses itself in fitting acts*. Whoever believes himself to have a correct general idea of a tiger, merely because he has an image of a tiger, has only to ask himself whether his general idea of a tiger is such as to permit him to believe that when you meet a tiger you pat him on the head and ask him to give you his paw, in order to see that his image of a tiger possesses what Professor James has so skilfully called a "fringe" — a fringe which at once excludes any such disposition to deal with a tiger as one does with a pet dog. One's general idea of a tiger includes states of feeling, which may indeed be represented to momentary consciousness only in the form of a general sense of familiarity with the idea or with the word "tiger," or only by the general confidence that, *if* one were asked to portray the nature of a tiger, one could in some respect fittingly do so. But these feelings of

U

quiescence in the presence of the familiar name or image are themselves indications of tendencies which tell one how one ought to act in the presence of an object of the class in question. If one's confidence, that one's general idea is a good one, is well founded, and if one then allows one's general idea of the object in question to become explicit and fully developed, instead of remaining a mere fragmentary image or word-memory, then one discovers that *the whole general idea involves what one may as well call "a plan of action," that is, a way of behaviour which is fitting to characterise and portray an object of the class in question.*

§ 112. The fact that too many psychological accounts of the nature of general ideas have resulted from confining psychological attention to the fragmentary images which may appear at any stage of the development or expression in consciousness of a general idea, instead of considering the total mental process which is needed in order to portray with relative completeness any general idea whatever, is responsible for the result that the traditional account of general ideas has usually missed this, their relation to our conduct. But if this relation exists, if *every complete general idea is a conscious plan of action,* fitted for the characterisation and portrayal of the nature of that of which we have a general idea, the psychological question regarding the genesis of general ideas is simply the question as to *how we could become clearly*

conscious of such plans of action.   For, as we pointed
out above, we are not usually clearly conscious of precisely those acts which have become most habitual, unless
special conditions call our attention to their constitution.

Our answer to the question thus raised has already
been stated.   The fact that all our general ideas have
been formed under social conditions, and that the ways
in which we describe, portray, and characterise things
have been throughout determined by motives of communication, by a disposition to imitate the behaviour of
our fellows, and by a disposition to compare our own
mental attitudes with theirs, this fact sufficiently explains why *the social contrasts and comparisons in
question have tended to make us and keep us conscious
not only of our own objects, but of our own modes of
rational behaviour in their presence.*

Meanwhile, the essentially *imitative character* of all
complex general ideas appears in all our most thoughtful processes, namely, in our more elaborate scientific
general ideas.   Such general ideas are best expressed
by drawing diagrams, or by going through the processes
of a scientific experiment, or by writing formulas on a
blackboard, or, finally, by describing objects in well-
ordered series of descriptive words.   From this point of
view one might declare that *all our higher conceptions,*
just in proportion as they are thoughtful and definite,
involve conscious imitations of things.   And these conceptions are general, merely because *the fashion of imi-*

lation that we employ in the presence of one object will regularly be applicable to a great number of objects.

Our *numerical ideas* illustrate this principle very well. They are more or less abbreviated expressions of *the motor activity of counting*, and of the results of this activity. The geometrical conception of a circle as a curve that can be constructed by fixing one end of a straight line, by leaving the other free, and by allowing this end to rotate in a plane, is another instance of a conception that is identical with our memory of a certain mode of portrayal by which a circle can be reconstructed. In brief, *we have exact conceptions of things in so far as we know how the things are made, or how they can be imitatively reconstructed through our portrayals.* Where our power to imitate ceases, our power definitely to conceive ceases also. All science is thus an effort to describe facts, to set over against the real world an imitation of it. Hence the vanity of endeavouring to describe the process of conception merely in terms of images, without remembering that mental imagery, when definite, is always related to our action. *But it is our social life that has made us conscious of our actions, and that has thus taught us how to form abstract ideas.*

§ 113. The mental process called Judgment is the second essential aspect of the thinking process. While judgment involves many other aspects, its essential feature lies in the fact that, when we judge, *we accept or reject a given proposed portrayal of objects as adequate, or as fitting for its own purpose.* The general conception, as we have just seen, is a portrayal, which one may compare to a photograph of a man. The act of judgment is comparable to the act whereby one to whom the photographer sends the proofs of a photograph, accepts or rejects the photograph as a worthy representation of the object in question. But our consciousness regarding the acceptance or rejection of proposed portrayals of objects has become critical, has come to involve a sharp distinction between truth and error, *because we have so often compared our judgments with those of our fellows*, and have so often criticised, accepted, or rejected their expressions, their attitudes toward things. Here again the conditions upon which the social consciousness depends have proved necessary to the formation of our thought.

§ 114. The process of reasoning, the third aspect of the thinking process, is in general *the process of considering the results of proposed conceptions and judgments*, of taking them, so to speak, as if they were themselves original objects, and of reading off from some new point of view the results which these conceptions or judgments, when once accepted, involve. The reasoning process is often regarded by students of psychology as in the main a case of the association of ideas. And that associations are concerned in every step of the reasoning process is indisputable.

Conceptions and judgments inevitably express habitual activities. Thought is a result of experience, and nothing appears in the thinking process which is not profoundly influenced, from the psychological point of view, by the laws of habit. But to regard a train of reasoning as merely an associative train of images is indeed to emphasise a true aspect of a train of reasoning, but is to neglect its most important aspect. So too, as we have before asserted, all thinking and so all reasoning, involves assimilation (§ 96). But we have also said that thought is much more than mere assimilation. As a fact, every act of reasoning involves new reactions of our own in the presence of a situation which we get before us as the result of former acts. The essence of reasoning, as of the whole thinking process, is that I am not merely concerned with the way in which images float before me, but with *my consciousness of what I am doing with these images, or with the objects that the images suggest*. When I reason, the object before me for consideration is principally represented by images of the results of former acts. My reasoning process involves a new judgment based upon these former acts.

Thus, if I am constructing a diagram, and upon a right line have placed a point *B* to the right of point *A*, and have placed a point *C* to the right of point *B*, I so far actually portray a situation which I may regard as representing the nature of some series of objects. If, hereupon, I observe that my construction involves as a fact that C, being to the right of B, must by so much the more be to the right of A, and if I hereupon note that this must hold true of the object which the diagram represents, then I reason. My reasoning thus consists *in finding out from some new point of view what I have meant by my former acts and judgments.* We bring out the essence of the reasoning process when, in an appeal to a careless child who has done some mischief, we say, "See what you have done." Reasoning is thus the reading off of the result of our former thoughtful acts from some new point of view. But it indeed involves no essentially new mental tendency. It is a continuation of the consciousness which characterises the whole thinking process, only of this consciousness on a higher level.

As reasoning involves a constantly more and more elaborate *consciousness of the nature and results of our own action* so again we see, from the whole history of the development of the reason amongst men, that *reasoning is a consequence of social situations, and especially of the process of comparing various opinions and connections of opinion, as these have grown up amongst men.* The whole method of the reasoning process has come to the consciousness of men as the result of disputation, that is, of processes whereby men have compared together their various ways of portraying things, and of taking accounts of the results of their own actions. *Nobody learns to reason except after other people have pointed out to him how they view his attempts to give his own acts of thought connection*, and to proceed from one act to another. Like the thinking process in general, the reasoning process develops out of conditions which at the outset involve a very rich, and in fact predominant presence of feelings and of complex emotions. That is, reasonings have resulted from what were at first decidedly passionate contrasts of opinion; and the dispassionate reason has grown up upon the basis of decidedly emotional efforts of men to persuade other men to assume their own fashions of conduct, and their own self-conscious view of how their various acts were connected together. If the process of conception is the formation of a plan of conduct, the process of *reasoning results from trying so to portray this plan as to persuade other men to assume it.* Persuasion and controversy, upon earlier stages of mental development, are always associated with passionate vehemence. The ineffectiveness of mere passion to attain its own social ends, the growth of ingenuity in the process of persuasion, and the gradual elaboration of social habits, formed through the successful bringing of men to agreement, — such are the motives upon which the development of the reasoning process has depended.

§ 115. It remains here very briefly to characterise the highest and most complex of all the intellectual processes, namely that one which has to do with what is called our "Self-consciousness" in general, that is, the consciousness which the Ego, the Self, possesses of its own life, activities, and plans. *The Self of any man comes to consciousness only in contrast with other selves.* There is no reason why one should be aware of his whole plan of life, or of his personal character, or of the general connections amongst his various habits, or of the value of his own life, or of any of the features and attributes which our present consciousness ascribes to the Self, unless he has had occasion to compare his behaviour, his feelings, and his ideals, with those of other men. It is true that when developed, this Self includes amongst its possessions all the states of consciousness that make up the inner life of which we spoke in our opening paragraphs, that inner life which we conceived as in some sense inaccessible to, and sundered from, the inner life of anybody else. But there is no reason why these states of consciousness should form, from our own point of view, a world by themselves, unless we had some world of other facts to compare and contrast them with. And the whole evidence of our social consciousness is to the effect that it is by virtue of our ideas of other people, and of their minds and conscious states, that we have come to form the conception of our own inner life as, in its wholeness, distinct from theirs.

The conception of the so-called Empirical Self, that

is, of the Self of our ordinary experience, is one which we find to be especially centred about certain of our most important organic sensations, and also centred about those feelings of pleasure, pain, restlessness, and quiescence, which are most persistent and prominent in our lives. But the mere possession of these organic sensations and feelings is not sufficient to explain why we regard them as peculiarly belonging to the Self. It is only when we see the importance that our social life with our fellows has given to these organic sensations that we recognise how we first have come to contrast our own experience with what we for various reasons conceive to be the inner experiences of other people, and then, by virtue of the prominence which our social contrasts and oppositions give to these organic sensations, have come to regard them as especially the immediate expression of our independence, and of that which keeps us apart from all other selves.

That the Self comes to consciousness in normal cases only in connection with organised plans of conduct, is obvious from what has already been said. Our social self-consciousness leads us to form such plans, and to compare them with those of other people. Our consciousness of ourselves as personalities is therefore simply an extreme instance of that relation between social consciousness and the higher intellectual development which we have already set forth in our account of the general nature of thought.

CHAPTER XIII

The Conditions of Mental Initiative

§ 116. In treating of docility we have everywhere had to take account of the presence of novelty both in our experience and in our conduct. But on the whole, such novelty has thus far been treated as something due, in the main, to the external stimuli, and to the order in which they come. A new habit, as we have said, may arise because certain stimuli A, B, C, D, act upon the organism. These stimuli have never been thus together before. The resulting brain processes, a, b, c, d, excited together, tend by the law of habit to become connected through repetition, so that they are more easily aroused.

We have indeed observed that, when new habits are formed, not all that occurs can be said to be due either to the external stimuli or to their repetition. For there is a certain internally conditioned tendency on the part of the gradually improving habit to grow more definite, to lose its useless elements, to involve less diffuse discharges. This tendency, as we have said, is due to the general adaptability of the organism. We left it to biological science further to explain the existence of such tendencies to the elimination of the unfit constituents of habits. But the rest of the process of the acquisition and the welding of habits involves features that were, as thus far considered, of one general type. This is the type which determines our whole docility, both in its intellectual and in its voluntary aspects. Assimilation, as we found, tends to minimise whatever novelties new disturbances introduce into the organism. Even the differentiation of conscious states we also found to be an exemplification of the law of habit. For differentiation is due to the fact that habits of successive action, when once acquired, determine our consciousness of the differences of simultaneous facts. The processes of the attention have appeared as further examples of the law of habit. The organisation of conduct follows the same line. So far there has therefore seemed to be no room left for any normal initiative which could be said to be due in the main to the organism or, on its psychical side, to the mind.

Yet as our introduction pointed out, there is at least the appearance of mental initiative in the phenomena of human ingenuity, in the acts which tradition has regarded as due to free-will, and in the processes of "self-activity" generally. This appearance we now need in conclusion to examine more carefully. We should come to the subject with no prejudice in favour of finding that this appearance of mental initiative either is or is not a well-founded appearance. We ought neither to be surprised to find the processes in question reducible to those which govern our docility, nor unwilling to admit that in some respects they are not thus reducible.

Modern biological theory, by its recognition of what have been called "spontaneous variations" as factors in evolution has, at all events, prepared the way for the recognition of the possible presence in the psychologist's world of *tendencies which are essentially disposed to the production of novel forms of conduct*, such as the environment does not wholly predetermine, *and to the formation of novel combinations of mental processes*, such as previous habits have not wholly rendered necessary. That such relative novelties should be possible in the psychologist's world, is in itself no more surprising than that variations of stature, of protective colouring, or of inherited functions, should occur in the world that the zoölogist studies. Certainly *a general view of the place which beings with minds occupy in the physical world strongly suggests that their organisms may especially have significance as places for the initiation of more or less novel types of activity.* That such novelty does not mean the absence of law, we have already pointed out.

We do not expect that the psychologist will ever be interested in events whose relations to previous events he regards as reducible to no sort of rule. Every science studies its facts for the sake of finding them instances that conform to rule. But nature furnishes us, even in the inorganic world, with numerous instances of what are called " critical points," viz., points where one kind of process ends, and a process of a decidedly distinct kind appears quite suddenly to begin. The advance of scientific theory does, indeed, depend upon discovering that, even at these critical points, there is no absolute discontinuity in the physical processes involved. But this fact does not deprive the critical points of their scientific interest. By so much the more might we expect to find that, in the development of a creature with a mind, there are indeed critical points, — places where something decidedly novel begins to appear; and where this novelty is not wholly determined by the relations between the organism and its environment, but is also in part determined by factors which are due to the organism itself, and which are not wholly reducible to the laws governing our docility. That such critical points in the development of an organism or of a mind involve no absolute discontinuities, we shall unquestionably admit. But that fact need not deprive the phenomena of mental initiative of their very considerable interest.

§ 117. We have heretofore spoken of the instincts, which lie at the basis of the development of our conduct, as if they were finished products of heredity. We have pointed out that, when external experiences arouse these instincts, the result is the performance of actions which leave traces in our central nervous system, and which therefore tend to the formation of habits.   But, as a fact, the phenomena of the appearance of instinct, either in infancy or later in the course of our development, are not so simple as this general formula would indicate.   In general, our most important instincts appear slowly, bit by bit, not as at all finished tendencies to specific kinds of reaction, but as at first crude and awkward tendencies *in the general direction of a given kind of action.*   The unfinished form in which the instincts appear in all the higher vertebrates seems to be of great importance for the development of the individual animal.   It gives opportunities to train the individual to special adaptations to his environment, such as are indicated by the special circumstances in which he finds himself.   Thus, the aquatic bird may have to learn, and that somewhat slowly, its first acts of swimming.   And still more obviously the human infant spends a long time in training the preliminary stages that lead it on the way toward creeping, climbing, and walking.   The reader of Miss Shinn's elaborate and highly instructive monograph on *The Development of a Child* will find in her account a remarkably minute discussion of the phenomena that appear in the case of the infant whom she studied. Every one of the acts that finally resulted in the attainment of the power to creep, to climb, and to walk, was very slowly reached as the result of a training whose details were nowhere predetermined by heredity, while on the other hand, every step of the process was indeed predetermined by hereditary constitution *to tend*, in the normal child, *toward a result that would give it, under the circumstances of its individual life, the powers of locomotion suited to a human being.* In consequence, the development of the individual child, with regard to such activities as those of locomotion, is at every step *subject to such modifications as tend to adapt the child to its individual surroundings.* The child does not possess its instinctive adaptations in any finished form, nor even in such form that habits, having a definite character, can at all rapidly be acquired. On the contrary, the early habits, in case of such complex processes as those of locomotion, appear for a long time in the form of very gradual and awkward acts, that do indeed, in some measure, adjust the child to its environment, but for a long time leave this adjustment very poor and ineffective.

§ 118. The same principle seems to hold true with regard to all the instincts upon whose modification and gradual training all our higher rational habits depend. *The higher we are in the scale of mental existence, the slower is the process of learning to adapt ourselves to the environment,* the more awkward are the intermediate stages, lying between the first signs that we possess a given instinctive tendency, and the fitting expression of the modifications of this instinctive tendency in the form of definite conduct. Hence the long continued awkwardness of the growing boy and youth. Hence the long apprenticeship through which many forms of professional skill and artistic ability have to pass. That, in the course of such a development, there should be *a constant tendency to the appearance of variations of individual conduct, whose precise details are not predetermined by heredity, and yet are not easily to be explained merely in terms of docility*, is fairly plain; for if our instinctive tendencies come to light only slowly as the nervous centres grow toward maturity, the external expressions of our conduct will be determined not merely by what happens to the organism nor by what the organism has inherited, but also *by the highly individual and unpredictable phenomena of the growth of the nervous centres themselves during our early life.*

As a fact, the brain of man which seems to be provided at birth with all its neurons, develops for a long time after birth, and especially during the first seven years of life, constantly new connections, structural and functional, amongst its various parts. The formation of these connections is determined not merely by the inherited tendencies of the organism, nor yet wholly by the laws of habit, but *by the circumstances of growth.* These circumstances are unquestionably affected by the actual conduct of the organism in question. But they are not in such wise determined by it as the habits are

x

determined by it in previous behaviour. It follows that there is a factor, hitherto neglected in our account, — a factor which tends to explain the appearance of unpredictable variation in the conduct of an immature organism of our own type. This factor is the organic growth. So far as this organic growth includes the appearance, at certain stages, of decidedly new instincts, such as those which appear at puberty, the phenomena have already been excluded, by our initial definition, from those phenomena of variability which concern us here. But in so far as the phenomena are determined by the growth of nervous centres and of nervous connections which are all the while undergoing training in accordance with the laws of habit, the consequences will appear in a type of variation such as our general account has already characterised. That is, *the results will appear in the form of a modification of habits in directions which are on the whole adaptive in their character, while they are not wholly to be explained on the basis of previous instincts, or as mere phenomena of docility.* The variations which determine the gradual organisation of the movements of the creeping child seem to belong in a considerable measure under this head.

§ 119. But closely associated with these processes there are others, whose significance for our whole organic life is very great, although they seem to be rather too generally neglected in theoretical accounts of the development of our conduct.   What especially attracts our attention, in following the development of the creeping child, is the fact *that it persists in a great number of its still unadaptive movements, in a great number of its still useless actions, despite their inefficacy.* As Miss Shinn expresses the results of her own observations in the case of some of these phenomena, the child seemed to take delight, or to persist, in certain processes, *because of the inner impulse to try them again and again.*

Professor Baldwin, in his work on *Mental Development in the Child and in the Race* has done no little service by laying stress upon the importance of such "try, try, again" activities for the development of imitative and of other intelligent functions.   Now all such actions may unquestionably be regarded as due to instinctive tendencies.   But the general instinct *to persist in trying,* is not like such a special instinctive activity as is the converging of the optic axes when the eyes are fixed upon an object.   For the latter, the special instinct, is, by itself, a directly adaptive instinct.   But on the other hand, the general tendency to persist in actions which are thus far *not* adaptive, is a tendency which does not, at the moment, or in any brief time, necessarily lead to results that are serviceable to the organism.   Nor, on the other hand, is this general tendency one that predetermines precisely what kind of act, whether adaptive or in so far ineffective, shall be

carried out. The eager child is disturbed by its environment, and hereupon is led somehow to a reaction which,
owing to the immaturity of the organism, is thus far
very imperfectly adapted to the environment. To the observer the child seems to be trying to do something, but
not to know what it wants to do. The particular act in
question may be the expression of some instinct not yet
completely developed. But hereupon there now appears the other instinct, — the mere tendency to persist,
— a tendency which has a decidedly generalised form,
and which may be described as *a tendency to do again
and again, with variations, whatever the child has once
begun to do*, without any especial regard to whether
the act is immediately adaptive or not.

That this tendency plays a considerable part in the
life of childhood, any observer may see for himself.
Miss Shinn's subject, during all the period of learning
to creep, to walk, and to climb, showed this persistence in manifold ways. It was not a persistence due
in every case to the child's observation that she had
already accomplished an important or otherwise useful reaction. It was frequently a persistence in what
was so far awkwardness. I have called the persistence a tendency of a more generalised kind, because
it seems to be a normal expression of the vigorous
activity of a growing organism. It seems also to be
an expression which may be applied in various directions, so that of itself it does not predetermine what

activities shall be persisted in, but only that any one of a large number of imperfect instinctive tendencies, if once begun, shall be repeatedly pursued. This tendency seems to be represented in consciousness by feelings in terms of which the child estimates the acts that chance experience, acting upon its immature instincts, may have so far initiated. Observers usually interpret these feelings as, in the normal case, predominantly those of pleasure. Professor Baldwin, who lays great stress upon the "heightened activities" of the organism as a basis for the acquisition of new special adaptations to the environment, regards these heightened activities themselves as, at the outset of the evolutionary process, the accompaniments of pleasurable feelings; and that this is to a considerable extent true is unquestionable. But one has only to take a somewhat wider view of activities of this type to see many cases in which, even when they first appear in the course of evolution, they seem to be inevitable, although they do not appear to be markedly pleasurable. From our own point of view, the feeling that consciously accompanies such early activities is *the feeling of restlessness rather than that of pleasure.*

Some act, due to a stimulus working upon a still immature nervous system, is awkwardly performed, and leads thus far to no satisfactory result. What shall be the consequence? The consequence of course may be, and often is, that *the mere activity of the*

healthy organism is itself joyous, whatever its result.
In this case the child will take pleasure in the act
and will repeat it. The repetition will be an expression at once of the general law of habit and of the
usual effects of pleasurable excitement. Professor
Baldwin finds at the basis of all such repetitions
a certain fundamental tendency of the organism to
what he calls "circular reactions," that is, to sorts of
reaction whereby any stimulus, if once presented, is, if
possible, again repeated. The "circular reactions"
thus include all acts that tend to be repeated over and
over. Granting the existence, in an organism, of inherited tendencies to such circular reactions, granted
the heightened activity with its pleasurable conscious
accompaniments, and granted the occurrence, in consequence, of any sort of reaction, however imperfect
or awkward; and *then, indeed, the tendency to try
and try again, may be regarded as a natural expression
of the whole relation between the organism and the
environment.*

Nevertheless when we ourselves are able consciously
to observe, even in maturity, similar processes, the conscious accompaniments need not be pleasurable. We
may find, in ourselves, at such times, simply the sense
that the result thus far reached *is unsatisfactory*, and
we may feel *a restlessness*. This restlessness may constitute either a painful, or a comparatively indifferent
state of feeling, so far as pleasure and pain are con-

cerned. But the feeling in all such cases will be a
distinctly restless feeling, and may accompany the
general organic tendency to persist in trying afresh.
This doing of something further may, for the reasons
upon which Professor Baldwin has insisted, *appear
predominantly in the form of a series of "circular reactions."* But the trying again may also *give place to
another sort of restlessness which leads to efforts at
movements in some new direction. The dissatisfied
creature may persist, but may persist in a restless
search for whatever else can be done under the circumstances.* And the trying again may be but a mere
incident of this restlessness, an incident due to the
fact that the repetition of the awkward act is one of
the comparatively few resources which recent experience has made available. In any case, the persistence in some sort of behaviour, which is involved in every
such activity, *tends to result in bringing the organism into
constantly new relations with the environment.* It may
also result, as is probable, *in hastening the growth
of those nervous connections which, in the immature
organism, will be necessary preliminaries to the acquisition of better adaptations.* In general, the result of
the disposition to persist, either, with pleasure, in trying
again the awkward act, or, with restlessness, in trying
anything whatever proves to be possible, will be a
tendency that at the moment when it most forcibly
expresses itself in action is not a directly adaptive

tendency. Furthermore, its results will not be wholly predetermined by heredity, nor yet by the kind of relation to the environment which the growing organism has yet attained. The most important consequence of this vague struggle for something more will be *that opportunities will be given to the organism to acquire adaptations which it never could acquire, unless this predisposition to endless experiment and to the trying of various relations with the environment were present.*

§ 120. The significance of the processes thus characterised will better appear if we hereupon consider two different classes of cases, the one much lower and simpler than is the case with the child, the other much more complex, but nearer to our own present consciousness.

Let us return to the case of the caged animal, or of the pet animal turned out of doors and anxious to get in again. Owing to the environment, such an animal is, at the moment, unable, on the basis either of instinct or of acquired habit, to make a desirable adaptation to its environment. It tries, struggles, and fails. What is the result? The result *may be* that, after a certain number of efforts, the discomfort of the struggle is so great that further effort is inhibited, and the animal passively resigns itself to the situation. So far no phenomena appear which are not generally explicable on the basis of sensitiveness, instinct, and docility. But now on the other hand, the animal *may continue* its attempts to escape or to get in. It may continue them in the form of constantly varied activities whereby it tries experiments, such as bring it into entirely novel contact with the environment. These experiments may *ultimately result in the occurrence of acts for which the animal's previous training had not prepared it*. When these acts finally occur, they will indeed be the result of a process of trial and error. They will indeed be instances of sensitiveness and docility. They may involve successful adaptations. They may thereupon establish useful habits for the animal's future conduct. But one feature of the whole process remains which is not fully explained in terms of the animal's special instincts (such as desire for warmth or for food or for comfort), and which is also not explained upon the basis of the animal's previous habits. This feature is suggested by the question : *Why did the animal persist*, under apparently hopeless conditions, and despite failures? *Why did it persist in activities which were so far not adaptive?*

The answer to this question may sometimes be stated in terms of the animal's painful feelings. One may say that the animal continued to long for food, or for other comfort, and to have some idea, based upon its former experience — some idea of the attainment of its ends. Its docility and its already established habits would then explain why, with such feelings, it persisted. But such an explanation in terms of the animal's feelings is, after all, ambiguous. For the struggle is painful, as well as the failure. The point may come where the pain of the struggle becomes greater than the pain of the lack. In case of a sufficiently hopeless struggle this point is actually reached, and the animal finally surrenders to fate. But what determines whether the one of these two pains is greater than the other? The answer is, of course, to be given in terms of the nervous constitution of the animal itself.

But when one considers this constitution, one has to take account of still another fact. *Some animals are actively persistent.* They are so by inherited disposition. However painful certain situations, *they will not give up until exhaustion sets in.* Other animals, which appear no more sensitive in many ways than are the former, are more quiescent. They surrender more readily. The difference between two such different animals may of course be described in terms of pleasure and pain. But this difference also seems equally to suggest a description *in terms of feelings of restlessness and quiescence, that is in terms of nervous predispositions which have to do, not so much with pleasure and pain, as with being disposed to persevere and to vary activity.* Such predispositions are themselves matters of the greatest variation both in ourselves and in the lower animals. Thus the horse can be broken to harness, because, in certain painful situations which are opposed in many ways to his primitive instincts, he erelong gives way. The zebra is said generally to escape being broken to harness, *not perhaps because he finds it more painful, but because he actually persists longer in his struggle.* In all such cases, where mere persistence in a certain type of action characterises an animal, and leads to a process of trial and error that finally results in adaptive reactions, one finds a factor which, for a time, may produce apparently useless activities; but it leads, in the end, to the establishment of fitting relations to the environment. Now this factor, this peculiar persistence, *belongs to the temperament of the animal.* The creature that has such a tendency is likely, in certain situations, *to form new habits, or to vary his old habits, in an adaptive direction. The heightened activities that lie at the basis of such tendencies are primarily activities of the restless type.* They may be pleasurable activities, or they may be activities that involve the effort to escape pain. But they are not to be uniquely characterised in these terms. It is best to characterise them as *the activities which lead to very various sorts of persistent experiment, that is, to repetitions and variations of such acts as so far prove to be maladaptations.*

§ 121. To turn now to a case that appears in the life of human beings. A problem baffles us. It may be a practical problem. It may be a matter of voluntary decision. It may be, in the main, an intellectual problem. The environment arouses us to action. But we are provided with no present adaptation. Our efforts to meet the situation prove abortive and disappointing. What shall we do? One in vain endeavours, at such times, to define our activities in terms merely of pleasure and pain. Of course our present failure is painful, and we indeed seek to escape from this suffering. Of course the thought of our thus far unattainable ideal arouses new desires to attain it. But there are various ways of escaping from such pains. The effort to escape by fresh attempts at winning the goal is itself painful. It involves renewed disappointments. Meanwhile, if we can once persuade ourselves to give up the struggle, the pain again diminishes. What shall determine whether we go on or not? Whatever does determine is something that lies very deep in our nature, that varies from person to person, and that is best expressed in consciousness in feelings not so much of pain and pleasure as of restlessness and quiescence. This deciding factor is *our disposition to persevere either in repeating with variations the particular acts that have so far proved abortive, or in searching elsewhere — anywhere — for a chance solution of our problem.* If this tendency is sufficiently predominant, we continue our efforts, and may do so when they are intensely painful. The result may be, in extreme cases, the "do-or-die" mood, which will end either in success, and in a novel form of adaptation to the environment, or else in our entire destruction. What is noticeable about this persistent tendency, when it appears, is that it is a very general tendency. It is the expression of an instinct, related to our special habits and instincts as the general experiences of orientation are related to our special experiences of the place of a point in space. It is aroused, not by a special stimulation, but *by our finding that we are in the position of having undertaken something, and of having thus far failed.* It predisposes us to no one kind of action, except to the general effort to try other reactions that may have to do with the task which we have begun. Thus, at first, it merely seems to dispose us *to persist in maladaptations.* In case of kindlier fortune this tendency may be very pleasurable ; but it appears in instances that cannot be explained in terms of Professor Baldwin's heightened reactions due to pleasure. Nor can I wholly accept the special explanations that Professor Baldwin has offered when he deals with the presence of such persistent activities as are, for the moment, painful. But what is certain is *that our power to learn decidedly new variations of our habits will usually depend upon the presence of this perseverance.* And this is what every moral counsellor of resolution practically recognises. The restless men may prove to be failures, but *the most successful of human beings are the men who are in some respects prodigiously restless.* These persist in doing what just now need not be done. They persist in trials despite maladaptations. Failure stimulates them. *What the environment cannot yet teach them, they teach the environment to furnish them, sooner or later, in a form that they can assimilate.*

§ 122. Now my thesis is that *the apparently spontaneous variations of our habits which appear in the course of life, and which cannot be altogether explained as due to external stimulation, have as their principal internal cause this restlessness.* The restlessness itself appears sometimes in more or less specific forms. But it is, on the whole, something very much more general in its character, than is any one of the specific instincts upon which our particular habits are founded.

The thesis that *the restless over-activity of the organism in carrying out its instinctive processes, or in seeking opportunity for the establishment of new functions, is the principal condition of every significant form of mental initiative,* may seem to reduce the province of mental initiative to a very modest and narrow range. But one has only to observe a little more closely our life, in order to see that the range thus left to mental initiative is, as a fact, very large. The environment and the inherited tendencies of an organism determine at any moment specific acts. The already acquired habits of the organism determine how these specific acts shall be based upon former actions. So far, however, the environment appears as the one source of whatever novelties are to appear in conduct; while the organism appears disposed to persist in its former modes of conduct, or to repeat such actions as its ancestral tendencies, its experience, and its docility, predetermine. But if, amongst the various reactions of the organism, *there are such as take the form of a restless search for novelty of environment and of conduct, then novelties will appear in the actions of the organism — novelties which are due, in an important measure, to the tendencies which the organism itself has inherited.* And yet the resulting acts will be not mere repetitions of ancestral acts, because they will have resulted from novel relations to an environment. It thus comes to be the case with the organism and with the mind, as it is with the emigrant to a foreign country. In the new country he lives a new life, and not the life of his ancestors. This result is indeed due to the new environment. *Yet the new environment would never have come to him if he had not wandered.* And he would never have wandered had it not been the result of a restlessness that was his own.

§ 123. The kinds of mental initiative which can result from the tendencies now summarised may next be briefly surveyed. First and most notable in the developments of early childhood are the forms of novelty in conduct, and of accompanying mental initiative, which are displayed in the *plays of children.* As Groos has shown in his monographs on the *Play of Ani-*

mals and *The Play of Man*, the value of play *lies especially in its relation to the future activities of the adult organism*. The various instincts which are manifested in play, whether in animals or in men, are indeed inherited instincts. But like all the higher instincts in vertebrate animals, they are inherited, as we have seen, in an imperfect form; and their expression is subject to much individual variation in consequence of the experience acquired by the individual animal or child as it plays. Just because the play activities are carried out at a time when they are not necessary to the preservation of the organism, they receive a free and manifold development for which there would be no opportunity if the same activities were postponed until the necessities of adult life called for the arts in question. The kitten, playing with sticks, and with leaves, and with other kittens, gets an expertness in pursuing and catching prey which it would not have time to acquire if it waited until hunger drove it to pursue food. Precisely the same principle holds with regard to the far more complicated plays of children. I have heard a sea captain tell how, in middle life, he saved his ship, in an emergency, through a device of navigation that he first learned, in a crude form, when, in boyhood, he was playing with his sail-boat in his native harbour. The same general principle holds regarding numerous arts which children acquire in connection with early and spontaneous plays. Now the most notable characteristic of the play activity, whether in the animal or in the child, is its apparent spontaneity. Yet every detail of a playful function can of course be interpreted as the result of the laws of habit, and of the immediate influence of the environment upon an organism, endowed with such and such instincts, and subject to such and such stimuli. Wherein, then, lies the peculiarly spontaneous character of the playful activities? Wherein does play most differ from any other activity, such as eating or as running from an enemy? *The natural answer is that the playful activity appears spontaneous because it is carried out when there is no necessity of carrying it out.* In other words, a playful activity is not an adaptation to the environment such as the momentary conditions imperatively call for. But to say this is to admit that the spontaneous aspect of a playful function lies especially *in the restless overflow of activities that the playful organism shows*. It seems to us, the spectators, as if the world did not require the child to play. Yet after all the child's play is like any other action, —a response to the environment, a response involving sensitiveness and docility, and dependent upon previous habits. Why do we make this comment on the apparent needlessness of the play? Because we recognise in the playful activities precisely the character of restless overflow, a character which we recognise, in other forms, in the persevering struggles of the imprisoned

Y

animal to escape, and in the equally persevering efforts of the inventor or of the reformer to solve the problems of his art or of his age.

In the case of the play of childhood we have, in fact, a collection of functions whose value lies *not in the immediate adjustments to the environment then carried out,* but in what we might call *the prophetic importance* of the activities in question. These are not only repetitions of ancestral activities, but they are in part (although indeed not altogether) an indication and foreshadowing of functions which are afterward to become important. And the playful functions acquire such importance in the child's life, not merely because the environment suggests them, and not merely because the child's special instincts and habits make the plays at the moment fascinating, but *because the child's restless eagerness, — his insistence upon trying over and over the playful activity until it wholly satisfies his own ideals, — because,* I say, *these tendencies of the child keep him at play with an earnestness which expresses his own initiative.* Consequently, as any close observer of childhood knows, children play, not merely because it pleases them, but *because they must play.* They often play to the point of exhaustion. They play, on occasion, distinctly painful, as well as, on occasion, agreeable games. Their playful activities may sometimes possess all the persistence of the "tropisms" that Loeb has observed in lower organisms. These considerations hold true not only of many social, but of some solitary games. The child may grow much overexcited in the pursuit of a self-chosen play ideal, even when he has no comrade to urge him to emulation. He may weep or rage over a failure to accomplish one of his own playful designs. He may insist upon one of his playful ideas with a seriousness and intensity that may weary all his family and friends. If such phenomena occasionally seem pathological, their normal equivalents are of the utmost importance in the life of every intelligent child. And my present insistence is upon the thought that *in this eagerness, in this perseverance, and in the restlessness with which the whole playful activity is pursued, lies the initiative which the child may himself be said to contribute toward the organisation of his playful functions.*

This initiative keeps him busy in perfecting old plays, or in searching for new ones. It makes him endure the criticisms of playfellows, and submit to the often severe discipline which the social forms of play early involve amongst the groups of children concerned. This initiative makes of the child very frequently a specialist in some form of childish art, or of amateur collection. And what such initiative may accomplish for the organisation of the child's mental life, becomes manifest when we for a moment consider the great variety of arts and ideas that chil-

dren teach themselves through play. The various
types of self-consciousness, such as appear during the
dramatic impersonations of early childhood; the various arts, such as drawing, manual training, sleight
of hand, skill with boats, or with other objects of early
play — these, together with a knowledge of nature,
and sometimes a certain literary inventiveness, are a
few of the mental treasures that childhood *may* win
from its various games. Such are some of the forms
in which what is often well called the "originality"
of a child may display itself. One sees, then, that
in the mere persistence of the playful child one has a
factor whose value for mental initiative it is hard to
overestimate.

§ 124. Second, amongst the regions where mental
initiative is displayed, we may name the *activities of*
youth as they appear at the point where youthful
productivity is most manifest and important. If we
ask why an original genius produces his first great
work, or why a man of talent first discovers his
mission, or why a man of mediocrity wins that control
over his powers which makes him the successful business man or professional person, our answer, so far
as we can give it at all, must of course take account,
in large measure, of features of which we have already
spoken when we discussed sensitiveness and docility.
What a man can do, depends upon what he can observe, upon what he can feel, and upon what he can

learn as his instincts are trained. And when thus regarded, a man seems to be the creature of his environment. *But there is one thing that his environment cannot determine.* Nor yet can his special instincts — for instance, the instincts that prepare him to be a painter or a poet or a politician or a good salesman — determine whether or no this one thing shall be present. This one thing *is the power of the organism to persist in seeking for new adjustments, whether the environment at first suggests them or not, to persist in struggling toward its wholly unknown goal, whether there is any apparent opportunity for reaching such a goal or not. Such persistence is the one initiative that the organism can offer to the world.* It appears, in the individual case, in the form of *passionate interests in apparently useless activities.* Such passionate interests may in some cases prove to be as decidedly injurious as they may in other cases be useful. Thus a passionate interest in gambling may lead straight to destruction. But the gambler's interests, where they appear, involve in their own way a sort of initiative which, destructive though it proves, has, in common with the nobler devotions, exactly the feature that makes all such devotion of such critical importance to the organism and to the mind. Without such insistent interests, restless in their manifestations, persevering in their tendencies to repeat over and over, and to vary, fascinating activities, the organism and the mind

remain the prey of the environment. With such interests mental initiative becomes prominent. What a
man is to learn still depends upon experience and
opportunity ; but the restlessly active man regards his
world as destined to express his purpose. He moulds
his environment accordingly. And in the long run
his life thus becomes not only a bit of the world's
life, but his own life.

§ 125. A third class of illustrations of this sort of
significance which persistent restlessness may possess
we find, on the social side of our activities, in a tendency
which we already mentioned, in an earlier chapter, in
describing the bases of our social docility. We there
pointed out that, as a social being, man is strongly disposed, on the one hand, to imitate his fellows, on the
other hand to set himself in opposition to them — to
lay stress upon the social contrast between his environment and himself. Now *the persistent tendency to establish a contrast between one's social activities and those of
one's fellows lies at the root of the social tendency called
Individualism.* Individualism may of course appear in
unhealthy forms. But where it is rightly connected
with social docility, it forms the most important aspect
of what may be called our Social Initiative. Now our
social initiative depends upon constantly using social
arts, upon our continually employing socially acquired
habits. On the other hand, the wisely persistent,
the restless although rational desire to be, as we

say, "ourselves," to "call our souls our own," this is *the continual mother of invention in all our social activities*. This it is which inspires repartee, which enlivens conversation, which, in childhood, leads to our endless questions, and which, in later life, makes us considerate and thoughtful as to our answers. This it is which provides the hostess with her devices for entertainment, the teacher with his plans to introduce novelty into school life, the literary man with designs for his new works. The enormously complicated mental processes involved in such successful activities are all of them subject to the laws of habit and of sensitiveness. They are impossible unless the environment continually suggests, and unless habit and training constantly support, the activities and the ideas of which inventive minds make use. But my present interest lies in pointing out that *unless this eagerness for the diversification of social life, this insistence upon individualistic desires, were persistently present, habit and environment would in vain provide the materials for inventiveness. Social inventiveness depends upon individualistic restlessness.* The latter, in its turn, depends upon vital activities that are as elemental as the "tropisms" of the organisms upon which Loeb experimented. The people who have such vitality of concern in social success, and who have such an elemental love of social contrasts, are the initiators. If you find a whole nation consisting largely of such persons, you stand in presence of the ancient Greeks

at their best.   Individualism always depends upon quite
elemental   tendencies, — upon   dispositions to pursue
social contrast-effects with eagerness, even where such
experiences possess, at the moment of pursuit, comparatively little adaptive value.   In short, "the kingdom of heaven is taken by violence."

§ 126. A final series of illustrations of the conditions
of mental initiative we have furnished to us *by the
ordinary activities of our attentive functions.*   It has
been common, in recent psychology, to insist upon the
active attention as a factor of great significance for the
understanding of the apparently spontaneous processes
of consciousness.   The school of Wundt have used the
name " apperception " to signify, not so much the
assimilative process upon which Herbart laid stress when
he used that name, as the process by which, from moment to moment, our attentive consciousness moulds its
own material in accordance with intellectual ideals, and
influences the processes of association, so that these
shall assume a definitely significant and thoughtful
form.   It has been objected to the partisans of Wundt
that the term " apperception," as thus used, seems to
signify a factor in mental life which can be explained
neither in terms of what we have called sensitiveness,
nor in terms of the law of habit.   It has also been
objected that the conception of a conscious process, engaged in influencing its own states, is a conception
which confuses together metaphysical and psychological

motives. The psychologist, engaged as he is, not in studying how Reason forms the world, but in observing and reducing to rule the mere phenomena of human mental life as they occur, is not interested, it has been asserted, in a power whose influence upon mental phenomena seems to be of so ambiguous a character as is that which the Wundtian "apperception" possesses.

It is far from my present purpose to enter into the subtle controversies to which this conception of Wundt's has given rise. This is the place neither to expound nor to estimate Wundt's theory. But it does here concern us to point out that *what occurs in mind whenever we are actively attentive is attended with a feeling of restlessness, which makes us dissatisfied with all those associative processes that do not tend to further our current intellectual interests.* On the other hand, the cerebral processes that accompany active attention are certainly such as *tend to inhibit many associative processes that would, if free, hinder our current intellectual interests.* Meanwhile, *our active attention itself is always the expression of interests which possess the same elemental character that we have all along been illustrating in the foregoing paragraphs.* The attentive inventor is eager about the beautiful things that he thinks of while he is trying to invent. The attentive hostess is eager about social success. The attentive caged animal is eager about whatever suggests a way of escape. In brief, *whoever is persistently attentive is*

*expressing an attitude of the organism which has the es-
sential character of the now frequently mentioned " tropisms" of the animals of Loeb's experiments.* Active
attention does not appear in our life as in any sense a
supernatural, or disembodied force. It appears as an
eagerness to get into some kind of relation to objects or to
ideas, — an eagerness which is accompanied with restless
feelings, and which while in itself not directly creative,
is continually selective. The organic conditions which
accompany active attention tend toward the persistent
bringing before consciousness of certain ideas and combinations of ideas, and to the equally persistent inhibition of other ideas and combinations of ideas. The
result of the continued influence of such a process is
*the constant moulding of our relations to our environment
and of our habits, in such wise that certain mental combinations appear, which would otherwise have been
impossible.* Thus it is that our active attention continually exemplifies, even in the ordinary processes of
waking life, mental initiative. But it does so in no other
way than in the way already exemplified when we spoke
of the play of children, of the constructive activities of
youth, and of the effectiveness of individualism.

§ 127. If the foregoing discussion is at all well
founded, we now have before us the bases upon which
the natural history of all "self-activity" must be
founded. Apart from the effects of experience, apart
from the influence of special instincts and of training,

what may be called the self-activity of an individual depends upon certain general instincts, — instincts which manifest themselves in a form of a restless tendency to a certain overwealth of persistent activities. These activities are pursued at times when the results are not immediately adaptive. All such activities especially involve a tendency to alter, in a relatively spontaneous way, our own relations to our environment. In the simplest form they appear as efforts towards a local change of environment. *In their highest and subtlest form they take shape from moment to moment in the processes of our active attention. All such activities are characterised by the feeling of restlessness. In their physical aspect they are examples of the "tropisms" of Loeb.* They may be abnormal and dangerous. In their normal form they work to produce *a continual and relatively spontaneous modification of our existing habits.* They cannot be referred altogether to that heightened intensity of organic processes which is due to pleasurable stimuli. For in general, *we have found reason to believe that the feeling of restlessness is decidedly independent of the feeling of pleasure.* In the most important part of our activities we are eager not for pleasure, but for rationally satisfactory change both of our environment and of our conduct. *Upon such rational eagerness is based all that is most characteristic of our mental initiative.*

The practical consequence is obvious. Nothing is

more significant for mental life than the cultivation of strenuous activity. Every sign of such a tendency should be encouraged by a teacher. It is equally true that every effort should be made not to confuse such activities with those which merely give a child pleasure. The purpose of a teacher is not merely to aid a child "to do what he likes to do." The purpose of the teacher is to assist the child *to become eager to do something that is in itself of a rationally significant tendency.* That this eagerness is pleasant, is indeed often the case. But the pleasure is by-play. *The restless eagerness is the essential.* And it is such eagerness that accompanies us into later life, wherein we may often be deeply interested in life, even when we find only very moderate pleasure in it. As Schiller states the case, "Passion flees, but love must remain." And in this chapter we have been discussing that elemental love of rational novelty upon which all mental initiative depends.

CHAPTER XIV

CERTAIN VARIETIES OF EMOTIONAL AND INTELLECTUAL LIFE

§ 128. Our general survey of the mental processes has not been determined by the usual division of mental life into Feeling, Intellect, and Will. But now that our survey of the conditions of Sensitiveness, Docility, and Initiative has been completed, we may, in a practical review of some of the varieties and defects of mental life, as they are likely to come under the observation of the teacher, return, for the moment, to the ordinary classification. While all our mental life illustrates sensitiveness and docility, and while all of it is subject to the conditions upon which we have found that mental initiative may depend, some of our mental life is most prominently characterised by the presence of feelings, some of it makes more prominent to our consciousness our power to know about the world, while some of it especially brings to light the organisation of our outwardly observable conduct. That portion of our mental life which was most characterised by the presence of feeling, constitutes the emotions. That portion of our

mental life in which our consciousness is most concerned with what we know, constitutes what we
usually call our intellect. That portion of our
mental life in which conduct consciously predominates is that of which we are chiefly reminded when
we ordinarily hear the word "Will" used. So far as
this latter word is concerned, we have indeed already
shown that the term "Will" refers rather *to the whole
significance of our conscious life,* viewed as our conscious response to our environment, or as our mental attitude toward our world; and that the word
"Will" is of little use, as a purely psychological term,
in the classification of mental life. The same is true,
in a less degree, regarding the word "Intellect." This
term emphasises a certain significant aspect of our
mental life, namely our power to have knowledge of
the world. But as soon as one begins to study the
natural history of the intellect, this significant aspect
loses its apparent separateness; and we find ourselves
dealing with special functions and processes, such
as those which we have illustrated under the head of
sensitiveness and docility. Even the term "Emotion"
suggests, at first, to our minds, rather the moral or
æsthetic significance of the objects that we love and
hate, than the natural history of the emotional processes. In consequence, our purely psychological study
has so far prospered all the better through keeping
somewhat in the background the terms here in ques-

tion, although we have by no means attempted wholly to avoid their use. But the practical student of Mind is frequently concerned with asking what sort of will or intellect or emotion he is dealing with in a given case before him. And it is now our purpose to connect the foregoing general exposition with a few questions such as the practical student of mental life may ask concerning the processes and variations of the emotions, of the intellect, and of the will. In the present chapter we shall first briefly deal with some of the phenomena of the emotions; and shall point out some of the variations and abnormities to which the emotional life may be subject. We shall then abstract that aspect of our mental life which we commonly have in view in making use of the term "Intellect," and shall speak of the practical study and of a few of the abnormities of intellectual life. Our next and concluding chapter shall be devoted to a brief review of the processes usually emphasised when one speaks of the will.

§ 129. Our feelings do not appear in our actual consciousness in simple and isolated forms as mere pleasures, pains, and experiences of restlessness or of quiescence. In our concrete consciousness, we possess what are called by the general term "Emotions." Amongst these there are some, the relatively calm and gentle emotions, for which the word "Moods" has been proposed. In addition there are the more vehement and intense emotions, such as anger, fear, strong love, and the like. The moods and the emotions have in common this feature, that, when we are conscious of them, we are aware, not only of feelings but of images, general ideas, thoughts, and external objects. And the feelings that are present seem either to colour these ideal states or to give value to their external objects. The moods and the emotions differ, however, very widely, both in intensity and in endurance. It is no part of our present purpose to present any catalogue of the various moods and more vehement emotions, or to describe them in any detail. We can mention, purely by way of illustration, only one or two typical instances. Let us take, for the first, the emotion of grief. Here feelings of a painful character, accompanied by states in which either restlessness or quiescence may predominate, give character to the emotion. But all these feelings are centred about certain objects and ideas. Without these objects and ideas, the emotion of grief would have no meaning. We grieve over the loss of a beloved object. Or again, let us take the widely contrasting gentle emotion, or mood, called Curiosity. Here certain feelings of restlessness, and of pleasure or slight pain, accompany and colour ideas whose relation to our attention, and to our processes of intellectual inquiry, is characteristic of the whole emotional state. Or finally, let us take the emotion of

Anger. Here the central idea is of some object that seems to be doing us an injury, while the accompanying feelings involve intense pain, sometimes also a certain pleasure, and restlessness, in very characteristic ways.

A glance at any such emotion shows the enormous complexity of the conditions upon which it depends. As soon as, following certain psychological interests previously discussed, we proceed to substitute for the emotion in question an analysed mental state, or a series of such analysed mental states, we find that a consciousness of certain bodily activities, a very complex consciousness of our relation to objects, and a very complex collection of more elementary feelings, come to take the place of the original emotion, which hereupon appears as an enormously complicated mental condition. The angry man has a swift succession of thoughts and beliefs regarding the object of his anger. He assumes a rapid succession of bodily attitudes toward it. He has very numerous states of restlessness, of pain, and even in some cases of pleasure as he faces the object. Our present purpose, however, lies not in the analysis of all these complications, but in the briefest possible indication of the nature of the conditions upon which our emotional life depends.

§ 130. In recent literature, much attention has been called to the fact that, whatever the other sources may be of the feelings that accompany our more complicated emotions, much depends for our emotional

z

life upon the fact that each emotion has certain characteristic bodily expressions.   The movements that
we make, the instinctive or voluntary expressive reactions which go on when we are under the influence
of an emotion, are in well-known ways characteristic
of the emotion.   For thus we can judge from without
whether a man is angry, afraid, loving, etc.   Now
as we already know, our consciousness is constantly affected by our sensory experience of our
movements, and of the organic conditions that accompany these movements.   If our emotions have characteristic motor and organic expression, it follows that
our emotional consciousness will itself be affected by
the expressive movements, and by the accompanying
organic states ; and thus much of our conscious feeling
is *actually secondary to what is called the expression of
the feeling.*   Thus our griefs alter their emotional tone
according to the sort of external expression that chances
to be forcing itself upon us.   Tearless grief is one
thing, tearful grief another ; and no doubt an important part of the inner attitude of mind which constitutes
the grief is determined by our very sensory consciousness of how we are expressing ourselves.   This manner
of expression is largely determined by our inherited instincts and acquired habits.   Reacting to a given environment in a given way, we then feel our own reaction.
In telling about the tone of one's own emotions one
often has to say, "My heart stood still," or "I felt a

choking in my throat," or "I found myself gasping." The poets are accustomed thus to remind us of emotional tones by mentioning their manner of expression, and by so suggesting how this manner of expression itself feels to one who finds himself giving way to it. Thus Bayard Taylor tells how, as the soldiers in the Sebastopol trenches sang "Annie Laurie," "something upon the soldiers' cheeks washed out the stains of powder." This importance of the instinctive or habitual expressive movement as a primary reaction to a given environment — *the emotion being the secondary sensory experience of this reaction* — has been of late especially insisted upon by Professor James.

Meanwhile, however, there can be no doubt that, in addition to all states of our organs of external and of internal bodily sense, *purely central nervous conditions have much to do with the tone and intensity of our emotions*. Brain-fatigue of all degrees, from the lightest to the gravest, is likely to show itself in altered emotional tones, even where it gives few other easily marked signs of its presence. There are known diseases of the brain (such as the extreme forms of nervous exhaustion known as Melancholia and Mania) whose principal symptoms are profound alterations of emotional tone. The phenomena of these disorders, as well as other known facts, have been regarded by some as indicating that the current conditions of the blood supply in the brain are direct causes of our emotional states.

§ 131. The practical aspect of the life of the feel-ings, and in particular of the masses of feeling and ideas called the emotions, is of great importance. Whatever their precise physiological explanation may be, we are in any case warranted in saying that in the feelings, and in their expressive signs, we have in gen-eral an especially useful *index of the current state of the nervous centres viewed as a whole.* The state of a man's present feelings may indeed, at first sight, throw com-paratively little light on his character or on his experience, except where one already knows what opportunities he has had to cultivate or to learn to con-trol just these feelings. It is notoriously unfair to judge any man by his momentary mood. The now violently angry man may be, in general, a person of amiable self-control. Especially absurd, as well as un-charitable, is, therefore, the habit of those who regard a character as best to be read by considering the most passionate or otherwise marked emotional excesses, or the weakest or most foolish moods which are known to occur in the life of its possessor. So to judge is to com-mit what may be called the scandalmonger's fallacy. But, on the other hand, for a good observer, an emo-tional reaction, regarded with due reference to its exter-nal causes, does tend to indicate the passing general nervous state in a way which is of great value for psy-chological diagnosis. Nervous exhaustion, mental over-strain, show themselves (as just pointed out) first of all

in emotional variability. This the popular mind generally recognises. What is not popularly so well recognised is the fact that this emotional variability of
overstrain is not by any means always equivalent to the
tendency to "black moods" or to ill-temper, but may
show itself — and in grave forms, too — in emotions of
a relatively cheerful or benign seeming. The sufferer
from nervous overstrain may have hours, or even peri-
ods, of abnormal vivacity, when his friends, remembering his former fits of gloom, feel that now he is surely
restored to himself, since he is so ambitious and ani-
mated. But *the symptomatic value of an emotional
state lies rather in the degree of its variation from the
normal mean of the individual temperament* than in its
agreeable or disagreeable seeming.

If emotional variability is often a useful index of
nervous overstrain, *the permanent common quality at the
basis of any man's normal emotions*, if once made out, *is
indeed also an important index as to the fundamental
type of his nervous temperament*. By this one does not
always mean his *predominant* emotions, which may
be made predominant merely by his business or his
fortune. One means something deeper. The emotional
undertone, as one may call it, of any given individual, is
always one of the most interesting features of his character. It must be made out by observing him in a
number of sharply contrasted passing moods, especially
when such moods are determined by circumstances

rather unfamiliar to him. One then finds it henceforth curiously independent of fortune. The fundamentally cheerful man is thus to be found, even in the midst of the keenest distress, and even when he cries out with his bitterest anguish, still, at heart, not really despairing, but in possession of a certain fundamental sense of satisfaction in living, which no mere fortune can overcome, and which only a serious brain disorder can set aside. There are other men, and often very resolute men too, who have withal a deep-seated emotional distrust of life, which never leaves them in the midst of the most joyous good luck. They may be enduring, patient, even heroic, but they are never on decidedly good terms with their own inner state.

Such undertones of emotion, when one has learned to observe them in any individual, remind one of the temper of an old violin, or of the quality of an individual's voice — facts which remain amid the greatest varieties in the music played or sung. Like the violin's temper and the voice's quality, this emotional undertone is unquestionably the accompaniment of a permanent physical organisation. In case of the emotional undertone, this is the inherited temperament of the brain — a fact which, when once thus diagnosed, may be henceforth counted upon with great assurance. The emotional undertone appears to be noticeable in many cases fairly early in childhood, although it is liable to great changes in the course of development, particularly in early youth.

§ 132. Abnormal emotions may occur in a great variety of forms. They appear not only as variations from the normal intensity or steadiness of the otherwise unobjectionable emotions, but as associations of emotions with objects, situations, or habits, with which these emotions ought not to be associated in a healthy organism. Our feelings, as we have seen, accompany certain nervous conditions which colour, and in part determine, our whole "adjustment to our environment." If the feelings are distorted, this indicates a distortion of these nervous conditions, and so this whole adjustment must tend to fail. Conversely, a failure of our adjustment, if determined by nervous conditions which express themselves in signs of feeling, is itself a proof that the feelings are worthy to be called abnormal; for our main test of the "normal" is the power of successful adjustment to one's world. All violent passions in ordinary life are therefore relatively abnormal emotional states. The man who adjusts himself well "keeps his head," whatever the temptations to passing moods of confusion. Just so, however, morbid fondnesses for dangerous objects or deeds (*e.g.* a craving for intoxicants or a love for unwholesome reading) demonstrate their unhealthfulness by the very fact that their results are instances of moral or of physical failure to adjust one's self to one's environment. But the mor-

bid emotion need not be either a violent or a special experience. The whole emotional undertone of any "perverse" character is, in its own degree, an abnormity;
and such an abnormity may calmly outlast years of
training, and thousands of broken and spasmodic resolutions. In fact, what is called "perversity" of character generally *means* simply an abnormity of the
emotional undertone, and is as hard to alter as the
latter.

Yet, of course, great and enduring emotional abnormities can be the result, not of heredity, but of training. Some of our emotions (*e.g.* our cheerful or gloomy
undertone) are principally due to heredity; but others
are very much moulded as they develop in our early
lives. Hence the importance of care as to guarding
the growth of such sorts of emotion as are subject to
the greatest degree of development during childhood
and youth.

A striking and critical instance is here the whole
world of the sexual emotions, including the romantic
and the "sentimental" tendencies. These, normally
absent or only sporadically hinted at in the emotional
life of childhood, develop with great rapidity at puberty
and for some years afterwards. They normally occur
at first as the phenomena of reaction to particular series
of facts in the environment, and they occur both with
and apart from more definite acts. But they also normally tend to spread through and colour gently one's

whole life to its very highest and noblest levels.   Religious emotion, for instance, has deep relations to them. It is the business of parents, teachers, and other guardians of youth, to see to it that these more subtle emotional reactions are controlled by duly controlling both this environment, and the youth's sentimental and passionate relations thereto.   The laws of brain-habit determine the principle that when experiences are keen and novel, any reaction then accomplished determines the brain's whole future to a degree never later equalled by other actions of the same sort and number. Does one early form an association between certain objects and certain vigorous emotional responses, one's emotions are thenceforth given what may prove a permanent "set."   This, as recent investigations have more and more shown, is peculiarly the case with the sexually emotional reactions.   Whether a youth is to be a libertine at heart or not, and whether or no his sexual imagination and feeling are to be definitely perverted even while they grow (perverted in fashions that are sometimes horribly grotesque and mischievous), is often determined by the earliest stages of his sexual experience, wherein must be psychologically included most of his youthfully sentimental experience, together with even his religious emotions. However convention, or resolution, or morality, may later teach him to control his more definite or more external acts, the "set" of his inner sexual consciousness, and of all that more or less unconsciously gets built up thereupon, the purity or impurity of his feeling as a whole, his capacity for honourable love, the whole colouring of even his highest social emotions, his love of honour, his truthfulness, his humanity of sentiment, may be made or marred for life by the emotional responses that he makes to a comparatively few situations in his early world of ignorant youthful sexuality — a world to him uncomprehended, and one where too often, alas, he is wholly unguided. It is one of the saddest of psychological blunders that even wiser guides often leave the young to fight this confusing battle of these inner emotional states alone, and so such guardians, entrusting the young to the mere chances of foolish companionships, subject some of the most delicate and momentous emotional functions of the youthful brain to a treatment that no man of sense would give to his watch, or even to his boots. To be sure, a false light, a deceitful guidance, an ignorant sort of terror at possible mishaps, would in these matters itself determine or even constitute a perversion. Guidance does not mean mere random meddling. And even a cheerful indifference accomplishes far more than a morbid anxiety. But one need not ask for a false artificiality of instruction, only for a cool and reasonable "symptomatic guidance" of the young, given confidentially, and treated as a matter of course, by watchful guardians; given, moreover, just when the charge is seen actually to need it. There is,

meanwhile, no one routine of instruction as to such matters. Each case ought to be watched for itself.

The mention of abnormal emotions leads to the practical problem of estimating their significance when once
they are present. Regarding the phenomena of any
given morbid emotional state, whether permanent or
transient, it is a general rule that, *of two morbidly emotional moods or individuals, viewed in general, and
apart from special causes, the cheerfully morbid is likely
to prove worse than the painfully morbid.* False
despair, within limits, is, psychologically speaking,
much more benign than false confidence or than vainglory. One sees classic instances of this in the case of
the before-mentioned fundamentally " perverse " characters. Such persons, in case their abnormal emotional
" undertone " is one of dissatisfaction (of gloom, or self-
distrust, of morbid conscientiousness), may be indeed,
in the strict sense, incurable, since one cannot provide
them with a new heredity. But they can often learn,
within their limits, how to get a very effective sort of self-
control, and to live tolerable or even nobly useful lives,
simply because they suffer for their frailties, and consequently strive for some sort of salvation. But the
cheerfully perverse, whose undertone is often one of
vainglory, and who accordingly revel in their own per-
versities, are much more hopeless cases. You may
give them the clearest sort of knowledge, and they
may have a high order of intelligence with which to

grasp it, to restate it in their own words, and even to preach it; yet at heart they understand their own perversity only, in secret, or openly, to admire it. The sole hope lies in getting them where they keenly suffer, not, to be sure, any external or arbitrary penalty, but what they can come to view as the natural result of their own characters. Even then, however, it is a ceaseless marvel to the onlooker how much they can suffer without either losing their false optimism or essentially mending their evil ways. They may change numerous special habits of conduct, but they still cling to the central enemies of their life. Self-induced anguish is often their only possible medicine, yet they tolerate it in simply enormous doses, and often go on as before to their doom, persisting that they have learned wisdom, but daily manifesting that they are fools.

A similar rule holds, as said above, regarding the judgment of even passing moods. A state of nervous fatigue which is extremely disagreeable, is in general nearer to the normal than a condition in which we are actually very tired, but feel extraordinarily vivacious. Cheerful insomnia is far worse than is even a decidedly painful sense of weariness when accompanied by sleepiness. Even anger that is uncontrollably violent, and that causes the keenest suffering to the angry individual, is less abnormal than that lucid type of fury which its possessor fairly enjoys and nurses. Temper

of the first sort quickly wears itself out in pathetically
helpless reactions.   Temper of the cheerily malicious
sort may make its possessor a criminal before it lets go
its hold.   After great calamities people are often
"dazed" into an ominous insensitiveness.   The return
to the normal is then marked by an anguish which the
sufferer himself welcomes as a sign that he is again
"coming to his senses."   Thus, in general, good observers are not easily appalled by the mere appearance
of suffering.   Mental anguish, viewed as a psychological phenomenon, and apart from any otherwise known
and serious external cause for sorrow, is always an
abnormal incident; but it is frequently, in its consequences, benign; in its direct indications, relatively
insignificant.

So much must here suffice for our study of some of
the practical aspects of the life of the emotions.   We
turn to our projected sketch of some aspects of the life
of the intellect.

§ 133. All the contents of the stream of consciousness, *in so far as they constitute experience,* — i.e. *in so
far as we learn from them,* — are contents of intellect.
When we view these contents from one side, we find in
them, everywhere present, a certain colour of passing
estimate, an immediate sense that they are worth something to us at any given moment, or that they then have
an interest to us.   When we view these same contents
in another light, we observe that not merely their pass-

ing interest as such has a real importance for us, but that this momentary value, as we feel it, is but a hint, and sometimes a poor one, of the real place that they have in relation to our adjustment to our environment. Not only that given states now pass, *but that certain former states have been*, guides us in our dealing with the world. *In so far as we either recognise or otherwise profit by this relation between our present and our former states, or in so far as, by virtue of such a relation to the past states, we are led to expect any future state, our mental states are said to be experiences, and they then have, in addition to their direct value as feelings, an indirect value as indications of truth, as sources of knowledge, or, once more, as intellectual conditions.* This "indirect value" we have already called their "intellectual value."

The laws of docility determine how our mental states come to get this, their intellectual value. The special processes of the intellect have been treated under that head. We are here concerned with practically interesting illustrations.

The practical study and proper guidance of the intellectual life constitutes one of the principal problems of civilisation. All efforts to deal with the problem must set out from the fact that the intellectual life is precisely the "organisation of experience," and that, on the other hand, both the expression and the very existence of the intellect are dependent upon the formation of rational habits of conduct, useful motor adjustments.

The first principle is itself twofold. It means that the intellectual life depends, as to its genesis in each of us, upon experience, and that, apart from experience, we have no sound intellectual guidance. It also means that *no experience is of importance unless it is organised*, and that chaotic or irrationally ordered experience is useless, and may be worse than useless. The second principle shows, in general terms, how experience is organised. It is organised by teaching certain fitting habits of conduct (imitative processes, constructive activities, language-functions, habits of attentive observation), such as are at once constant, familiar, and accurate as to their general types, and at the same time plastic, adaptable, and controllable, with reference to the novel circumstances that may arise. That this complex object may be attained in case of healthy brains is itself a matter of experience. How to attain it belongs to the art of the teacher—an art whose rules, so far as they can be stated abstractly at all, must be founded on the laws of habit, of interest, and of inhibition—all of them laws which can best be stated in terms of the physical functions of the brain. At all events, he teaches in vain who does not in some way organise the activities, the intellectually expressive deeds of his pupils. Thought is either action or nothing.

§ 134. The abnormities of the intellectual life are more manifold and sharply definable than are those of the emotional life. The common formula for them all is a failure of due imitative adjustment to the environment, conditioned either by defective sense organs or by defective or by hindered intellectual habits of brain. This failure, whether its cause lies in hereditary temperament, or in early training, or in acute or in chronic disease, is very generally a matter that shows itself more or less plainly to every close observer. The intellectually abnormal person seems "queer," or is called a "fool" or a "crank," or makes a "failure of life," or, in cases of acute acquired malady, "becomes stupid," or "loses his memory," or otherwise "breaks down." Such things, in a general way, one constantly hears. Intellectual defects and disorders, if considerable, do not easily escape notice, because the keen struggle for existence sets every man busily adjusting himself to his environment, and a serious failure of the brain to display useful habitual functions is sooner or later pretty unsparingly exposed.

On the other hand, the diagnosis of what is the actual failure present in any individual case is much more difficult. There is, one must remember, no such thing as "foolishness" in general, unless, as in case of the extreme idiot or of the patient suffering from advanced *dementia*, one means thereby simple absence of all significant cortex functions. Otherwise what gets called

"foolishness" or "crankiness" is some particular group
of defects; and then the question is, each time, What
group? It is regarding this question that careless
judgment, in general, hopelessly errs.

Here it must be noted, in the first place, that many
intellectual defects and disorders are but secondary
phenomena, due to disorders whose primary manifestation lies rather in the realm of the feelings. The grief-
stricken, the anxious, the worried, the exhausted man,
or the victim of violent physical pain, may have, for a
longer or shorter period, an almost complete suspen-
sion, or else an extensive degradation, of all the higher
intellectual functions. This sort of thing, in case of
sufferers from acute nervous exhaustion, may assume
an outwardly very formidable aspect, and may give the
sufferer and his friends numerous fears of impending
insanity, even where the whole trouble is of relatively
very superficial character. The nervously exhausted
are likely not only to be, for the time, intellectually
inefficient, but to be keenly aware of the fact, so that
their fears of disorder may often tend to aggravate
what disorder they have. It is important, therefore, to
distinguish the false fire from the real mental danger
in these regions.

In cases of simple nervous exhaustion, the attention is
usually one of the most easily affected intellectual functions. It grows unequal — spasmodically intense as to
some matters, uncontrollably helpless as to others. A

sense of confusion overtakes one in the midst of business complications or of other intellectual tasks. One's favourite mental work grows unaccountably distasteful, or else morbidly engrossing in its portentousness, so that one cannot lay it aside during the hours of rest. One forgets in the middle of a sentence what one was going to say, and is terrified accordingly. One then talks of entire mental collapse. Memory may become more or less unequal or helplessly uncontrollable before the case has progressed far. A complaint of the " total loss of memory " — a complaint, to be sure, often absurdly unfounded — is very common with nervously exhausted patients. Over all these things, however, "the sense of inefficiency," a collection of feelings, may easily be seen to preside, if one observes more closely. And a noteworthy characteristic of this whole state is that the nervously exhausted man can often do all, or nearly all, that he declares himself unable to do, can perform nearly all the brain functions that he regards as impaired, can speak coherently, can avoid confusion, can attend closely, can remember very fairly, if only, without his express expectation, you engage him in a conversation that gets him for the time " out of his ruts," and that so temporarily frees his essentially intact brain from the emotional cloud that is hindering his habits from their natural expression. This is, of course, an objective proof that the clouded functions are not yet destroyed. So that the question of mental diagnosis is not here what the nervous patient can *not* do (when he is left to his anxiety or confusion), but what he still can do when for the time you get his thoughts " out of himself."

§ 135. This may serve as a suggestion of the nature of a secondary impairment of otherwise intact intellectual processes. But we must proceed to exemplify the intellectual disorders proper. A striking example of disorders directly intellectual in type is furnished by the morbid phenomena, of a sensory character, called " Hallucinations," or false perceptions, which have no foundation in external facts. These occur normally in our dreams, often also on the borderland of sleep, and in a great variety of mental disorders. Sporadically, as single brief waking experiences, they occur also in the lives of healthy people. But they are never present in any considerable number or persistence in a wide-awake person without a decidedly serious nervous cause. This may be a cause seated in part in the external sense organs; but it generally involves those portions of the brain where the sensory nerves of the sense affected have their central stations. An hallucination is, in any case, *prima facie* evidence of an abnormal form of central excitement. Yet hallucinations, as morbid phenomena, may occasionally exist for a good while in a comparatively isolated form in the mind. The patient may then be quite cool about them, may reason correctly that they are only hallucinations, and may be in all other intellectual respects apparently un-impaired. But this clearness can seldom thus last long. The strangeness of the hallucinatory experience fixes attention upon it. The physical cause of the trouble is usually pretty general. In the further development of the case either a general delirium follows, or the intellectual habits, even if they remain relatively intact, are gradually but dangerously modified by these sensory intruders. The delirium of fevers, and of a number of other nervous conditions of toxic origin is largely characterised by the presence of manifold and massive hallucinations, along with great emotional dis-turbances.

The hallucination, in itself alone considered, is a fair example of a special disorder of the intellectual life. But another form of intellectual impairment appears in what are technically called Delusions. Delusions are morbid derangements of one's habits of judgment. These may be, like sporadic hallucinations, phenomena confined to a decidedly limited region of the intellectual life. But this seems to be seldom the case. If a man suffers from one delusion, he commonly falls a prey to more than one, although then his delusions may still relate, for the most part, to some one class of topics. Yet the psychological mechanism is such that delusions, from their nature, tend to influence all of the sufferer's intellectual habits, and nobody can be trusted to remain long "insane on one topic only." One can never tell when the false habit may not show itself in some unexpected region.

While the phenomena of insanity proper belong elsewhere, this sketch mentions delusions simply because of the practically interesting psychological problems of diagnosis which they suggest. As to the name, the psychological usage differs somewhat from the popular usage. The latter often confounds hallucinations with delusions. The psychologist means by delusion a morbidly defective type of opinions, while hallucinations are false perceptions. When a man groundlessly and morbidly accuses his family of trying to poison him, this is a case of delusion. When a patient hears unreal voices talking about him, this is a case of hallucination. Of course, phenomena of both kinds may be combined; and in many forms of insanity they always are combined. The distinction, however, is important; because, from a purely psychological point of view, a delusion is, in general, the sign of a deeper derangement than is a mere hallucination. The latter may be due to transient conditions of cerebral excitement. The former, the delusion, stands at once for the distortion of one of the most significant of our habitual functions, namely, the function of judging our relation to our environment. And it is a universal rule of psychological diagnosis that the more general the habit of brain which has been really deranged (and not merely hindered by temporary emotional disturbances), the worse is the abnormal indication. To forget a familiar name is possibly an abnormal, but is so far a decidedly superficial incident. To hear a voice when none is really speaking may be a very grave matter, if it becomes chronic; but of itself, as a single incident, it indicates merely a state of excitement which may soon pass away. But coolly to insist, without any objective ground, that you are indubitably aware that your wife means to poison you — this indicates an established "set" of brain which (unless the cause is an acute and transient delirium) is likely to prove serious in proportion to the number and the generality of the altered habits which must lie at the basis of the perversion. (On the "general" habits of the brain, compare what has been said in § 28 near the end.)

On the whole, other things being equal, the cooler and less emotional a delusion is, in the tone with which it is held and expressed, the worse is the indication, because the more does this state of things indicate a direct perversion of the more general "set" of the brain. The delusions of a fever delirium are largely secondary to violent emotions, and so in their contents they are confused, and they may soon pass away, when the temporary brain-poisoning is relieved. The wild, fleeting, and scarcely utterable delusions of an ether-intoxication are as massive as is the stormy emotional outburst of the intoxicated condition, and they vanish with recovery. But an experienced insane patient may hold to his chronic delusions with considerable coolness and clearness of head. His power to do so may of itself indicate the hopelessness of his state. Especially grave is the tendency of cooler delusions to get thought out, or " systematised," by the patient. For thus all of a man's habits of brain get wrought over into the service of his delusion, and then he can never even conceive the way out. All of the foregoing indications must of course be modified by the circumstances of individual cases, but these suggestions may serve as hints of the principles of psychological diagnosis.

A morbid delusion, for the rest, is by no means the same thing as a foolishly false opinion. When one gets superstitions, or other absurd views, by hearsay, and from the tradition of the social order to which one belongs, the process of acquiring the false belief is then normal, however false the faith. There is no view so ill-founded that perfectly sane men may not hold it, given a sufficient weight of social tradition and of popular ignorance. But the peculiarity of the morbid delusion is that a man does not get it by normal methods, *e.g.* by accepting current social traditions, but comes upon it alone, as a matter of his private experience. The exceptions to this rule are, for our present purpose, insignificant. Moreover, the morbid delusion has always a characteristic reference to the patient's own private fortunes or dignity, instead of being, like the socially acquired tradition, a matter which concerns others quite as much as himself. A morbid delusion may, indeed, assume a philanthropic seeming, but a closer inspection always shows that the deranged man is to an abnormal degree at the centre of his false world. It is he who, of all men, is most persecuted or exalted.

§ 136. So much must here suffice as a mere hint as to the greater intellectual abnormities. Very common, however, is another problem, viz., that of the diagnosis of mere eccentricity of intellectual life, apart from any specifically manifest perversions. It is normal for us to acquire the most of our intellectual habits, by imitation, from the society to which we belong. Our social experiences are normally the most potent of all our experiences. Speaking, reading, writing, investigating, the knowledge of our profession or business, the thoughts of our daily life — these are all determined for us, in great measure, by our guardians and teachers in early life; by our friends, comrades, rivals, and other fellows in later life. Hence the most of our intellectual habits ought to be of a sort that we have in common with many of our fellows. When one's intellectual life varies, however, from the average intellect of his tribe or of his class, then, according to the degree and the noticeableness of the variation, one is called "striking," "individual," "original," "independent," "a man of parts," "a genius"; or, in less kindly speech, one is declared "eccentric," "queer,"

"quaint," "odd," "a fool," or "a crank."   Now it is
manifest that variations from the average intellectual
type are, within certain degrees, advantageous both to
the individual and to the community.   The best commu-
nities cultivate certain types of originality.   One habit
that ambitious young people often catch by imitation
is the very habit of seeming not to imitate, *i.e.* of
striving to be original.   On the other hand, there is a
good deal of intellectual originality in the asylums,
and certain forms of eccentricity are of themselves
abnormal.   The question of diagnosis often offers itself : Is this particular sort of intellectual eccentricity
(*e.g.* in this young man) a mark of wholesome talent
or of dangerous crankiness ?

The answer must be founded upon principles, some
of which can easily be stated.   Conformity to one's
environment is, as we must insist, in the end the test of
normality.   But some original men first win their environment over to conform to them ; and herein they
show, even through an early conflict with the environment, their higher sort of capacity to find a place in
their world.   Moreover, all young men have to spend
some time in learning what they are fit for before
harmonious life becomes possible.   Thus the test of
the conformity of a given intellectual life to a given
environment must be applied, especially in early life,
very cautiously.   Some eccentric young men are so
because they are "ugly ducklings," who will turn out

swans. Still others, however, are rather geese among
swans. The psychological observer is therefore not
afraid of the mere show of eccentricity, even where
it is great in degree. It is the *sort* of eccentricity
that such an observer tries to consider more carefully
before he judges. And now a general test of the
abnormally eccentric intellectual life, where it involves
as yet no graver disorders, — no delusions, no violently morbid emotional states, is to be found in
much the same region as the one in which the morbid
character of true delusions was just seen to manifest
itself. The morbidly eccentric intellect is one in which
the interesting experiences are to an extraordinary
degree centred about matters which have too little social
concern, and too much private concern for the morbid
individual himself. This test is not applicable, of
course, in childhood, since all young children are extremely self-centred. But it is, despite the normal sel-
fishness of youth, already fairly applicable in the later
years of youth. A young man may indeed be very
extremely and grossly "self-centred" and intellectually
commonplace *at once*, without much mental danger;
for he belongs to his herd, and his herd will take care
of him. His socially submissive instincts may, and
probably will, offset the selfish grossness of his conscious aims. He will live, like the rest of his kind, a
poor intellectual life, but a normal one. He will think
mostly about his private concerns, but still society will,

after all, determine *what* he shall think about them. Not so, however, is the eccentric or "original" mind fatally protecte̠ ̠y the instincts of the herd. And where an intellectually eccentric or original mind is extraordinarily devoted to thinking over, dwelling upon, planning, the private success, the exalted dignity, the selfish preferment, of just this individual, then, *in the combination of intellectual eccentricity and selfish narrowness of personal aim*, there are strong marks of danger. To be sure, even such a being might have the brain of a Napoleon; but that is, to speak mildly, uncommon. On the other hand, a naïve eccentricity of intellectual life, sincerely, not falsely, devoted to objective concerns (mathematical problems, scientific pursuits, the study of nobler literature, the pursuit of a modest but effective philanthropic career), is consistent with a true promise even where the anomaly is relatively great. A noteworthy test, then, is *whether the anomalous young person really looks rather without than within.* One need not add that to apply such a test needs often a pretty close scrutiny. Selfish greed may wear many cloaks and may use noble phrases.

CHAPTER XV

The Will, or the Direction of Conduct

§ 137. The life of the Will has already been characterised, as we have repeatedly seen, at every step of our
whole inquiry. We here confine ourselves to such illustrations of the growth of the will, and of its variations,
as will help to render our foregoing discussions more
easily applicable to the facts of life. It is therefore
possible to be here especially summary in our method
of treatment.

By the term Will in the narrower sense, one very commonly means so much of our mental life as involves the
attentive guidance of our conduct. How such guidance
is possible we have in this practical study, to summarise.

All definite brain processes tend to express themselves
without in movements by which we adjust ourselves
to our environment. Many of these movements pass
more or less unnoticed by ourselves. But all of them,
in proportion as they are marked and effective movements, tend not merely to result from brain processes,
but to influence, in their turn, the very brain whose
processes have initiated them. If one's arm moves, the
movement is itself a fact in the world outside the mind,

and, like any other outer fact, it may be once more perceived and remembered. One sees the arm move, feels
the sensations of muscular contraction, and is in still
other ways advised through one's sense organs of the
processes which the arm's movement involves. Moreover, if the arm, by moving, accomplishes something
definite, such as an act of grasping, one perceives the
resulting movements of the object grasped. If the arm
is engaged in writing or in drawing, one sees on paper
the lines which the moving hand traces. In all such
cases one observes, then, the results of one's doings.
And so, in short, *one's own activity constantly becomes
itself a part of one's experience.* If an experience is any
mental state in so far as its relation to past states guides
our present thoughts and deeds, and if all of our mental
life accompanies those expressive movements, or tendencies to movement, which the brain initiates and directs,
it follows that *every mental state has an aspect in which
it may be regarded as involving an experience of our own
fashions of action, or of our own attitudes toward our
world ;* for at every instant we are acting, or tending
to act, and so at every instant we are experiencing the
results of our own activity, or of our own tendencies to
action. So far, then, there is an aspect in all of our
mental life which constitutes this life *a series of experiences of our own doings,* a series which can take on, by
the laws of intellectual growth, a highly organised and
rational character in proportion as our habits of conduct

become themselves regular, uniform, and complex, and are observed by ourselves for what they are.

But just as our activity has its intellectual aspect, in so far as we constantly learn what we have done and are doing, so, too, this activity has also its passing value for us in our direct feelings. It either gives us pleasure or pain; or else it makes us either restless or quiescent; or possibly it combines pleasure or pain with restlessness or quiescence. What we are doing at any given moment is thus *satisfactory or unsatisfactory to us.* Action which, by virtue of its passing character as a felt mode of action, relatively satisfies us, we call an expression of our desires. When an action is such that the feeling which estimates it is one of predominant dissatisfaction, the act opposes our ruling desires, and tends to be inhibited accordingly. *Thus, then, every mental state tends to have, as a fact of feeling, an aspect which embodies our current relative satisfaction or dissatisfaction with our own momentary doings. A desire means a tendency to action, experienced as such, and at the same time felt as a relatively satisfactory tendency.*

So far, then, we see : (1) that our own activity forms constantly a part of our experience ; (2) that this same activity constantly results in a modification of our feelings of satisfaction and dissatisfaction in what we are doing. If one combines these two aspects of our inner life, one can say that together they involve *a vast experience of our own desires and aversions, of our own doings and inhibitions, and of the inner results of these doings and inhibitions, together with a constant play of feelings of inner content and discontent with our own motor processes, and with the tendencies or attitudes which accompany our partially suppressed movements.*

Thus we briefly characterise that aspect of our inner life which constitutes the world of desire and of its outcome. Thus viewed, our minds appear as full of passing impulses, of tendencies to action, of passions, and of concerns for what we take to be our welfare. All these impulses and concerns get woven, by the laws of habit, into systems of ruling motives which express themselves without in our regular fashions of conduct. The whole of our inner life, viewed in this aspect, appears as the *purposive side of our consciousness, or as the will in the wider sense.*

§ 138. But it remains to lay stress upon one further aspect, by virtue of which the world of the more or less organised impulses, concerns, passions, and other desires gets its fully developed character as the world of the will in the stricter or more narrow sense. We not only observe and feel our own doings and attitudes or tendencies as a mass of inner facts, viewed all together, but in particular *we attend to them with greater or less care,* SELECTING *now these, now those tendencies to action as the central objects in our experience of our own desires.* For the process of attention often has as its objects not only external facts, or facts of sense perception, but also desires, actions, inhibitions, tendencies to action, concerns, feelings, passions — in brief, whatever constitutes the active side of our nature. But to attend to anything is to emphasise that object, to give it "relief" as against the rest of what is in our minds. *To attend to any action, or to any tendency to action, to any desire, or to any passion, is the same thing as "to select," or "to choose," or "to prefer," or "to take serious interest in," just that tendency or deed. And such attentive preference of one course of conduct, or of one tendency or desire, as against all others present to our minds at any time, is called a voluntary act.*

The will is, in its more complex manifestations, *the attentive furthering of our interest in one act or desire as against another.* The act or desire is in itself of more or less interest to us. If we attend to this act or desire, we further our interest in it. The furthered interest results in a clearer consciousness of the act or tendency in question. But the very existence of such clear consciousness implies (by the principles indicated in § 33), that the condition of brain which naturally expresses itself in just this form of outward activity is, at the moment of clear consciousness, a predominant condition of the brain. The furthered interest, if intense enough, therefore means, on the physical side, that the form of activity in which we are interested gets an actual outer expression *just as*

*soon as our attention sufficiently prefers the thought of
this act to the thought of any other act.*

To think of any sort of activity, therefore, already
implies a tendency to this form of activity. And
actually to will a given act is *to think attentively of that
act to the exclusion or neglect of the representation
or imagining of any and all other acts.* Whenever
one idea of action or one type of desire becomes
really predominant in consciousness through attentive
consideration, then the action or desire in question at
once gets carried out, until some restraining idea arises
and in its turn gets attended to. Choice bears, therefore, the same relation to actions that intellectual
attention bears to images, ideas, or thoughts; and in
discussing the phenomena of attention (see § 103 and
§ 126), we have already discussed all that is essential
to the comprehension of an act of will.

§ 139. It remains to note here only one or two
considerations of no small practical moment. The
first is that, strange as the statement may seem, *we
can never consciously and directly will any really
novel course of action. We can directly will an act
only when we have before done that act, and have so
experienced the nature of it.* The will is as dependent
as the intellect upon our past experience. One can
indeed will an act which is sure to involve, in a given
environment, absolutely novel consequences; but the
act itself, so far as one wills it, is a familiar act. Thus

2 B

a suicide can will an act which results in his own death, and so far he seems to be willing something which wholly transcends his past experience. But, as a fact, the act itself which he makes the direct object of his will (*e.g.* pointing a pistol and pulling a trigger, or swallowing a dose) is itself an act with which he is long since decidedly familiar. One can will to visit a far country, to engage in a new sort of speculation, to choose a still unfamiliar profession, to marry, or to do anything else whose consequences one cannot foresee. But it is the consequences that are novel; the act which one directly wills is not novel. What one does at the decisive moment is to buy a ticket, to sign one's name, to say "Yes," or otherwise to repeat deeds whose contents are already perfectly familiar, while the circumstances under which they are willed may make them to any extent momentous. But, on the other hand, one cannot will to fly, because one has never learned how. *We can thus will to do what we have learned to do.* "Control yourself," says the stern adviser to the spoiled child. But the adviser upbraids in vain. How *can* the spoiled child will to control himself if nobody has ever shown him, by an appeal to his imitative instincts, what self-control means? Our choice, psychologically viewed, is thus an absolutely unoriginal power. It gives back what experience has taught it. But, on the other hand, the will, if not in itself original,

may be to any extent *originative*, because to repeat
such an unoriginal act as signing one's name, or saying "Yes," may, under given conditions, begin a new
life for the doer. Moreover the voluntary process is
always bound up with the conditions which determine
Mental Initiative (see Chapter XIII).

Closely connected with the foregoing consideration
is the further principle that, before we can come to
possess a will, we must first perform numerous and
complex acts by virtue of the inherited tendencies of
the brain. Such original tendencies of the brain are
the source of our human instincts. The will is based
upon instincts. These get moulded by experience.
The resulting acts, gradually organised by the laws
of habit, come at last to our notice, in so far as our
doings are themselves a part of our experience. The
accompanying feelings colour our acts so that they are
also expressions of desire. Then attention fixes now
on this, now on that conceived act, tendency, or desire,
according as our interest plays over the whole series
of such experiences of our activity. The emphasis
which attention gives, in the end, to the ruling idea of
action is the inner and psychological aspect of our
current act of will or of choice.

§ 140. The growth of language in any child is an
excellent example of the evolution of the will. Inherited instinct expresses itself in the infantile actions
known outwardly as cries, and later as more vocal

sounds — babblings, primitive efforts at wholly mean-
ingless articulation.   Then the child begins to observe
these acts of his own, to feel satisfaction in them, to
desire their repetition.   The result, so far, is the development of a chaos of vocalised expressions, but not yet
anything resembling true speech.   However, long before this process is completed, another inherited instinct
intervenes.   The child is imitative.   This instinct involves complex processes which result in making the
child's vocal noises tend to resemble those which he
hears from other people.   This resemblance, once
more noticed by the child, also becomes a much-desired
ideal; and hereby the child first gradually learns and
then definitely wills to reproduce the utterances of
others.   Then there is added, while these processes
are still under way, the intellectual experience that
many of the sounds uttered by other people mean
something — are names for things, or for feelings, or
for purposes.   This, erelong, shows the child that he
too can express his meaning by using the right sounds.
Now he becomes selective, attentive to speech as such,
desirous of harmonising what he says with what others
say or understand; and finally, upon the basis of all
these elaborately moulded instincts and habits, the intelligent will to talk takes form; and henceforth the
child says whatever he predominantly and attentively
desires or chooses to say, whenever he is thinking of
speech rather than of any other mode of activity.

§ 141. While the expression of our minds in and by our conduct is the one great tendency upon which all our knowledge of mind from without, and all the serviceableness of mental life for the interests of society, depends, it is nevertheless the case that the practical study and training of the will are almost always regarded as secondary to the practical study and training of the feelings and the intellect. The reason for this current view is obvious. Apart from intellectual training, the life of our desires is mainly the expression of our inherited instincts, which nobody can hope to eradicate altogether, or to enrich by the addition of any entirely novel instincts. *What can be done for us is to organise our planlessly numerous inherited instincts in such fashion that there shall result valuable and consciously directed habits.* The devices for accomplishing this aim are largely appeals to our universal human love of social imitation. Hereby we "learn how" to act aright; and unless we have "learned how," one appeals to our will in vain. Hence what appears as an intellectual acquisition — a "learning how" to be good, industrious, skilful, self-directing, etc. — is always prior to the successful moulding of the will as such. As every such "learning how" involves interests, the feelings are appealed to at every point. But the will itself, whose proper moulding is indeed in one sense the goal of all education, seems to be capable of only this indirect

approach.   Or, again, to teach one to will involves
teaching him first to take note of his own conduct.
But to teach him this you must first establish in him
the desired conduct.   You must get him to do before
he has consciously willed this particular sort of doing.
The involuntary conduct must precede the voluntary;
but the right sort of involuntary conduct you can
only establish through appeals to the feelings, and
through presenting the fitting objects of knowledge
to the intellect.

For the same reason disorders and defects of the
will never exist alone.   They always involve alterations either of the feelings or of the intellect, and
must be studied in connection therewith.   It is noteworthy that insanity, in the popular mind, is usually
conceived as primarily an intellectual defect rather
than as primarily a defect of the will, and this despite
the notorious fact that insanity can only manifest itself
through some sort of " queer " or " wrong " expressive
action.

Nevertheless, it is often important to consider mental
defects or disorders from the side of the will.   So
viewed, what are usually and practically named the
" disorders of the will " may be said to manifest themselves in three general types.   The first type is that of
the absence or serious impairment of the ability to
carry out important voluntary acts, when such acts
have already been in the past learned as well as often

performed. This first defect is often known by the rather vague name of "weakness of will." A technical name is "Aboulia," or morbid will-lessness. The second type of defects of will is that of the chaotic or "segmented" will, whose plans do not hang together, whose action is morbidly impulsive, capricious, inconsistent, or inwardly anarchical. The third type of defects of will appears in those morbidly perverted persons (*e.g.* in morbid criminals) whose activity, without being confused or chaotic, is still steadfastly such as fails of any tolerable adjustment to the environment, and especially to the civilised social environment.

§ 142. The first type, aboulia, is sometimes a manifestation of the temperament as such. In such cases one naturally looks for its cause in the emotional "undertone" (cf. § 131). The deeply hesitant or morbidly indecisive man, who, despite having learned how to do a given thing, and despite his clearly knowing that it is to his interest to act, still remains permanently fast bound in a Hamlet-like incapacity to will anything for himself at the important moment, has become a favourite topic for literary portrayal. Hamlet notoriously refers his own defects of will to intellectual causes. His "native hue of resolution" is "sicklied o'er with the pale cast of thought." But such defective will may appear with a less obvious intellectual basis than in Hamlet's case. Then, however, the defect would probably be definable, in emotional terms, as the pretty constant presence of some emotion of painful timidity or scrupulosity, in the presence of which all very decisive action seems in general unsatisfactory. "Apathy" of temperament — *i.e.* an enduring state of abnormally depressed emotional sensitiveness — might have the same effect.

But aboulia is a frequent acute symptom in cases of more or less transient nervous exhaustion. In a measure, every one can occasionally notice such a defect of will as an incident of normal weariness. At such times we may find it especially hard to make a decision, even when we seem to ourselves clearly able to see just what decision ought to be made, and even while we feel that, as we say, we "want" or even "long" to decide. The feeling of helplessness is then itself often extremely painful. If by chance we actually begin a decisive course of conduct, then the feeling that we are "committed" gives a great sense of relief, and the defect of will may at once, for the time, vanish altogether.

In cases of nervous exhaustion, such aboulia is an inconvenient complication, in so far as it tends to set a habit of indecision which may long survive the period of exhaustion itself. In itself, however, this acute aboulia is apparently no very alarming incident. The nervously exhausted man should be carefully relieved, so far as possible, from every necessity of making difficult choices. He should, therefore, if possible, "resign his will" into the hands of some one, or at most two or three competent and harmonious advisers; and he must be protected from every confusing variety of plans. On the other hand, whenever decisions are really necessary, he should always be gently but firmly helped to a quick and irrevocable choice, since hesitancy is a very exhausting incident in his experience, and since even a poor choice is often better for him than doubt. But if such care is taken, the aboulia itself is no very serious symptom. Sometimes one meets with light cases of weariness where such aboulia is, in fact, almost the only discoverable morbid symptom, and these cases are actually encouraging as to the outlook for quick recovery.

Much more manifold are the chaotic disorders of the morbidly inconsistent or capricious will. Temperaments abound which are characterised by phenomena of this kind, and in both acute and chronic disorders the disorganised will is a well-known symptom. This, for example, is especially true in hysterical disorders. But ordinary nervous exhaustion is frequently burdened with enemies of the kind. One often sees, for instance, the man who forms morbidly one-sided resolutions for the conduct of this or of that portion of his life. He means to permit only this or this train of thought, or to exclude wholly this or this possibility of temptation. Over the well-meant but possibly useless resolution he grows morbidly conscientious, and upbraids his friends for not sufficiently appreciating and aiding his efforts.

Meanwhile, however, he freely indulges himself in graver defects than the one which he is so elaborately correcting, and inconsistently encourages even the very tendencies which he is fighting by giving them a false importance through his over-wrought self-scrutiny. In more hysterically disposed cases such defectively insistent broodings will be subject also to vast changes of plan, so that the sufferer alters his religious faith, or the whole ideal of his life, without any clear reason, and throws to the winds a whole system of good resolutions in favour of some other equally useless scheme. The habit of mere fickleness may thus become finally prevalent over all other habits (cf. § 28, p. 69). One thus finds people who acquire a " mania " for changing their religious faiths or their callings.

Simpler, but often very stubborn, are the phenomena of disorganisation of will in case some one more or less generalised motor habit becomes rebelliously insistent — *e.g.*, the habit of counting or of examining gas-jets, locks, etc., to see whether they have been safely adjusted, or of asking useless questions about some sort of topics. Disorganisations of this kind appear in many patients on the basis of a defective hereditary constitution. But in children and quite young people they are also often present as mere disorders of development, which pass away with maturity. And nervous exhaustion can bring them on as acute symptoms in otherwise unburdened people. A surprisingly large number of such morbid habits can often exist without destroying or even seriously endangering in other respects the general capacity of the brain that suffers from them; and the fears of an impending general insanity which they often arouse are therefore very frequently unfounded. On the other hand, they are certainly grave inconveniences, and are not to be trifled with. They are best treated, apart from the medical care of the patient's general health, through a discreet moral support, given by a competent adviser, who can often help the patient to or towards a relatively effective and cheerful ignoring of his enemies.

In estimating all such defects the rule holds here, as in case of the defects of the intellect, that the stronger the attendant emotional colouring of the disorder, the more hopeful, other things being equal, is the outlook. The cooler the emotional tone of the sufferer from a defective will, in so far as concerns his immediate feeling about his disorder, the fewer are the means of influencing his morbid state. And this finally suggests why the morbidly perverted characters whose wills are relatively well organised, firm, and cool, but whose behaviour is intolerable, are in general incurable. In consequence, we may as well here abandon the task of further describing such characters, whose mission in the world seems to be to illustrate the variability but not the healthy docility of our human nature.

INDEX

[In use, this index should be supplemented by the analysis of the text in the Table of Contents.]

Aboulia, 375.

Æsthetic experiences, as instances of the harmonious relation of the unity and variety present in consciousness, 89; æsthetic values of musical chords, in relation to analysis, 111.

Affection, and the affective aspect of consciousness, 163. See **Feeling.**

Analysis, the, of conscious states into elements, 97–107; question whether the doctrine of mental elements is right in its interpretation of the facts, 107–113; what the facts, upon which the doctrine of mental elements is founded, really show, 113–115; analysis as a substitution of analysed for naïve states of consciousness, 114; the process of analysis in the course of the actual differentiation of consciousness, 242–257. See **Differentiation.**

Animals, lower, experiments upon, and the relation of such experiments to the general methods of psychological study, 16; signs of mental life in animals, 22, 25, 34; questions as to the value and interpretation of such signs, 23, 28–30; the pigeon when deprived of its cerebral hemispheres, 63; animal activities as indicating mental initiative, 43, 312–315.

Apperception, Herbartian doctrine of, 236; Wundt's definition and doctrine of apperception, 328, 329.

Assimilation, 229–247; physical basis of, 231; illustrations of, 235–247; relation to perception, 235; to memory,

237; to thought, 245. See also **Sameness,** and the analysis of Chapter X.

Association, as the representative in the conscious process of the results of the law of habit, 203–205; forms of association, 210; explanation of cases where the law of habit seems not to explain the associative process, 205–208; association of mental elements, 208; criticism of this last doctrine, 209; factors which determine the actual course of association in our ordinary consciousness, 210–217; association in its relation to assimilation, 229–247; active attention in relation to association, 262, 328–330.

Attention, its general relation to the field of consciousness, 84, 85; to the feelings, 190, 191; definition of attention, 261; discussion of its principal characteristics and conditions, 258–264; active and passive attention, 190, 191, 261; relation of attention to habit, 263, cf. 226, 227, 235, 236; fluctuations of attention, 263, 264; social conditions that determine us to regard attentively our own acts, 283–285, 290, 291, 297; relation of attention to mental initiative, 328–332; active attention as dependent upon "tropisms," 331; as an instance of restless persistence in advance of adaptation, 329. Attention in relation to voluntary action, 367–369. Attention in nervously exhausted patients, 353.

Auditory type, of mental imagery, 156,

Baldwin, Professor J. Mark, on imitation, 276; on heightened activities and the conditions of mental initiative, 307, 309, 310, 311, 317.

Brain, as seat of the nervous processes that condition mental life, 11; the study of the relations between brain processes and mental life as one of the methods of psychology, 15; complexity of brain structure, 65; general way of functioning of the brain, 65; the law of habit in relation to the brain, 66, 198, 200–203, 219, 231–235; localisation of cerebral functions, 67; the law of habit in relation to the distinction between general and special habits, 68, 69; " set " of brain, 69, 72, 78, 79, 214, 215, 263; relation of the brain to lower centres, 70; inhibition as a cerebral phenomenon, 70–75; hierarchy of the functions of the brain, 70, 74; the higher cerebral functions as especially inhibitory in their relations to lower functions, 73; relation of the functions of the brain to consciousness, 80, 81; inadequacy of the conscious process to correspond to the complexity of the brain processes, 199, 205; formation of new habits, under the influence of new combinations of stimuli, 200–203; influence of inherited temperament of brain upon prevailing emotional tone of the individual, 342.

Browning, Robert, 187.

Change, as present in the stream of consciousness, 83; in relation to the unity of consciousness, 95–97; significance of change and succession for discrimination, and for the differentiation of mental life, 248–257; change in relation to our direct consciousness of temporal succession, 95–97.

Childhood, mental phenomena in, difficulty of diagnosing certain mental defects in a child, when these involve sense organs, 27; sudden appearance of the signs of inherited tendencies at certain points in childhood, 52; inhibition in childhood, 75, 78; visualisation in childhood, 155; mental imagery as related to conduct in children, 161; conflict of feelings in the sulky child, 173; perception in infancy, 219–221; the expression of interest in a child in the form of repetitions of acts, 260; fluctuations of attention in childhood, 264; social tendencies in childhood, 275–279; the development of language in childhood, 281, cf. 371; initiative in childhood, 303–312; plays of childhood, as examples of initiative, 319–324; further passages, 332, 342, 344 sq.

Clearness of consciousness, defined, 93; how attained in practice, 94, 95; results from attention, 261, 262; its relation to social conditions in case of the thinking process, 283–285, 290, 291. See also Difference, Differentiation, and Discrimination.

Conation, 193. See Will and Conduct.

Conduct, in its general relation to docility, 33, 37, 197, 198; in its general relation to initiative, 39–55; in its general relation to the signs of sensory experience, 24 sqq.; in its relation to mental imagery, 159–161; in its relation to the feelings, 172–176, 182–191; in its relation to perception, 218–228; in its relation to the assimilative process, 234, 242. The two fundamental social types of conduct, 276–279; social conditions that tend to make us conscious of our own conduct, 283–285, 291, 295, 297. The variations of conduct, and the conditions of mental initiative, 300–319; illustrations of initiative, 319–331; relations of conduct to attention, 328–330, 367–369; relations of conduct to intellect, 350, 351; to discrimination, 251–258. Defects of conduct, 347, 348, 373–379.

Consciousness, see also Mental life. The general features of conscious life discussed, 81–117; the " stream of consciousness," 82–85; the unity of consciousness characterised, 85–89; variety essential to consciousness, 89; what processes in the cortex are accompanied by consciousness, 81, 82; consciousness inadequate as a representation of the complexity of the habits and functions of the brain, 199, 295; psychological results of this inadequacy, in case of our associations, 205–209; consciousness as not consisting merely of a complex of mental elements, 84, 85, 97–117; the analysis of consciousness as a substitution of analysed states for unanalysed ones, 114, 115; when the unity of consciousness too much predominates over the variety, consciousness tends to cease, 89; where the unity and variety of consciousness, and the samenesses and differences present in consciousness, support one another, consciousness possesses what is called clearness, 93; how this clearness is practically attained, 94, 95; how the differentiation of consciousness occurs in the course of our mental development, 248–258.

Contact, sensory experience of, 133.

Cortex of the brain, as the seat of the nervous processes that are attended by mental life, 11; what one amongst the functions of the cortex are so attended, 81, 82; complexity of the structure and functions of the cortex, 65; inadequacy of the conscious process to represent the wealth of the functions of the cortex, 199, 205. See also Brain.

Counting, as a motor process of an imitative character, 292.

Delusion, 356.

Dermal sense, 133.

Description, why inferior to narrative as a method of portrayal, 255.

Description, scientific, conditions of success in, 5.

Desire, 195, 186, 187. See also Restlessness, Pleasure and Displeasure, Feeling, Will.

Difference, as a relation always present amongst the various states that are found within the unity of consciousness, 90; difference inseparable from sameness, 91; if the consciousness of difference too much predominates over that of sameness, the nature of the difference becomes problematic for our consciousness, 92; the samenesses and differences must support one another if consciousness is to be clear, 93; relation of difference to variety in consciousness, 93; how we teach pupils to take definite notice of differences, 94, 95; successive differences of conscious states, and their relation to discrimination, 95–97; an increasing consciousness of differences accompanies mental development, 230, 248 sqq.; perception of simultaneous differences develops, on the whole, on the basis of habits formed through the consciousness of successive differences, 249–257; differences in the spatial positions of objects come to consciousness on the basis of a certain general extensity of our sensory experience, due to our total experience of orientation, 141–147; the perception of differences of sensory stimulation is a perception not of absolute, but of relative differences, 264–267; the psycho-physic law, 267–273; the consciousness of the differences between our own activities and those of our social fellows, and the importance of this consciousness for our thought and for our self-consciousness, 282–285, 290, 291, 293, 295, 297.

Differentiation, of consciousness as a process occurring during mental development, and determined by the laws of docility, 248–273. See the analysis of Chapter XI in Table of Contents. See also Difference, Discrimination, Attention, Psychophysic law.

Discrimination, discriminating sensitiveness as a sign of mind, 21; its manifestation in the signs of feeling, 22, 23; in the signs of sensory experience, 24–28; its relation to unconscious reactions and tropisms, 28–31; its importance in all grades of conscious life, 31, 32. Discrimination of simultaneous facts is aided by habits formed through the discrimination of successive facts, 249–257; practical consequences of this principle, 258; relation of discrimination to attention, 258 *sqq.*; discrimination in relation to the psycho-physic law, 264–273. See also **Difference.**

Displeasure, feeling of, 168–176, 179, 180. See **Feeling, Pleasure and Displeasure,** and the analysis of Chapter VII in the Table of Contents.

Docility, definition of, 38; outer expressions of, 32–38, 198; forms of, 218, 229–281; General laws of, 197–217; law of cerebral habit in relation to law of mental association, 198–208; perception as an instance of, 218–228. Assimilation as one aspect of, 229–247; differentiation as an aspect of, 248–273; the higher forms of, 274–298; relation of Docility to initiative, 41, 51, 303, 318; relation of docility to intellect and will, 198, 199, 334; Docility in relation to habit and association, 198–208. Docility often sufficiently explains the appearance of spontaneity in conduct, 41. See also the analysis of Chapters VIII, IX, X, XI, and XII, in the Table of Contents.

Dramatic element in all successful instruction, its relation to the general process by which differentiation takes place in consciousness, 255.

Elements, mental, the doctrine which maintains that consciousness is composed of such elements discussed, 97–117; the doctrine as applied to associative processes, 208, 209.

Elements of the nervous system, 58, 59.

Equilibrium, sensory experiences of, in relation to orientation, and to our consciousness of space, 144.

Exercise, physical, its value as furnishing a relief from inhibitions, 78.

Experience, the signs of an animal's relation to its own former experience, 32–38. See also **Consciousness, Mental life, Sensitiveness, Sensory experience, Docility, Intellect, Habit, Association, Assimilation, Differentiation, Perception.** Relation of any new experience to the immediately previous and subsequent states of consciousness, 83; relation of experience to the intellectual life, 351.

Experiment, upon nervous functions as an auxiliary method in the study of mind, 16; psychological experiment in the stricter sense, as a leading method of psychology, 18, 19; as in particular an aid to psychological analysis, 100, 103; interpretation of the results of experimental analysis, 112–116; experiment as a means of isolating and studying sensation, 105, 106, 122, 131, 133; Wundt's experimental study of the feelings, 176; experiment and the psycho-physic law, 267; experiments on fatigue, 217; experiment upon the movements by which we acquire our consciousness of space relations, 253.

Experimental psychology, 18, 19; see **Experiment.** See also Preface.

Expressions, and **Expressive acts and movements** as signs of the presence and the processes of mental life, and as means by which mental life is studied, 6–9, 14; their relation to the introspective study of mind, 17; their classification, 21–57; difficulty of interpreting them with certainty, 14, 15; their value as evidences that consciousness is present at all, 21, 23, 28–31; the expressions that are signs of feeling, 23; the signs of sensory experience, 24-27; of docility, 32-38; of initiative, 38-58; the physical conditions of expressive movements, 9, 10, 58-79; the inhibition of expressive movements, 70 *sqq.* See also **Feeling, Docility, Perception, Initiative, Conduct, Will,** for the various types and characters of expressive movements.

Fatigue, 217.

Faust, Goethe's, as illustrating certain aspects of feeling and desire, 183, 186.

Fechner, and the psycho-physic law, 267.

Feeling, the signs of, 22 *sq.;* general nature of, defined, 167, cf. also 163-165 for preliminaries to this definition; classification of feelings: traditional classification, 168; Wundt's classification, 176; author's classification, 178; definition of the feelings of pleasure and displeasure, 168-173, 179; of restlessness and quiescence, 180-182; mixed feelings, and their types, 182-189; relation of the feelings to the attention, 190, 191, 259, 261, 329, 331; to conduct, 172-176, 182-191; to the emotions, 335-349; practical significance of, 340-349. See also the analysis of Chapter VII in the Table of Contents.

French Revolution, mental phenomena of its popular excitements, 216.

Functions, see **Expressions** and **Expressive movements.** See also **Nervous system, Brain, Sensitiveness, Docility, Initiative, Will.** Higher and lower nervous functions, their distinction, 11, 33, 34.

Galton, Francis, on mental imagery, 152 *sqq.*

General ideas, see **Ideas,** general.

Geometrical ideas, as imitative in character, 292.

Goethe, 183, 186.

Groos, on play, 319, 320.

Habit, law of, first stated, 66; restated, 198; generalised habits, 68; special habits, 69; general relation of cerebral habits to consciousness, 199, 205; the process of the formation of a habit, 200-203; habit and association, 203-208; habit and perception, 219-228; the assimilation of new habits by old ones, 231-235; consequences for mental life, 235-247; the habits by which the power to discriminate between simultaneous facts is cultivated, 251 *sqq.;* our social habits and their significance, 276-298; novel habits, how acquired, either in a growing brain or in one already possessed of habits, 242-244, 302-332; abnormal habits, 343-348, 374-379.

Hallucination, 355.

Hartmann, Fritz, on orientation, 141.

Hearing, 135; relation of, to our consciousness of space, 140, 141, 145; analysis of sensory experience of the sense of hearing as an instance of psychological analysis in general, 104-106, 108, 111.

Heliotropism, as an instance of outwardly observable sensitiveness that need not be attended with mental life, 29.

Herbartian doctrine of apperception, 236.

Idealism, 2 *note.*

Ideas, general or abstract ideas, nature and social conditions of, 285-292; definition of the term, general idea, 286; general ideas are in one aspect indeed images, 286, cf. 157, 158; but this aspect is never dissociated from our consciousness of our acts, 286-288, cf. 159, 193, 194; and we become conscious of the details of our acts, especially under social conditions, 283, 291; correct general ideas expressible only in terms of fitting deeds, 289; feelings that accompany and colour our consciousness of ideas, 288, 289, 290; imitative character, especially of our more elaborate scientific ideas, 291; ideas and language, 280-284, cf. 371, 372; language not the exclusive expression of general ideas, 284; ideas as attitudes, 288; as plans of action, 290.

Images, and Imagery, the general nature of mental images indicated, 148; their relation to sensory disturbances, 148-150, 158; differences between sensory experiences and images, 150, 151; the variations of mental imagery in different individuals, 151-157; the types of mental imagery, 156; the relation of mental imagery to higher mental processes, 157; to our motor activities and to our conduct, 159-161.

Imagination, 161.

Imitation, as a fundamental social tendency, 276; its relation to the tendency to social opposition, 278; combination and balance of the two tendencies as a social ideal, 279; imitative character of our more elaborate general ideas, 287, 291; numerical and geometrical ideas as examples of this fact, 292; judgment as acceptance or rejection of proposed imitative portrayals of objects, 293; imitative aspect of processes of judgment, 257; language and imitation, 281-284, cf. 372; imitation and originality in intellectual life, 361.

Impulses, insistent, 378.

Inertia of cerebral processes, and relation of this inertia to consciousness, 83.

Inherited tendencies, see Instincts.

Inhibition, 70-80; definition, 70; importance of, 71; the "set" of the brain in relation to, 72; examples of in processes of high grade, 73-75; practical results of the doctrine of, 75-80. Relation of attention to inhibition, 264.

Initiative, definition of, 50; signs of in general, 38-50; many signs that appear to be those of spontaneous initiative on the part of an organism are to be explained as due to sensitiveness or to docility, 39-42; but not all such signs can be thus explained away, 42; illustrations of initiative, 43-46; the term "spontaneity" not the best to define such activities, 46; analogy of such activities to variations in the process of heredity, 48, 49, 301; initiative always closely connected with docility, 51-53, 303 sqq.; initiative and self-activity, 53-55, 330; initiative appears both in the intellectual and in the voluntary life, 55; the problem regarding initiative restated, 300 sq.; the development of our inherited, but at the outset very imperfect, instinctive tendencies as giving an opportunity for initiative, 302-306; persistence in actions, and in the variation of actions, in advance of adaptation, as the principal source of initiative, 306-319; illustrations of the results of such persistence, 319-330; the persistence as based upon tropisms, 331. See also Table of Contents, Chapter XIII.

Inner and outer worlds, contrast of, 1, 2 sq. See also Mental life.

Insistent impulses, 378.

Instincts and inherited tendencies, 34, 35, 44, 52, 125; the tropisms of orientation and their importance for our consciousness of space, 141 sqq.; inherited tendencies at the basis of habits, 200 sqq.; as related to perceptions, 219 sqq.; the instincts that lie at the basis of sociality, 275-279; inherited tendencies in relation to initiative, 302 sqq.; tropisms that support initiative, 306-331. Other inherited tendencies, 341, sqq., 375.

Intellect and intelligence, relation to discriminating sensitiveness, 31, 32; to docility, 37; to initiative, 55; to will, 37, 164, 165, 334, 351; to experience, 351; to the feelings, 164, 165; to the attention, 259-262; perception in relation to the intellect, 218 sqq.; assimilation in relation to the intellect, 234 sqq.; differentiation in relation to the intellect, 248 sqq.; higher intellectual processes, 274-

298; social aspects of intellectual life, *id.;* general ideas, 285 *sqq.;* judgment, 255–257, 292, 293; reasoning 293–296; practical aspects of the intellectual life, 350–363.

Interest, in its relation to feeling, and to the process of attention, 259.

Introspection as a psychological method, 16; its uses and limitations, 17; was not the exclusive method of Aristotle, nor of the other greater psychologists of former times, 17, 18.

James, William, on instinct 'in human beings, 35; on the "specious present," 96; on discrimination, 250; on "fringes," 289. See also Preface.

Judgment, in relation to the general process of differentiation, 255–257; in relation to the social conditions under which the process of judgment has come to our own consciousness, 293.

Language, its development in the child, 371, 372; its development as indicating its relation to thought, 280–285; its relation to imitation, 281, 284; it is not exclusively the function in which thinking gets expressed, 284, 285.

Loeb, on tropisms, 29, 30, 141, 322, 327, 330, 331; on orientation, 141. See also Preface.

Memory, in relation to the assimilative process, 236–241. See also **Habit, Docility, Association.**

Mental life, general definition and character of, 1; relation of this definition to philosophical opinions of author, 2; problems as to the possibility of studying mental life, 5 *sq.;* solution of problem indicated, 6 *sqq.;* relation of mental life to its physical expression, 6 *sqq.;* general relation of mental life to its physical conditions, 9–11, 15, 59, 64 *sqq.,* 70–78, 81–83, 100–103, 107, 110; relation of mental life to physical conditions in case of sensory experience, 117, 121–

129; the organs of sense in their relations to mental life, 130–135, 137; the conditions of spatial consciousness, 139–146; relation to physical conditions in case of mental imagery, 148–150; relation to physical conditions in case of feelings, 179–182; the relation of the associative processes of mental life to their physical conditions, 203–208. Classification of the processes of mental life, 55–57; more detailed discussion of the signs of mental life, 20–57. See also **Consciousness, Sensitiveness, Docility, Initiative, Perception, Assimilation, Differentiation, Will.**

Methods of psychology defined in general, 14–19.

Mob, mental phenomena of the, 216, 276.

Moral Law, its relation to the processes of inhibition, 75–77.

Motor imagery, and the motor type of persons when classified with respect to imagery, 156.

Motor nervous processes, 61–65, 67, 68; their inhibition, 70–75; their relations to the law of habit, 66, 67, 198–205; how they come to be represented in consciousness, 127; their relations to mental imagery, 159, 156, 157. See also **Conduct, Habit, Will.**

Movement, see also **Expression** and **Expressive movements.** How we become aware of our own movements, 127, 365; of our movements of orientation, and, through them, of our spatial relations, 141–147. For the significance of our movements for consciousness in general, see also **Conduct, Perception, Discrimination, Will, Tropisms, Motor nervous processes.**

Multiplicity of conscious states, in relation to the unity of consciousness, 89. See also **Consciousness.**

Münsterberg, Professor Hugo, 3.

Narrative, why more interesting than description, 255.

Nervous system, its general relation to mental life, 10. Distinction between nervous processes that are, and those that are not, attended by mental life, 11, 33, 34, 64, 81, 82; the study of the nervous processes that accompany and condition mental life as one of the methods of psychology, 15; general characterisation of the structure of the nervous system, 59-61; possible nature of the transmission of nervous excitation, 60; sensory and motor nervous fibres and functions, 61-64; adjustments to the environment as determined by nervous functions, 64; complexity of higher nervous processes, 65; localisation, 67; habits of nervous centres, 68-70; the hierarchy of nervous functions, 74; inhibition, 70-75. Nervous conditions of habit and association, 198-203. Inertia of the nervous processes, 83. Some phenomena of nervous exhaustion, 353-355, 376. See also **Brain**.

Neurons, or "elements," of the nervous system, 58, 59, 305.

New Testament, positive precepts in, 77.

Numerical, general ideas, as imitative in character, 292.

"**Old-fashioned winter**," the, as an example of an idea due to a characteristic defect of human memory, 239-241.

Opposition, as a social tendency, nature and significance of, 277-279; its relation to imitation, 278; to argument and reasoning, 296; to individualism and to the social forms of initiative, 326-328.

Organic sensation, 131, 132; in relation to orientation, and consequently to the bases of our consciousness of space, 141-147; in connection with the emotions, 169, 337-339; in relation to our consciousness of our movements, 127, 365.

Orientation, the functions of, in relation to our consciousness of space, 141-147; reactions of orientation, 141, 142; their representation in our sensory experience, 143; all our sensory experiences related to our acts of orientation, *id.;* result as to any special sensory experience of which we become conscious, 144; the primal experience of extensity, 145; consequences for the nature of our spatial consciousness, 146, 147.

Pain, sensations of, 132, 170; feelings of, 168-173, 179. See **Pleasure and Displeasure, Feeling**, and the analysis of Chapter VII in the Table of Contents.

Perversion, of character, 344, 347, 348, 375, 379; of emotion, 343-346.

Physical conditions of mental life, 9; always include conditions involving the nervous system, 10. See also **Brain**, and **Nervous System**. Controllable physical conditions in experimental psychology, 18.

Physical expressions of mental life, see also **Expressions**. Every physical expression of mind, direct or indirect, interesting to the psychologist, 12, 14. The physical signs of the presence of mind classified, 20-57.

Physical facts, the general nature of the contrast between physical and mental facts, 2 *sqq.*

Plasticity as a sign of mind, 32-38. See **Docility**.

Pleasure and Displeasure, feelings of, their signs, 22, 23; the traditional theory, which regards all feelings as of these two types, stated, 167-173; application of the theory to the case of the emotions, 169-171; relation of pleasure and displeasure to conduct according to this theory, 172; doubts concerning the sufficiency of this theory, 173-176; Wundt's view as to the classification of the feelings, 176, 177; the author's classification, 177 *sqq.* Relation of pleasure and displeasure to other feelings, on this basis,

179 *sqq.* See also analysis of Chapter VII in Table of Contents.

Positive and negative precepts, their psychological relations to inhibition, 76, 77.

Practical applications, of the study of the signs of sensory experience, 27 *sq.;* of the relations between the various special habits of the brain, 70; of the facts relating to inhibition, 75–79; practical results of excessive inhibition, 77; the relief from inhibitions as one use of physical exercise, 78; the practical significance of the phenomena of worry, 79, 80; practical consequences of the doctrine regarding the relations of sameness and difference, 94; the significance of the proper training of the senses for the development of any and all grades of conscious life, 127 *sq.;* the life of the senses not a lower life, but an auxiliary of the highest mental processes, 128; the relations of mental imagery to conduct, 159; need of considering, in guiding minds, the individual varieties of mental imagery, 162; practical application of the doctrine as to the relation between perception and conduct, 226–228; of the doctrine of assimilation, 236; of the doctrine as to the differentiation of consciousness, 257; of the doctrine of the social factors of the higher forms of docility, 279; of the doctrine of mental initiative, 331. Practical suggestions concerning the life of the emotions, 340–349; concerning the intellectual processes, 349–351; concerning some intellectual disorders, 353–355, 358–360, and anomalies, 360–362. Considerations concerning the will, 364–379. See also **Conduct**, and the analyses of Chapters XIV and XV in the Table of Contents.

Present moment of consciousness as not indivisible, 84; but as of finite length, 95–97; what is present to consciousness at any one moment, 85.

Psychology, defined, 1; how possible as a science, 5 *sqq.;* essentials of all psychological study, 12, 13; how related to neurological science, 10–13; the methods of psychology, 13–19; the business of psychology restated, 112, 113, 116, 117; psychological analysis as a process of substitution, 114; as a further carrying out of the tendency of the developing consciousness towards differentiation, 230, 257. See also **Consciousness** and **Mental life**.

Psycho-physic law, 138, 264–273; as a law regarding the limitations of our docility, 269.

Quiescence, feelings of, 178, 179; their relation to feelings of restlessness, 180, 181; of pleasure and displeasure, 182, 183; quiescence as a positive state of consciousness, 185; the quiescent pleasures, 185; the relatively quiescent experiences of displeasure, 188, 189; despair as an instance of such union of displeasure and quiescence, 189; relation of quiescence to passive attention, 190, 191, 261; the feeling of familiarity as a relatively quiescent feeling, 224; the feeling of confidence (which sometimes takes the place of a general idea) is of the quiescent type, 288.

Reasoning, nature of the reasoning process defined, 293, 294; illustrated, 295; the reasoning process as the result of social training, 295, 296; its relation to the devices of social persuasion, 296.

Restlessness, feelings of, 178 *sqq.;* their general relation to feelings of quiescence, 179, 180; to feelings of pleasure and displeasure, 182, 183; the four resulting mixed types of feeling, 179, 185–189; the relation of these mixed types of feeling to desire and to conduct, *id.;* the relation of restlessness to the active attention, 190, 330; the relation of restlessness to the conditions which determine the persistence in and the variation of types of action, in advance of adaptation, 306–331; resulting theses as to mental initiative, 318, 331; the relation of restlessness to desire, 195.

Rhythm, as an example of the presence of unity and variety in consciousness, 84, 89, 93; relation of rhythm to the duration of the present moments of consciousness, 96.

Sameness, as a relation always present amongst the various states in the unity of consciousness, 91; sameness and difference are inseparable facts, 91; each may help us to become aware of the other, 92; if sameness too much predominates, consciousness tends to lapse, 89; relation of sameness and difference to unity and variety, 93; relation of consciousness of sameness to clearness of consciousness, 93; the consciousness of sameness as a factor in the process of thought, 245; the consciousness of sameness in relation to our power to observe objects, 235.

Science, descriptive, conditions which make it possible, 5; problem as to how a science of mental states is possible, 5–13; the relation of scientific inquiry to the discovery of law, 43.

Self, and the consciousness of self, in relation to the social conditions which determine self-consciousness, 296–298; see also 283–285, 291, and the analysis of Chapter XII in the Table of Contents. On the self as the sole observer of mental states, see 1–5. On the character of feelings as states referred especially to the self, 166, 167.

Self-activity, see Initiative.

Sensation, definition of, 122; the signs of the presence of, 24–28; the classification of, 129–136; the attributes of: intensity and quality, 136–139;

extensity as an attribute of sensation, and its relation to our experiences of orientation, 139–147; consciousness not a mere complex of elementary sensations, 120–122.

Senses, the physiology of the senses, 16; the classification of the various senses indicated, 129–136; the life of the senses plays its part in all grades of consciousness, 123–129.

Sensitiveness, discriminating, as the most general sign of the presence of mind, 21; the forms of this sensitiveness, 22–32; why called discriminating, 21; relation of sensitiveness to habit, and to plasticity or docility, 27, 36; to apparent spontaneity, 39. The outer appearance of discriminating sensitiveness as not an unquestionable sign of the presence of mind, 23, 28–30; but of great importance in the interpretation of mind where we know that mind is present, 31. The appearance of spontaneity often only a phase of sensitiveness, 39. The first form of sensitiveness: sensory experience, its relation to consciousness of all grades, 121–129; its classification, 129–136; the attributes of sensory experience, 136–147. The second form of sensitiveness, mental imagery, 148–161. The third form of sensitiveness, feeling, 163–195. See Table of Contents, Chapters V, VI, and VII.

Sensory Experience, the signs of, 24–28; the interpretation of these signs not always certain, 28–30; but these signs are of great importance for the interpretation of all grades of mental life, 30–32. See further the analysis of Chapter V in the Table of Contents.

Sensory nervous processes, 61–65.

Sequence of states in consciousness, see Change and Succession.

Sexual emotions, 344–346.

Shinn, Miss M. W., on early habits in childhood, 303, 307, 308.

Sight, 135, 136; relation of, to the consciousness of extensity, 139 *sqq.*; to perceptive processes, 219 *sqq.* Imagery of objects once seen, 152 *sqq.*

Signs of mental life, see **Expression** and **Expressive movements.**

Similarity, see **Sameness** and **Difference.**

Simultaneous association, see **Association.**

Simultaneous facts, how the differentiation of such facts comes to consciousness, see **Differentiation.**

Simultaneous functions, how affected in case of the formation of habits, 202, 203.

Smell, sense of, 134.

Social conditions and tendencies which determine the higher forms of docility, see **Imitation, Opposition,** and the analysis of Chapter XII in the Table of Contents.

Space, consciousness of, its relation to our consciousness of sameness and difference, 92; its basis in our general experiences of the orientation of the organism, 139–147; differentiation of this consciousness of space through our experiences of movement, 252–254; the perception of single objects in space, 219–223.

Spontaneity, appearance of, in the nervous functions that attend mental life, 12, 22, 39; apparent spontaneity as often but a phase of sensitiveness, 39 *sq.*, or of docility, 41; but some forms of spontaneity not easily thus to be explained, 42–46. Spontaneity does not mean a lack of causal connection, 47; objections to the use of the term, *id.*; the term Initiative substituted, which also see for further facts of spontaneity.

Static sense, 144.

Stern, William, on the "present moment" of consciousness, 96.

Storch, on our consciousness of space, 147.

Succession, in the stream of consciousness, 83; in relation to the unity of consciousness, 95–97; the significance of our consciousness of succession as a means of developing our habits of discriminating simultaneous facts, 248–258. The consciousness of succession as related to the consciousness of difference, 97. See also **Time.**

Suggestion, negative, in relation to inhibition, 76.

Synthesis, 256, 258.

Taste, sense of, 134.

Temperature, sensory experience of, 133.

Ten Commandments, the, as examples of appeal to inhibitory tendencies, 77.

Thinking process, see **Thought.**

Thought, in relation to our sensory experience, 123–129; in relation to the assimilative process, 245–247; in relation to the process of differentiation, 255–257; in relation to our social habits and training, 280–296; thought and language, 381–285; thought in relation to conduct, 351.

Time, our consciousness of the present moment always a consciousness of a finite duration, never of an indivisible present moment, 95–97; temporal succession as significant for the formation of our habits of discrimination, 248–258; temporal sequence an essential character of the stream of consciousness, 83; our memory of past time affected by assimilative processes, 237–241; the relation of our feelings to our consciousness of time, 180,181.

Touch, see **Dermal sense.**

Tropisms, of Loeb, general usage and definition of the term, 29, 30 (see also Preface); see also 141, 322, 327, 330, 331.

Unity of Consciousness, see **Consciousness** and **Mental life**; the unity of consciousness generally characterised, 85 *sqq.*

Variations in the race as analogous to the appearance of initiative in the functions of the individual, 48, 301.

Variety as an aspect of mental life, 89; see also **Consciousness, Mental life, Change, Differentiation.**

Verbal-motor type of mental imagery and of persons when classified with respect to imagery, 156, 157.

Visual type, of mental imagery, 153 *sqq.* The variations in visualising power from person to person, 153, 154. The relative predominance of visual imagery over other imagery in the "visualising" type of persons, 155, 156.

Volition, see **Will.**

Voluntary acts, as resulting from attention, 367–369; in what sense voluntary acts are never, as such, original, 369–371; the growth of language as an instance of the development of a voluntary function, 371–372.

Wagner, Richard, 187.

Weber, and the psycho-physic law, 267.

Will, in the wider sense, as our total consciousness of our activity, and of our own attitude towards our world, 194–196, 364–367; in the narrower sense, as the process of the attentive selection of one way of action as against another, 367–369; will in relation to intellect, 37, 164, 165, 334, 351; the term "will" as of little use for purposes of purely psychological classification, 196, 334; will in relation to feeling in general, 164, 165; in relation to the special types of feeling, see **Feeling.** For the practical aspects of the life of the will, especially in reference to the narrower use of the term, see analysis of Chapter XV in Table of Contents.

Worry, phenomena of, 79, 80.

Wundt, Wilhelm, on the classification of the feelings, 176, 177, 180; on the association of mental elements, 208, 209; on the early stages of the development of language, 281; on apperception, 328.

THE CONCEPTION OF GOD

A philosophical discussion concerning the nature of the Divine
Idea as a demonstrable reality

By JOSIAH ROYCE, Professor of the History of Philosophy in Harvard
University; JOSEPH LE CONTE and G. H. HOWISON, Pro-
fessors in the University of California; and SIDNEY EDWARD
MEZES, Professor of Philosophy in the University of Texas.

Cloth   **12mo**   **$1.75 net**

"The subject is a tremendously interesting and important one, handled
by all the disputants with great ability. The book can be warmly recom-
mended as an intellectual gymnastic of the most exacting quality." — *New
Unity*.

"It is a model of calm, judicious, respectful polemic writing, and every
reader must lay it aside with the impression that he has been in good
company and has received numberless suggestions toward a better understanding of the various ways in which the human mind may approach the
conception of God, the idea of individual freedom, and the 'vital principle
of all personality.' We commend the book to students as one eminently
worth careful examination." — *Independent*.

"The book is the record of a remarkable occasion and a notable
moment in the history of philosophy in America." — *Hartford Post*.

66 FIFTH AVENUE, NEW YORK